Sensational and lo[illegible] every drop. A Wow.

–Kate Ritchie

Every parents go to… .

–Angela Schwartz

Wise truths in every turn of the page… a must have.

–Kalunda Freud

RAW FACTS FROM REAL **PARENTS**

How to parent children, teens and adults
in the 21st Century

DR. MICHAEL ACTON

Psy. D., M.Ed. (Psych.) Hons., M.A. C.Psych.

MPA
mind.com
Michael Padraig Acton

Published by Life Logic Publishing LLC 2022

Text © Michael Padraig Acton 2022
Illustrations © KS Turner 2022
Cover Design © Helen Braid 2022

The author has asserted their moral right under the Copyright, Designs and Patents Act, 1988, to be identified as the author of this work.

All rights reserved. No part of this publication may be reproduced, stored in retrieval system, or transmitted, in any form or by any means without the prior written permission of the publisher, nor be otherwise circulated in any form of binding or cover other than that in which it is published and without a similar condition being imposed on the subsequent purchaser.

A CIP catalogue for this book is available from the British Library.

Paperback ISBN 978-1-8383527-4-5

Typeset in Garamond Classic 11.25/14.5 by Blaze Typesetting

Also by Dr. Michael Acton

Power of You: Learning How To Leave*
Narcissism & Codependency: Walking You Away From Toxic Relationships
Narcissism & Codependency: Both Sides of the Coin

*also available on audiobook

My deepest heartfelt thanks to the families, couples and individual clients and patients that I've worked with over all of these decades. I also want to give special appreciation to all of my colleagues, peers, clinical supervisors and scholastic mentors. Your journeys with me made this book possible!

ACKNOWLEDGEMENTS

I thank every one of you amazing people who contributed to this important work: *Raw Facts from Real Parents.*

To Patricia Velasquez, thank you for being an inspirational force for good in this challenging world: as founder and president of the Wayuu Taya Foundation; through *Straight Walk*, your revealing book about life, recovery and coming out as gay, and through co-parenting a daughter whilst managing life as supermodel and actor. Patricia, you have come through great adversity and shown true leadership in all areas of your life. Inviting you to write the foreword to this book is my way of showing my appreciation of and admiration for you as a parent and as a unique and genuine soul.

To Sharon Pursey OBE, mum and co-founder of the SafeToNet app and SafeToNet Foundation. You have made two powerful contributions to ensuring the safety of all of our children in our modern virtual village. We could have talked for days, weeks, months snd still not had enough time.

To Kathy Davis, who has provided readers of this book with a wealth of knowledge compiled from 40 years as a licensed child carer. Thousands of children have experienced your calm, safe, encouraging and loving nature - you are everyone's wish for a mum.

To Dawn Biggers, school inspector turned mother extraordinaire. Since bringing triplets into this world, you have navigated family, school and work challenges with passion and pragmatism. Parents of multiple births would do well to follow your example. You lead by example, a true gift.

To Alyssa D. Honickman, your experience, as a former public prosecutor and family lawyer, is invaluable.

As a mother to two pre-teen girls, your desire to educate people about the reality of the law - which is often not what they think - comes from the heart. Your contribution will steer our readers into the reality of the legal role and the reality of a family lawyer's role.

To Sharon and Billy (Chapter 40: Family Lost), as a hard-working Canadian mom and son, who put your trust in the medical and educational services, readers will relate to you. Your loving family was ripped apart by misdiagnosis and deathly pharmaceuticals - an all too common occurrence. Your choice to tell your heart-rending story could save others from experiencing your pain. Thank you! Thank you!

To Dietlinde Turban Maazel, you keep the musical dreams of your late former husband Lorin Maazel alive in Castleton, Virginia, while expertly managing the challenges of a modern day blended family. I am so pleased that you and your husband Tony Wood, financier, trauma survivor and amazing father, agreed to write the foreword to the second part of this book. Who could be better qualified to comment on the reality of managing adult children?

I am truly grateful to each of you for your time and the open way in which you have expressed your truths.

Finally, a sincere and heartfelt thank you to all those parents I have worked with during the past three decades. Your trust in me and your hard work, strength and motivation is so humbling. I am proud to be able to share the vast knowledge I have learned from each of you. Every one of you has helped me grow personally and professionally beyond my dreams. I will leave you with one of the most powerful of those lessons:

"The way our children behave or treat us, generally, has very little to do with how we parent them... nor is it a true measure of our parenting ability. They are their own CEO."

FOREWORD

Many people know me as an actor and a supermodel. Fewer people know me as a philanthropist and caring, loving mother. I'm so thankful, in many ways, that Michael and my paths' crossed. I am honored to support Michael in helping you, parents, that want to do better and need help navigating.

They say that all it takes for a person to become a successful human being is for just one person to believe in them. That can then lead to us believing in ourselves. Through Raw Facts From Real Parents, Michael helps all parents to trust and believe in themselves.

Parenting isn't easy, and there is no training for such a crucial role. We are the future of our children. The feeling of loneliness is one that we all live with, especially when confronted with situations we don't know how to react to. I remember cutting my baby daughter's fingernails and cutting them too far. She was bleeding so much we ended up calling the doctor. Fast forward to now, and we find ourselves with a teenager, not knowing how to negotiate boundaries, consider healthy options and tread the fine line between child and adult.

Michael writes with a lot of passion and clarity. He also writes with a lot of science, knowledge and insight. He takes very complicated scenarios and delivers simple, very understandable pathways. He tells us that he cares and he's 'got us' - we're not alone as parents. That's extremely important. This is a book that connects with you at a very deep, sincere, person-to-person level. It makes us feel that we're being listened to and that Michael has got our backs. There's advice that can help with any and all situations.

I love how Michael starts every chapter with a thought, then the problem, then a solution and finally a list of resources for you if you need to dig deeper.

Chapters are small, concise and very powerful; he really hits the nail on the head. It's a wonderful guide that goes straight to the heart of each point.

Nowadays, our lives are so crazy, and we can panic when we encounter a parenting issue that we haven't dealt with before. Michael first helps us to identify the situation. He says, 'Let's put this in perspective. This is what you're going through. This is what our child needs. And now this is how we're going to find a solution for it and navigate through it, again together.'

It is also an inclusive book about parenting. I am a gay parent, and our family is atypical because we are basically four moms. Any parent can relate to the messages inside because Michael talks at a simple but profound level. After all, the truth is simple: you love, you feel, you have emotions. We just overcomplicate things most of the time; Michael's great at unraveling.

One of the things I truly love about this book - maybe because I am Latin, and Latin people often feel self-conscious about their parenting style - is the chapter on dictatorial and negotiating language. I admit that, out of desperation, I sometimes find myself using the demanding language style. I've always admired my daughter's other mom who sits and plays with her and listens to her for hours. She is so engaged, and that's admirable. Michael recommends we take a similar approach to help our children understand why we are making certain choices and putting in healthy boundaries. But he also points out that there is a fine line, and you sometimes have to change from discussion to instruction (i.e., from coercive, loving and nurturing to dictatorial, hardline instructions). Where health, wellbeing and education are in jeopardy, you will find the keys and confidence to do a good enough job.

Michael brings up these three 'non-negotiables' (health, wellbeing and education) over and over again.

I run a foundation for children, and we're dealing with very basic situations there, where the children have very little access to education. There is a lack of food and medical provision also. Taking into consideration these three non-negotiables, and integrating them into the vision of my foundation, leads to a happier, healthier and more structured pathway to cared for children. As parents, we would have the ability to elevate society in general if we were all to listen to Michael's three principles.

I also love how Michael talks about the value of spending quality time with our children in this chaotic, digital 21st Century. My daughter is going to be 16 soon, and I have realized that we share a lot of quality time in the car, while I am driving her to places. Michael has already advised me that we will need to create new routines and traditions in our family to replace that lost 'car time' when she becomes a driver, goes to college, gets her own home, etc.

The theme of communication is repeated over and over. One of the strategies I have picked up from Michael's book, which I am already using with my daughter, is the use of open questions. I love that! Simple but powerful. There's one example question from the book I'm going to ask her very soon: "How do we compare with parents of other children at school?" I'm very curious about how she sees herself in relation to other kids.

That's what I think is great about this book for all readers. In addition to inspiration and emotional solutions, Michael provides very practical help. I resonate with all levels, but other parents might connect with just the practical part.

The book is enriched by discussions between Michael and experts from other fields. For example there are chapters on the legal system and technology. Michael and his contributors provide constructive criticism, highlighting areas where society needs fixing for the benefit of our children.

Whatever type of parent you are, you have made a wise choice with this book because Michael covers all elements of parenting. The content is easy to digest, but it goes beyond Parenting 101. I would say it sits somewhere between a parenting bible and a practical guide. You will want to keep it permanently on your bedside table. It is a parenting book for your entire career.

If you have any sort of parenting issue, you will find a chapter on how to handle it. For example, if there's an issue with bullying, there it is. You can move quickly from understanding the situation to how you can practically help your child. There is also a list of additional resources for each chapter should you need them.

This book is very much needed in this world. It fills a void. It reminds me of that incredible book you have when you're pregnant which tells you exactly what to expect every month. I always gift a copy to people I know who are having a baby. I am now also going to buy loads of copies of Raw Facts From Real Parents to gift them once the baby has arrived. I know it is going to be the ultimate gift, parenting companion and comforting wisdom.

For me, the most important thing about this book is that Michael is asking us to listen to our children - and to be there for them, especially in those times when we want to run away the most. I am delighted that Michael is going to build on Raw Facts From Real Parents and is developing a parenting course based upon this book because this is definitely something special.
Patricia Velasquez
Actress, model and founder of the Wayuu Taya Foundation

CONTENTS

THE SERENITY PRAYER

Since my childhood, in which I was originally groomed to be a priest, I have drawn comfort and solace from the Serenity Prayer. I have used it with the people I have worked with throughout my career, bringing relief and understanding of limitations and abilities.

Grant me the serenity to accept the things I cannot change,
Courage to change the things I can,
And wisdom to know the difference.

PART I

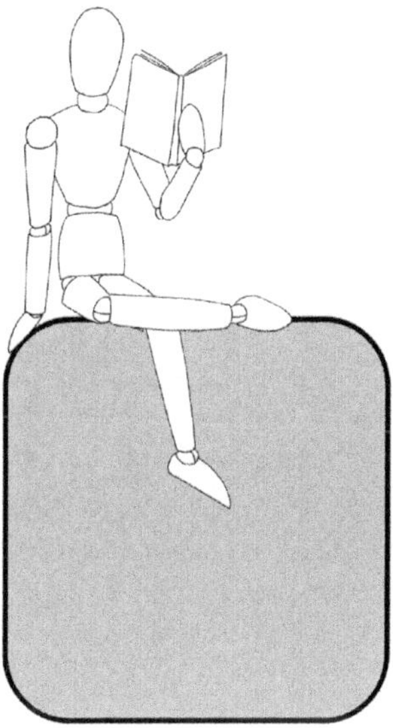

WHAT YOU REALLY NEED TO KNOW ABOUT PARENTING YOUNG CHILDREN AND TEENAGERS TODAY

"These are raw facts learned by parents from real families I've worked with over the past 30 years. And signposts to effective parenting that I had to learn the hard way through being a dad and a grandpa, and through growing up and being parented and grandparented."

- Michael Padraig Acton -

WHY WRITE THIS BOOK?

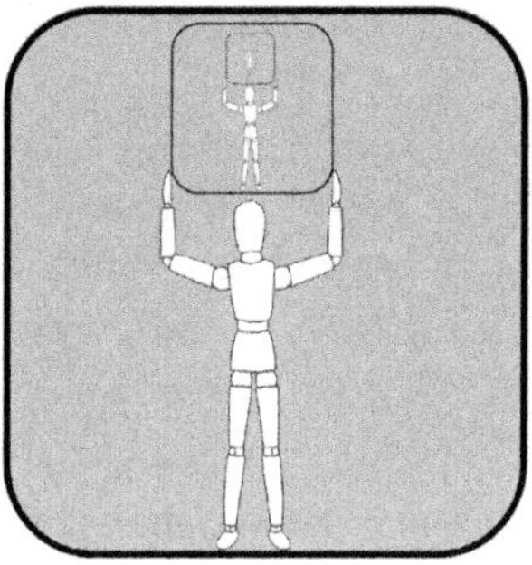

"I can only write about things I'm passionate about. And giving children a voice and safeguarding them is my priority. An equal priority to safeguarding children is for me to help you, parents and grandparents, not burn out doing your best, and to equally be treated fairly along the way, whatever your family situation may be."

- Michael Padraig Acton -

I am always humbled to be invited into the worlds of my patients and clients, their loved ones and their families. Over the past 30 years, I have worked with some very difficult, tragic and extreme circumstances that have needed thought, ideas, navigation, support, care, love and acceptance from me as a practitioner and for those that I work with.

I came into this field as a calling. Not only was I going to be a priest as a teenager, but I also came from my own story of Hell, and I've used all of my personal and clinical experiences, working with real people and real situations in our world, to bring you this book. It delivers small but powerful ideas and tips on how you may navigate your life as a parent through the stages of infancy, toddling, adolescence and adulthood. It is my hope that this will serve as a co-parent guide for all who read it, whether you're a grandparent, parent or caregiver.

I'm always learning and growing. It's something I treasure and embrace in my life. I would really welcome any feedback from you on how we may improve, modify or add to this work in progress, because as a book on parenting, this will always be a work in progress!

As a parent for 36 years myself, and a grandparent for the last 16 years, it's been a journey.

I am and was the worst parent in the world! I chastise myself, even now, 36 years later. Was I too strict? Do I still cave in too much, etc?

This is a good place to start this book for you: we learn only from recognising our mistakes and we choose to learn because we fear we won't do a good job. And parenting is a job; it is work. The healthy result of that work is to be able to say that our kids bring out love that we never knew was possible before we had them. Grandchildren are an even more special miracle of love.

Believe me; being able to say, "I am/was a good enough parent" is an A+ grading.

People like you, who read parenting books, know there are better ways. My fear is for those parents who believe they are good enough already. I always tell people who access work with me in therapy or life coaching that they are the smart people and not the crazy ones. It's the same for parents: the smart and healthy parents want to learn and improve.

In my clinics, and life in general, I find so many families, couples and individual parents suffer for too long. There are many reasons why. . .

First, most people don't feel there is a problem within their family. They seek help only when things get to a crisis point. By that time, they or their children may have suffered immensely, and unhealthy patterns of behaviour and thoughts have set in.

Second, there is an absurd lack of information about real relationship, family and child management issues. The news only reports and comments upon matters of political or fashionable interest.

Third, some of the most heart-breaking enquiries I get happen when I have a wait list and no room for intakes. They are from parents worried about their children, begging me to help. The only thing I can do is give them a ten-minute phone call or an intake session and an appropriate referral to somebody who might best help them.

Finally, therapy for your child should be the LAST resort. If there is severe trauma or mental illness, then specially trained therapists do help but generally it is best to be cautious. It's difficult enough to manage a triangle between parents and child (or even a single parent scenario) let alone introduce a third party, which can be the biggest monster of all: "But my therapist told me," "That's not what we decided in therapy, etc., etc. It is much better to help resolve issues through the parent/caregiver structure than have a third element, which can damage your child's template for their life or disrupt their moral compass.

Hopefully, this book will serve as an alternative vehicle by which I can reach some of those parents, children and family members I am unable to see or communicate with directly.

Disclaimer: This is not an exhaustive book about parenting. It is my personal pick of the most helpful parenting ideas from more than 30 years of clinical work across every imaginable situation. Neither I nor any of the contributors to this book can be held liable for any negative impact perceived to have been caused by anything I have written or omitted in this work. By reading this book, you fully indemnify the writers and contributors for any claims that may be made against them in connection with the provision of this contribution including legal costs incurred in defending any such claim.

How I work: one, two, three

A large part of my work is re-educating people. About what they are able to or not able to do. About what they are able and not able to accept. And about how they can (or maybe cannot) accept difference. I take them by the hand and help them to 'do relationships' differently.

Simple and genuine communication is always effective.

In my work, I often draw upon transactional analysis, using a three-step model:

Step 1. The feelings: why you are feeling those?

Step 2. The evidence: is it for or against those feelings?

Step 3. What are we going to do to resolve the issue?

That's the core of all of my work with families and couples (and with individuals where the family or partner doesn't attend).

I learnt very early on in my career, over a quarter of a century ago, that if we work with an individual, sometimes they will go back to old behaviours. To prevent this, we need to really think about changing that core process within a person: their behaviours, their thoughts, their coping mechanisms. We look at what's real, breaking down their fake stories.

Sometimes, when working with an individual, I realise that healing lies not just with them. I may then invite them to bring in their mum, dad, partner or child (but only if they feel it would help and only for a limited amount of time). I make it clear that this is an aid to help shift the context they live in.

This type of systemic work has proved to be some of the most rewarding work I've ever done.

A dangerous method: beware!

More and more people come to me after having already been in therapy with somebody who is not trained in systemics or relationship work. More often than not, they have had their bad behaviours or unhealthy positions in relationships supported rather than challenged and changed.

In addition, trained counsellors know that when there's risk of harm within a relationship (e.g., if there has been violence or betrayal) we talk about how we can manage those risks before we do any work. Our professional ethics now require us to agree a contract: there must be no risk, or we will stop working. If we continue to work with a couple or family where abuse or risky behaviour is taking place, we are saying that behaviour is 'OK.'

Unfortunately, somebody without training or experience in relationship or family therapy wouldn't understand how to assess risk or manage it appropriately.

In the world of psychology, psychiatry and counselling it is becoming harder to understand what qualifications, experience, tools and training people have and to decode the names given to trendy popular therapies.

Of late, mindfulness is a hot topic: I don't think anyone should practise helping vulnerable people unless they have mindfulness but I find that teaching mindfulness for therapy in four-week counselling courses is dangerous. Where is the practical support?

As therapists, we are the gatekeepers of mental health, family trauma, children at risk, elderly at risk and people's deepest, darkest secrets. We need to be effective, supportive and trained.

If we don't truly understand - and therefore can't help a person to see - the reality of their situation, then we have no business helping that person move forward at all!

A guide for everyone, kids n' all

So back to why I'm writing this book.

I've learnt a lot over the last quarter of a century. I've worked with people from all backgrounds, countries, faiths, genders and sexualities. I've gathered a wealth of ideas, knowledge, wisdom, skills and theoretical underpinnings.

But whenever I read new books on family systemics or relationships they are complicated! They are like the bible in Latin. Luther changed the Bible to make it readable by mums, dads, kids, the elderly and the less educated. That's what I'm doing with this series of books.

You can dip into this book, you can use it as a reference point, or you can read the whole thing. Either way, this book will give you a good grip on everything you need to know to help guide and manage yourself as a parent as well as support your friends and loved ones.

The practical skills and ideas to follow are proven to be applicable across all lifestyles, circumstances and belief systems. But you must apply them if you are to change your circumstances for the better. One of the central themes of this book is about pivoting as a parent. That is, in a nutshell, realising that something is not working and having the courage to change it and start moving in a different direction. By pivoting, we can break unhealthy behaviour patterns and shift the dynamic within the family, often in a profound way.

We start our book proper with the issue of control. The balance of power between parents and their children begins early in their childhood and extends into their teen and young adult years.

In my work, I have come across a common theme whereby controlling parents have become estranged from their children and are desperate to reconnect but don't know how. Before we can make that pivot away from controlling behaviour, we first need to recognise we are behaving in that way and then accept that our behaviour isn't working.

CHAPTER 1

CONTROL FREAK DOESN'T WORK. AM I A CONTROL FREAK?

"We can let go of control when our children are able, at any age. We can tighten the control when our children are less able. . . drugs, mental health issues, illness, etc. However, we can let go of control and at the same time not let go of loving and caring for them."
- Michael Padraig Acton -

The battleground of parent versus child control is common to most families. This chapter looks at the many cases where one or more of the parents have a habit of trying to control everything around them. The popular term for such parents is 'control freak' although this label suggests that there is something innate about the need to control. This is not normally the case. Most of the time, this behaviour is a learned habit and can be worked with.

For some parents, and you may be one of them, we only realise that our 'control freak' habit isn't working for us when our children have cut themselves off. Young children may distance themselves emotionally; adult children may make that distance physical. Sometimes they might cut themselves off completely.

How controlling behaviour affects our relationship with our children

As children become older and more independent, they are more likely to resent their behaviour being controlled. As the emotional tension builds, they may choose 'fight' or 'flight'. For a child living at home, flight might include disengaging (the silent treatment), spending lots of time in their bedroom or even 'running away'.

Adult children (and even younger teenagers, in some circumstances) can make the choice to leave home. If they have the skills to manage a parent's controlling behaviour from a distance, the relationship can work. However, if they lack these skills, physical distance can turn into estrangement.

When we realise we have become estranged from our adult children, we can feel angry but beneath that anger is often a cocktail of other emotions: guilt, hurt, shock and more. We might also feel judged by friends and family, as we imagine what they might be thinking or saying about your parenting.

Where control freak behaviour comes from

The need to control is based on the fear of what happens when we let go. No human is comfortable with complete chaos but we all have different thresholds when it comes to how happy we are to 'go with the flow'. This comes from both individual psychological and biological differences as well as our lived experiences.

Rarely, controlling behaviour is part of a personality disorder such as narcissistic personality disorder (NPD) or borderline personality disorder (BPD). Or there may be an underlying mental health condition such as obsessive-compulsive disorder (OCD) or generalised anxiety disorder (GAD).

However, in most cases, 'control freaks' have learnt this behaviour as a general coping mechanism for feelings of anxiety.

The symptoms of being a control freak

Control freaks are rarely at peace with themselves. Since they feel that they are responsible for everything that happens around them, they can never let up, even for a minute, in their management of people and environments.

Here are some of the common signs that someone has an unhelpful need to be in control:

- They don't work well in teams. They either prefer to work on their own or to dictate what everyone in the team is doing.
- They hate delegating as they feel they will need to spend even more time fixing what goes wrong. When they do delegate, they micromanage the person carrying out the task.
- They are unforgiving of mistakes, in themselves or others.
- They often appear busy yet may not be very productive.
- They often seem irritable or stressed.
- They catastrophise, fearing the worst is about to happen.

Dealing with your need to control

One of the first things you can do to curb your controlling behaviour is to recognise when the impulse to take charge rears its head. This can be hard to do, especially at first, so congratulate yourself when you do recognise it and gently, with compassion, ask yourself whether you really do need to exert control.

Knowing the difference between what needs to be controlled (taking your son to school on time or making sure your adult daughter pays the rent) and what you want to control (telling your daughter what book she should read next or making your adult son come back home before ten o'clock) is key.

As you waste less energy trying to control the people and things around you, you will find you have more to spend on what really matters.

If you do feel overwhelmed with uncertainty, learn to calm yourself with small areas of control. Choose which restaurant you want to go to or which outfit you will wear. Make lists and choose which tasks you can delegate.

Getting your child back

If your child has chosen not to engage with you because of your controlling behaviour, trying to make them change their mind through guilt-tripping or manipulation is like throwing fuel on a fire to put it out.

Recognise that they have made a choice to disconnect and that blaming them–or your parenting–for that decision is not going to change that.

What can you do to help repair the relationship? Here are some tips:

- **Don't cut them off to spite them.** Often, 'cutting off' is an immature response to emotional intensity. As an adult, it is more constructive to be a role model for how to repair a damaged relationship. Reach out to them occasionally in a non-intrusive way. Leave them messages, remind them that you love them and want to fix things. Send them birthday cards and gifts.
- **Get support.** Talk to friends and relatives you trust about what you are going through. Join a parents' support group. Avoid the temptation to dwell on anger or your feelings of betrayal.
- **Hear your adult child.** If your child does talk to you about the reasons behind their estrangement, then be prepared to swallow your pride. Even if they have misunderstood the situation, there may be grains of truth in what they say. Accept their perception of what has happened and work with them on a way forward that suits everyone.
- **Change yourself.** Whatever happens between you, know that you can never change your adult child. You have to accept them as the adult child they are and not the idealised child you may have been trying to mould. Your focus has to be on changing your own behaviours and thought processes.

When the time is right, your child may surprise you by responding positively to your olive branches. They may realise that the only way to inner peace for them is to face the issues between you and untie those knots.

In the meantime, the best thing you can do as a parent is to let them live their lives while letting them know that the door is always open. You will never let go of loving them, but you can make a space for yourself to live in peace.

For more guidance, read:
Eyes Wide Open: Help! With Control Freak Co-Parents - D. Wingfield
Stop Being Controlling: How to Overcome Control Issues - B. Gain
Recovering from Control Issues: How to Rebuild Your Self-Esteem and Confidence - C. Loving

CHAPTER 2

TRUTH IS POWER OR IS IT A LIE?

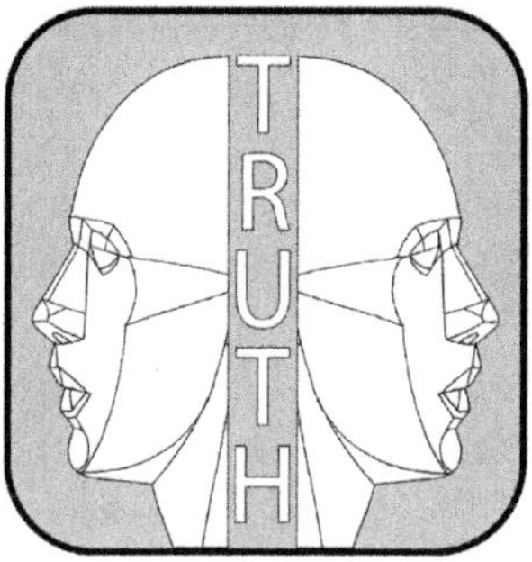

"It is important to be real and truthful with children. Children can smell deceit. Deceit leads to chaos and chaos leads to trust and survival issues."
- Michael Padraig Acton -

Let's be clear, being honest does not always mean giving our children unfiltered access to the truth. That can be dangerous to their mental health. The truth about a situation has to be managed and each parent (or caregiver, friend, auntie, counsellor, therapist, psychologist) is a manager of that situation.

To help our children with their struggles, we also need them to tell us the truth. If the child doesn't give us the truth, how can we get the data to make an informed decision on the way forward?

Part of the role of the truth 'manager' is helping the child to express their truth in words. Sitting opposite them and just telling them to talk to you might not be the best way to get reliable and helpful information.

With a physical problem we have health services, which can check vital signs and look for the source of any trauma. We can't do that psychologically, so how do we get the truth out of an eight-year-old or teenager? How about a child who's scared, in shock or in trauma?

We need some techniques for gathering helpful, informative data. Here are some of the therapeutic skills that psychologists and counsellors use that will help you to draw the truth out of your child:

- **Check your own anxiety.** Parents need to check their own anxious feelings first because anxiety is contagious and will cause your child to freeze up.
- **Use a shared activity to open a door.** Therapists teach their patients to create a relaxing, simple activity: drawing, baking, walking on the beach, tidying a garden or cleaning a room are some examples. Tell the child you are really interested in finding out truthfully what's happening with them or ask them if they could tell you the truth about why they have blood on their hands, etc. And then, be silent so that the child can think about the question. What we do with the data depends on the context but setting up a peaceful, simple activity creates a safe space that can help a child feel ready and able to open up.
- **Describe the positives.** Describe the benefits for the child of telling the truth. Use language they understand. For example, you might say, "If you tell me you like strawberry jam, I am going to keep on buying strawberry jam. If you tell me you don't like strawberry jam, we can look at buying a different type of jam." Explain that the truth can reduce fear and worry and lead to resolution. Tell them that the world is very difficult at times but 'we' have to find a way forward.
- **Keep things simple and relevant.** Always remember the limits of a child's life experience and stage of development. Don't expect them to make decisions based on adult understanding. We can't talk about complex grey areas with children when they haven't had enough life experience to make sense out of what we're telling them. Likewise, when they agree to tell us the truth, we have to understand that the language they have to express their thoughts and feelings will be limited.
- **Suggest a third party.** As a last resort, if the child is struggling, perhaps because the truth is embarrassing for them, you could ask

them if there is someone you both know that they might be more comfortable talking to and telling the truth to. This could be a family member, priest, teacher, etc.

Accurate data in the form of truthful information is critical. If we don't truly understand a child's situation and can't help them to see the reality of their situation, belief system, thought or behaviour then how can we justify trying to help that child move forward?

For more guidance, read:
I didn't do it. A book about telling the truth - S. Graves
Teaching your children to tell themselves the truth - W.D. and C. Backus
Lying Up a Storm - J. Cook

CHAPTER 3

HOW CAN I HELP MY CHILD WHO IS DESPERATELY LONELY?

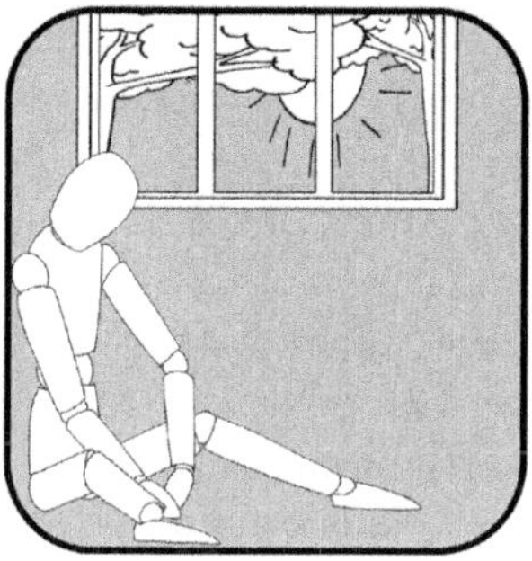

"Attention! Loneliness kills people, pure and simple. Loneliness leads people to hopelessness. Hopelessness leads people to killing themselves. If your child is experiencing loneliness as depicted below, you need to–and must–take action."

\- Michael Padraig Acton -

Can you remember how loneliness feels? Everyone has been there. If you can't think of a time you've felt lonely, you're either lying or you're dead because every human experiences loneliness.

We're pack animals; we like to be in a group and need safety in numbers. If we don't feel part of a collective, something is desperately wrong. If your child feels this way, this is a massive warning sign for any parent or caregiver.

Here are some simple steps which may help if your child is feeling or appearing lonely:

- **Bring back fun, laughter and activity.** We're all so busy with our smartphones, reality TV shows and soap operas, we forget to spend meaningful time with our children. So, strike up conversations with them. Plan regular one-to-one fun time with each of your children. Watch an age-appropriate comedy programme or cartoon.

- **Make sure they feel they belong.** It may be a dying concept because of the competition between humans but if your child does things for others, it will help them feel they have a purpose and are contributing. Within the home, projects like baking are ideal. Anything where there's an end product that can be shared with the family will work. Outside the home, consider a volunteer group (conservation or litter pick group, etc.). Find out what your child's real passions are and search for a group they would like to be part of. It's also very important to regularly tell your children that they are loved and are important.
- **Encourage them to attend to personal hygiene and dress.** Image is very important when building and keeping friendships. It's very important to make sure they have a chance in this world by presenting cleanly and neatly and showing table manners when eating. They can, of course, express their own personalities but in a clean and acceptable fashion rather than giving off 'stay away' attitude. This may seem shallow, but it is how relationships work in our society.
- **Explore self-nurturing activities.** Lonely children can develop low self-esteem and lose confidence quickly. Discuss with them the benefits of activities such as yoga, guided visualisation, mindfulness meditation and even jigsaw puzzles, or sitting down and listening to relaxing music–anything they can do on their own and that can help relax the mind. There is a plethora of ideas out there, most of which are free.
- **Change up their mood.** Some lonely children delve into social media sites, music or activities that are depressing and encourage anger, self-harm or even suicide. Limiting access to the Internet is vital in child welfare and mental health but there are other ways you can help. You could maybe rock out a happy beat with them before dinner, work on changing the social media sites they're

engaging with or put on something funny or upbeat–something the family can dance to or that brings up good memories.

- **Spend mealtimes together.** This should not be an option. Don't make your child talk about their problems. Instead, talk about fun, light-hearted stuff. Talk about hope, the future, etc.
- **Get professional help if needed.** Where there has been a severe tragedy or trauma in the family and you're not yet accessing help through the medical or psychological fields then find an appropriate, qualified therapist or counsellor.

Don't expect any of this to be plain sailing. All children act out. They will rebel. They will push away from ideas. Hormones will fly.

The main message is to act. To change it up! Even if your child is smart and says they're not lonely and they're coping, change it up! Be a parent! Be directive! Save your child!

For more guidance, read:

Loneliness in Childhood and Adolescence - K.J. Rotenberg and S. Hymel
How to be Alone - S. Maitland
Mama, I'm Lonely! - R.C. Sood and D. Joglekar

CHAPTER 4

DRUGS AND ALCOHOL: DO AS I SAY

"Alcohol and drugs consumed in large quantities over a long period of time will likely kill your child.
If it doesn't kill them, it will damage and destroy their life."
- Michael Padraig Acton -

When you are a parent, there should be no negotiating regarding health, wellbeing and education. When a child is under 18, we've got to manage these three areas. Clearly, drug and alcohol abuse are a threat to all three of these areas.

Children can be good at hiding their problems with drugs and alcohol so be vigilant for any unusual behaviour or evidence of drinking or drug-taking.

If you are concerned your child may have a problem, here are some simple steps to assess and start fixing it:

- **Make sure they are abusing.** It can be challenging to uncover the scale of substance use. Many kids tell stories or invent things to beef themselves up and sometimes parents find minor evidence of experimentation and blow it out of proportion. On the other hand, young people may not realise what constitutes a problem.

In my own experience, a kid will say they aren't doing very much but when you get down to it, the amount is absolutely massive.

- **Avoid addiction centres.** Whatever the local services and programmes for young people's drug and alcohol abuse are, whether public or private, you are going to be introducing your children to characters who are also abusing. That is sometimes like putting children in prison and teaching them how to make friends with difficult people who have an assortment of problems. It is best for them to go through the cycle of change with you at home. If progress isn't made, reach out to a therapist trained in drug and alcohol abuse.
- **Use the cycle of change.** The cycle of change is used worldwide as the most effective way of helping somebody reduce or stop using alcohol, drugs or any habit that is damaging to mind, body or spirit.
- **Find your child's motivation.** Sit your child down and find out their motivations for both continuing and stopping. Acknowledge the reasons for abusing but reinforce the reasons for stopping. Sometimes it is the friendship base or school that needs to change. You may need to move home. Read the opening sentence of this page again if you think that is an overreaction.
- **Consider substance-induced psychosis.** This can occur as a result of substance abuse, but symptoms usually subside if the abuse stops. Be aware of the possibility of mental illness and see your family doctor if you have concerns.

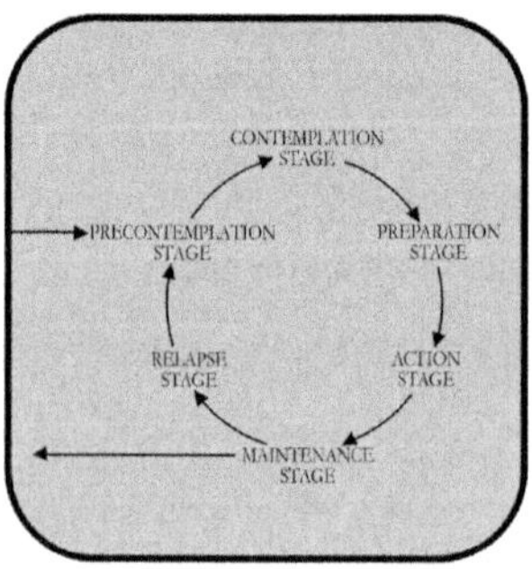

The Stages of Change Model (1)

For more guidance, read:

How to Tell When Kids are in Trouble with Alcohol/Drugs - Parenting for Prevention Information Series

Teens, Alcohol and Drugs: Adventures in Single Parenting - L. Mooney

Parenting for Prevention: How to Raise a Child to Say No to Alcohol/Drugs - D.J. Wilmes

Teenagers, Alcohol and Drugs: What Your Kids Really Want to Know About Alcohol and Drugs - P. Dillon

CHAPTER 5

PROTECTIVE PARENT TO CYBER POLICE: Sharon Pursey OBE, co-founder of SafeToNet, and Michael Padraig Acton discuss

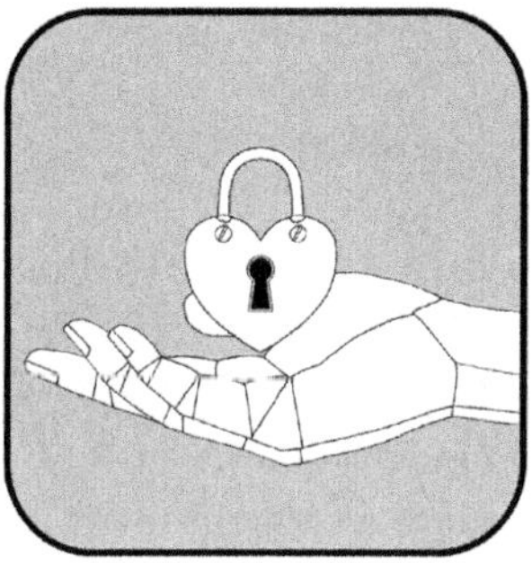

"To wish safety for children and give them a voice is commendable but to do something about it is most honourable."
- Michael Padraig Acton -

Sharon Pursey OBE on the birth of a new concept in safety tech: We sit down today in our commercial roles but also as mums and dads. If you ask me to stand up and talk about our deep tech and AI, I can't do that very easily, but I can talk about being a mum of four children and I can talk with confidence about understanding why parents want to keep their children safe.

I'm a co-founder of SafeToNet with my husband Richard, who has a background in behavioural analytics. I'm a people person so I've always been in sales/customer-facing roles. About seven to eight years ago, we were asked to work with a young social media company. The owner was a second-year student at Manchester University who had created this platform and was earning an insane amount of money. He wanted us to analyse his business to help him monetise it. So, we took a deep dive into the world of social media, and it was clear it was a massively growing industry.

At the same time, our two older kids had just got on Snapchat. We asked them to share their experiences with us in order to get a better understanding. Our eldest was in her early twenties at the time. They were telling us that Snapchat was basically a sexting tool.

We could see that there was clearly a gap in the market for online child safety, so we decided at that time to start our own social network that would be a safe environment for children to socialise and explore. We called it 'Avanatta', which you have to pronounce with an East London accent. It was about having a chat, a good old natter, and exchanging short video clips but it was to be a safe environment where you could connect safely. It was a bit like TikTok actually, so looking back, maybe we should have stuck with that! At that time, we were focused on stopping predators from getting on to our platform and quickly realised that we would have a better chance in protecting children than stopping the predators. One of the unintended outcomes of an arcane piece of UK law is that, as we cannot intercept messages without the permission of the sender–you have to have a predators' consent– you can't actually stop them from sending messages to children. In addition to this, messages are encrypted, which makes interception technically impossible, and we also don't have 'intercept powers' so it would be illegal anyway.

So, we pivoted our whole business about 18 months later and decided to create a safe way for children to access the Internet and use social media. We realised that just having an app of our own wouldn't work because we weren't going to compete with Twitter, Facebook, Snapchat, Instagram and the rest. We needed a piece of technology that was platform-agnostic, that worked across every application. We created the SafeToNet safeguarding and wellbeing app.

A smart keyboard that protects children in real time

The SafeToNet app has, at its core, an intelligent keyboard that is installed on the child's device. The keyboard then guides and advises the child in real time while they are typing messages. It looks for harmful conversations and offers real time advice and guidance to children. We built into this advanced digital wellbeing features.

When it comes to online child safety, it's important to include parents, so we also provide parents with information, so that they can have informed but not intrusive conversations with their children about their digital lives. And it's this combination of real time safety interventions, digital wellbeing features and the drawing together of parents and children for conversations, which makes SafeToNet unique.

Our youngest daughter, at the start of our mission, was about 11 and she and her siblings were all completely mortified! Can you imagine? Your parents setting up a safety tech company aimed at children. From her point of view, we were doing the worst job in the world!

Our daughter became the Young CEO of our Youth Advisory Board, and they were brutally honest about our tech, which was actually very helpful. Through the Youth Advisory Board, we've consulted with more than two thousand young people while developing SafeToNet. Through that, we understood about children wanting their privacy and in order for SafeToNet to be accepted by children and young people, we had to respect that. We're not about 'controlling' children, we're about guiding and supporting them in real time. We never show parents the actual messages or their content; we indicate to parents if there are signs of risk in their child's behaviour and help guide them in how they help their children.

Our app is aimed towards children from the moment they get that first smartphone or device, typically eight, up to around 16. That's when children say, "I don't want this on my phone anymore."

In 2020, we launched a collaboration with a mobile network operator in the Middle East that is five times bigger than BT. We're also working in the Caribbean with the mobile network operator. Can you believe, we do a deal, during lockdown, in the Caribbean and don't get the chance to go over there and meet them face to face!

So far, we have raised about £23 million investment to develop our solution. We have a B2B(2C) strategy and sell to mobile network operators and handset manufacturers, as well as being in the Android and Apple apps stores to reach consumers directly.

Alongside the business, we have set up a UK registered charity called The SafeToNet Foundation. The Foundation ensures, among other things, that we can gift our software to families who may not be able to afford it: children in children's homes and socially deprived areas. Online safety should not be only for those who can afford it.

Taking on the tech 'elephant'

Getting heard is the challenge of any tech start-up. One challenge is that we are a new technology that you wouldn't know to look for while Googling for something to protect your children online. You wouldn't know that a solution exists to safeguard what your child is typing in real time, which guides them away from risk. You would probably search for 'parental control', and we don't see ourselves in that market. We don't 'control' children; we 'safeguard' them.

Our mission is to become the *de facto* online safeguarding solution worldwide. The only way that we're going to reach millions of children is by working with network operators, handset manufacturers, enterprise companies, governments, alongside selling directly to consumers via the app stores.

What we're having to do is move the needle. Right now, children aren't protected on their devices, and they've had unfettered access to the Internet and social media. So, parents adding this type of software have had to negotiate with their children. I think, as time progresses, installing safety tech will be easier as children realise it doesn't compromise their privacy. As a mum, I know it's very difficult to retrospectively introduce device protection for older children. Our vision is, moving forward, that you should not be able to buy technology for children unless it comes with safety tech already embedded.

Hopefully, the Online Safety legislation [the draft bill was published after this interview, on May 12th, 2021] will mean that UK Government will impose a duty of care on digital service providers to moderate user generated content in a way that prevents users from being exposed to illegal/harmful content online. OFCOM will be the regulator for this legislation. We are hoping this will open up opportunities for safety tech companies like SafeToNet to ensure that social media apps are safer for children and to help social media service providers meet their duty of care. We would like to see handset manufacturers and mobile network operators pulled into scope, so they take responsibility too.

If you listen to the big tech companies, they always say it's not possible to analyse harmful content in real time. We've shown it is possible. In these big organisations they struggle to balance the commercial driving force and the wellbeing of their customers.

Making Internet access safer for children is like eating an elephant: you've got to do it in little bite-size pieces. This whole world of online harms is extremely complex, and you've got to decide which bit you're going to eat first. We've stuck our stake in the ground by being on the child's device and looking at the harms of cyberbullying and sexting in real time and balancing this with mental wellbeing support. We offer in-app breathing exercises and audio practices to help children better understand the emotions they experience. Often these emotions are directly linked to experiences in the digital world.

We also have a prototype that's coming out of our R&D team in Ottawa, Canada that analyses real time streaming of video content. According to IWF's annual report 2020, more than 44% of child exploitation content is self-generated: that is children taking and sharing intimate images of themselves on their smartphone, often from the privacy of the locked family bathroom. We are very keen to develop and use our technology to disrupt this alarming trend.

There are other organisations that look at managing screen time, location services, age verification and that sort of thing. For example, Yoti is a brilliant age verification company doing stuff that you wouldn't believe is possible. They can verify a person's age extremely accurately by analysing images. We had a meeting, a long time ago, with a global gaming company with a reputation for older adults changing their age to ten and joining younger children playing. Yoti's technology can help solve that. Age verification was expected to be in the Online Safety Bill and many people are puzzled as to why it wasn't.

While we work with all of these organisations, we focus on the device with the child and the parent. So, we're not actually going head-to-head with the big technology companies. What we're doing is providing a service for parents and providing an added value service for mobile network operators or education tech companies to offer this additional tech safety feature. That's how we've positioned ourselves.

Intercepting abuse and 'Dark Thoughts'

We can't intercept incoming messages because messages are encrypted, and we don't have 'intercept powers' so this would be illegal. Our software contextualises the outbound side of children's messages and our AI can pick up children who are including sexual references or aggression in their conversations, so we're sometimes able to pick up those parts of the conversation and raise the alarm for the parents and the child.

Suicide ideation and self-harm references are classified as 'Dark Thoughts' for us. Incidentally, there was a young girl in California whose parents were testing our software. They thought they had a fault with the software because it kept showing high risk for one of their daughters. When they talked to her, which is one of the fundamental aims of our app, they realised she was self-harming and they had to rush her into hospital. So, the SafeToNet app gives parents an insight, but it doesn't tell the parents 'x' is happening. They might see 'high risk' on the dashboard on, say, a Friday afternoon and they can then join the dots, connecting what's happening in the real world with what's happening on the app.

I believe parents do think real time online child safety is a brilliant idea and they do worry about their children online but many of them think that bad things aren't going to happen to their child because they're good kids and they 'know what they're doing.' But the sad reality is that social media allows anyone from anywhere to contact their children at any time. All children are equally at risk.

Towards 'safety by design'

We've recently acquired a company in Germany and now own and operate 77 high street stores called 'SafeToNet Family Stores' that sell mobile phones and contracts. However, most importantly, the stores also offer our suite of safeguarding products. Parents will, for the first time, be able to buy phones which are safe out of the box for their children.

These days, no one would buy a car without seat belts or an airbag. No one can buy leaded paint. These changes for safety in society were brought about by legislation and we think there has to be some sort of online safety legislation. Mobile network operators and handset manufacturers, along with social media service providers, have a responsibility to their consumers and the children using their platforms and networks.

A vision for the future

I think the answer is in parents realising that this happens to all of us. For every child that's being bullied there's a bully and all of our children are capable of being hard work one minute and angels the next. That's what kids are like. I think it's about taking away that 'safety stigma' and being able to talk to your teenager. That's a whole chapter on its own and with hindsight, now my youngest is 18, I could probably write my own book on my experiences. But when you're going through it, it's a real struggle.

Technology is wonderful. It helps our children learn in ways that we couldn't: learn the piano, learn a language, visit the world. . . When we were children, we only had the Encyclopaedia Britannica and if it wasn't in that, you had to try your luck at the library.

If only children could go online without fear of predation. There are a lot of good people working in this ecosystem, all doing different things. Together, we are actually all working towards the same common mission. We should help and support each other because it's going to take all of us to move the needle.

To watch a video of this interview, go to https://mpamind.com

Michael Padraig Acton: My thoughts on gaming and devices

While the technology developed by SafeToNet, Yoti and the rest is still in its infancy, therapists like me will continue to do what we can to help parents keep their children safe through raising awareness and giving practical advice where possible.

So, what is gaming and why should it be such a big concern for parents?

Gaming isn't a single type of activity as there are different forms. A natural division can be made between social gaming, where players work with or against others, and solo games where the player is pitched against a computer program.

Social gaming

Social gaming can be dangerous.

I once worked with a 14-year-old child and his parents who had a friend on the gaming circuit who lived over 5,000 miles away. The two children had very different demographics and the parents couldn't understand why, within six months, their child was smoking dope, had tried to kill himself with an overdose (while filming it on social media) and was threatening to try the same again unless they took him to see this friend.

After much digging, we discovered that this friend was from a government housing project in an inner-city area. His parents were drug abusers. His siblings ranged in age from thirty to two. This family's child had been learning all the 'tricks of the trade' to get attention.

During our therapy, the child reported his parents, accusing them of physical and sexual abuse leading to the home being raided and months of investigations.

Knowing your child is playing an online game should not be good enough for you as a parent or caregiver. There are further questions due. Who are your children playing these games with? Where are these children from? How is the influence developing?

I don't claim that online social activity is not as rewarding as real-world social activity. However, we can more easily control the friends our children see and the social impact they have in our local neighbourhood. We can't do this with online games.

It must be remembered that online predators use mass online tactics to hook children through online games.

To repeat, social gaming can be dangerous. We need to monitor our child's online activity even more so than we monitor friends in the neighbourhood or at school.

Repetitive solo games

Most solo games are not purely skills based. Instead, they rely upon the randomisation of scoring, and this is the key to their addictive nature. One moment you are doing well and the next you are not. Children are actually competing with themselves and are always looking for the crumbs of achievement.

Another issue with games, as a whole, is that they often provide a black and white world. In gaming, if you do x, y and z you tend to get x, y and z back. Real life is not like that: there are shades of grey.

Mobile devices: a special kind of addiction

Spending time on a mobile phone may not seem in the same league as taking a drug or smoking but consider the following:

- Mobile devices are a portal to potentially dangerous social gaming and addictive solo games (see above).
- Social media sites are designed to promote judgement and are often competitive (how many likes did your last comment get? How many followers do you have?).
- A mobile phone call or text alert has been shown to trigger the release of dopamine.
- Some young people suffer from anxiety when they can't use their mobile device (e.g., through misplacing it, losing Wi-Fi or running out of battery power).
- A University of Illinois study linked addictive mobile phone use with high levels of anxiety and depression.
- 61% of kids admit that smartphone use has negatively affected their school grades. Excessive device use can also reduce extracurricular activity and other social activities.
- Children can become obsessed with checking their mobile devices (78% check every hour with 72% feeling an urgent need to immediately respond to texts).
- Older addicted teens may use their mobile phones while driving and they have a 400% higher chance of crashing than adults who text and drive, partly because they are less likely to respond to traffic events.

- 52% of teens talk on their phones and 32% text while driving. A quarter respond to at least one text each time they drive. Texting while driving causes 11 teen deaths per day. 21% of teens who died at the wheel were distracted by mobile devices while distraction is a factor in 58% of crashes involving teens. While 94% admit the dangers of texting and driving, 35% admit to doing it. Mobile phone use while driving reduces the brain's driving related activity by 37%.
- A University of Utah study found that the reaction time of a teen using a mobile device was the same as a 70-year old's.
- 44% of teens use their mobile device at the dinner table, disrupting valuable family bonding time.
- Sometimes, children constantly check their phones despite wishing they could stop. This is compulsive behaviour. Those at risk of OCD may use the mobile phone as a focus for this behaviour, which often gets worse.
- Listening to videos and music via headphones can become addictive.
- Half of the teens surveyed by Common Sense Media felt they were addicted to their mobile phones. A third had tried to cut down but most had failed.
- 59% of parents believe their children are addicted to their devices while 77% feel that the distraction of mobile devices leads to antisocial behaviour at home (specifically not paying attention to others during family events).
- Mobile devices can cause arguments. 30% of teens and parents admit having daily arguments about them.
- Excessive mobile phone use can affect a child's ability to sit quietly and experience the present moment. It can also reduce their ability to reflect and to empathise with others. This can eventually lead to a disconnection from fellow humans, depression and the fraying of the social fabric that holds us together.
- Excessive mobile phone use leads to decreased neural connectivity, harming teens' ability to control their emotions.
- Mobile phones can be used as a way to escape reality, warping

perception and putting up a barrier between the young person and the 'real' world. They look like 'walking zombies'.

- Teens can also develop 'text neck,' a type of chronic strain from looking down at their mobile phone. Other common physical issues include eye strain, blurred vision and poor nutritional health. This is because when teens branch off into their own worlds, away from parental guidance and advice, a high proportion will start eating more junk food.
- Nine out of ten mobile phone users experience phantom vibrations where they feel their phone going off even when it isn't present.

What is gaming disorder?

While not all psychologists, psychiatrists, parents, children or therapists agree that it exists, gaming disorder has been defined in the ICD-11. The World Health Organisation (WHO) have set out three characteristics that define gaming disorder:

- Impaired control over gaming activity
- Prioritising gaming over other activities
- Continuing to play games despite negative outcomes

A diagnosis of gaming disorder may be made if the impact is severe enough to affect personal, family, social or educational functioning and, normally, if problems have persisted for a year or more.

Specialist gaming disorder centres have been set up to tackle this issue, including the NHS National Centre for Gaming Disorders in the UK, which comes under the wing of the National Centre of Behavioural Addictions, more commonly used for the treatment of problem gambling.

The centre takes both self-admissions and referrals and has worked with teens of all ages, as well as adults. Treatment does not begin until a young person reaches the age of 13. Nevertheless, parents of children as young as eight have contacted the centre for help.

As of 2022, over 300 referrals to the centre had been made, 89% male, and 200 of those in 2021 alone. Some of those children were spending up to 14 hours a day playing video games. This is clearly excessive, but it can be tough for parents to decide where to draw the line.

Is my child spending too much time on devices?

As clarified by the WHO, if the child is functioning in all other areas of life (having dinner with the family, doing their homework, exercising, socialising, doing chores and sleeping), a moderate amount of gaming is fine.

However, if they struggle to stick to limits on their gaming, choose gaming over every other activity and persist with gaming despite being frustrated or otherwise feeling bad about the game, you will need to act. Gaming might be your child's priority, but their education and wellbeing is yours.

Parents should be consistent: if a child is playing on a game for seven hours during a car journey, this may be easier for the parent, but it is teaching double standards. That same parent can't then insist that this behaviour is wrong at home.

Parents should not take the ability of games to be addictive lightly: children have been known to beg and steal for a spare device so that they can play games in secret.

If you have any strategies that work in this arena, I would be very interested to hear them. Please go to mpamind.com where you can email me or share your ideas with my followers on social media.

Let's come together and be a village, because it really does take a village to take care of and bring up all of our children. In the 21st Century, that village looks very different. Our village is no longer the few streets we live in, the church hall and the school our children go to. Our village is the whole world, and the caregivers of that world are, unfortunately, the tech giants. They embrace and bring in our children to play without safeguarding them enough. Safeguarding is improving but we have to work as a village to bring up our children and truthfully care for them. If someone in our village were getting our children hooked on gambling.

If someone were putting our children in the vicinity of sexual abusers, predators and pedophiles. If someone were helping our children to experiment with drugs and alcohol or run away from home. If somebody in our village were a bad influence on our children by saying, "Well, in actual fact, you can kill yourself by doing this." If somebody in our village were to teach our children how to throw their parents under the bus to get whatever they want because they've been doing it for years, would we stand for it? Would we just stand by and let all that happen? Because that's exactly what's happening in the tech world. That's exactly what's happening to our children in our global village, and we have to stop it. We have to say 'no' and now is the time.

Thank you Sharon Pursey for contributing to this book. We value you immensely in what you are managing to do and are attempting to do, and your vision is part of the village I want my children to be part of.

For more guidance, read:

21 Lessons for the 21st Century - Y.N. Harari

The Tech Diet for Your Child and Teen: The 7-Step Plan to Unplug and Reclaim Your Kid - B. Marshall

Are Your Kids Naked Online: How to Protect Your Tech-Savvy Kids from Online Self-Destruction - C. Good and L. Good

CHAPTER 6

SEXOPHOBIA: THE SCARY WORD

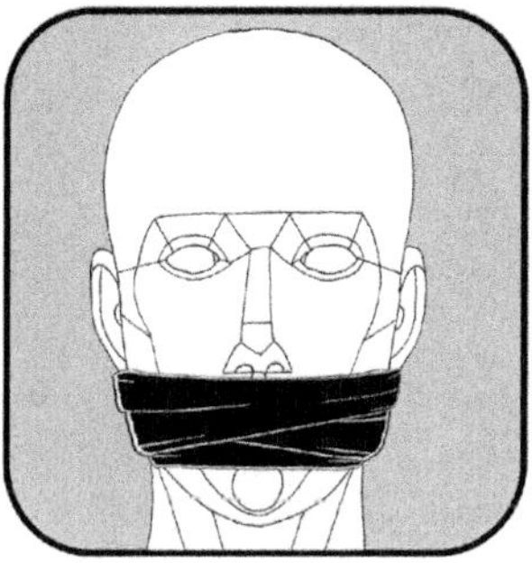

"Sex education needs to be the responsibility of each and every family member and caregiver. No one is going to do this for you! The advice below comes from me having to sort out the messes of families where the children knew nothing about safe and healthy sex."
- Michael Padraig Acton -

Having worked for the British NHS for a Young Person's Service in Morley Street, Brighton, UK as well as a hospital in Brighton, I saw everything that could be possible to see. Children were referred to my psychological services with pregnancies as young as 10 years of age. These were not about children in the sex trade or from abusive families or unhealthy environments. They were from every demographic and were children who had been unfortunate to become pregnant on their first time of having unsafe sex.

This involved me with educational nurses, gynaecological services, termination services, parents, the police at times and the child protection unit to make sure the children were being supported to be safe and well. This was just a small fraction of my work and doesn't include same sex issues, STIs, UTIs, attacks to future welfare and health, rapes or paedophiles.

Sex can be very healthy providing a young person understands what sex is, is aware of when sex is safe and healthy and has a door open to report anything that concerns them. Sex education needs to be the responsibility of every family member or caregiver.

Children and pornography exposure

If you are thinking that your child is too young to have been exposed to pornography, consider the results of several recent studies which found that more than half of adolescents have seen porn (either accidentally or deliberately), with the average age of first exposure between 11 and 12 years. As Dr. Amanda L. Giordano, assistant professor of counselling at the University of Georgia, correctly points out, it only takes a friend to pass over their smartphone in the playground and ask, "Have you seen this?"

If you have liberal views on children viewing porn, you should be aware that there is scientific evidence linking exposure to pornography to negative consequences. With no category (or 'schema') in their minds with which to compare what they see, how can developing teen minds understand what's normal and acceptable and what's fake and abhorrent. For example, unsafe sex and non-consensual sex are frequently depicted. With their lack of experience, knowledge and mental maturity, how can young people be expected to realise this is not the norm?

While some online porn is 'mainstream', much involves violence, fetishes and group sex. Over a fifth of US teens have seen violent porn, and this has been specifically linked to teen dating violence. With rape, choking and name-calling normalised through Internet porn movies, this is not surprising.

Porn can also affect children's self-esteem as they compare themselves with porn actors whose appearance and performances may be enhanced or faked. Viewing porn can also lead to young people objectifying themselves and others as sex objects. It is normal to be sexually curious and even aroused through porn, but teens who have been exposed to it often feel ashamed or guilty, and often keep it to themselves.

For example, one study found that over 70% of New Zealand teens had accidentally viewed porn, but that most didn't tell an adult about what they had seen. Therefore, parents and caregivers need to be proactive in talking to their children about porn and sex. It is their responsibility to promote healthy attitudes and behaviours around sex and relationships. Highlighting the misleading and damaging nature of online porn is an important part of this. Children and teens need a safe space where they can talk openly without feeling judged.

Parents can promote safe and healthy sex in the following ways:

- **Prepare your children.** Don't keep putting it off or assuming sex education at school is enough. You must find the language and prepare to go through this with your child.
- **Give them a condom.** Just as it's normal to give a girl a period starting kit well in advance of their first period, it's not a bad idea to give them a condom. You can still tell them you think it's too soon for them to have sex but if they get into a situation where they just can't stop themselves, they absolutely must be safe. Remember: sex doesn't have to happen at night or in a bedroom. It can happen in two or three minutes behind the bike shed or at a bus stop.
- **Don't discredit love.** Make sure your children know they will be loved and accepted no matter when they have sex and who with.
- **Be gender neutral.** Be mindful not to use the terms boyfriend and girlfriend as your child may be lesbian, gay, transgender or questioning. Using pronouns or ideas which prejudge how a relationship should be could traumatise them. This can lead to suicide.
- **Be aware of inappropriate touching.** This is not always obvious. For example, it can involve a friend or family member becoming excited when a child is sitting on their lap. If the adult then starts bouncing that child around this is not only scary for the child, but it is also sexual abuse. You need to find a way to make your child understand that if it feels wrong it probably is. It's a good idea for your child to have an exit strategy!

For more guidance, read:
Where did I Come From - P. Mayle
It's NOT the Stork - R. Harris
21st Century Guide to the Birds and the Bees - B. Messer and R. Luik

CHAPTER 7

HELP: HOMEWORK IS NOT JUST FOR KIDS

"A good 90% of children are not naturally scholastic. What do we need to do as parents to help the process?"
- Michael Padraig Acton -

As I said earlier, there are things that are negotiable with a child and things that are non-negotiable. Health, wellbeing and education are non-negotiable. How do we healthily instil the need to do homework? Most children (probably a good 90%) are not naturally scholastic; they're not interested in sitting down for two to three hours a night and sometimes during the weekend to be A-star students. What do we need to do, as parents or caregivers, to help the children in our care?

Parents can help by:

- **Making homework enjoyable and interactive.** Homework can be a social event. Excluding your child from the pack by making them work alone in their bedrooms can be counterproductive, especially if they are struggling and need help with understanding.
- **Leading by example.** Parents need to always take an interest in their children's homework. Sometimes this means putting other concerns to one side and sitting and helping them.

- **Removing devices.** Although a lot of homework is now done online, when this does not apply, turn off the router (and the TV) and remove smartphones and tablets. If you don't have a split router, plan your day around your child's homework too. That's the investment you should be prepared to make.
- **Finding ways to motivate.** Older, more studious children may be motivated by simply reminding them of the importance of homework for grades and success. Others may need more tailormade motivational tactics such as challenges, competitions and rewards for effort.
- **Making sure they're comfortable.** Children won't perform at their best when they are uncomfortable. If they need to have something to eat or go to the toilet, they should do this first. Their surroundings need to be quiet, well-lit and conducive to work.
- **Watching out for demotivating teachers.** Teachers should be encouraging in their attitude. Be aware of how your child is reacting to teacher input and arrange a meeting if you have any concerns.

For more guidance, read:

Calmer, Easier, Happier Homework: The Revolutionary Programme That Transforms Homework - N. Janis-Norton

Ending the Homework Hassle: Understanding, Preventing, and Solving School Performance Problems - J.K. Rosemond

Homework Help for Mums and Dads: Help Your Child Succeed - K. Dolby

CHAPTER 8

WHEN SUPPORT BACKFIRES: ENABLING

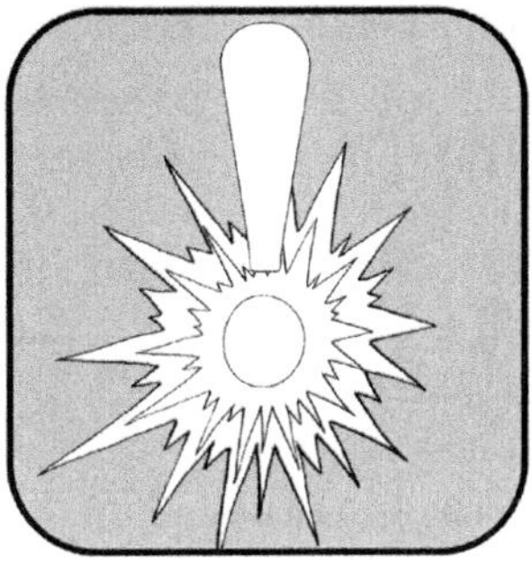

"When does helping your children mess them up? When you're throwing them fish rather than teaching them how to fish!"
- Michael Padraig Acton -

When does support end and enabling start? Support is having a step-by-step process or guide to help your children to achieve their goals. Enabling is achieving their goals for them. That is your barometer.

Where there is a set aim, support is helping your child move towards that goal. For example, if your child is doing gymnastics, you are supporting them by driving them to classes, paying for classes, helping them with their clothes, offering healthy encouragement and prompting social interactions.

Enabling is pandering to your child by doing things for them that they should be doing for themselves. It is going over and beyond what would be expected from a support framework. It happens more at the opposite side of the scale where a child is not moving towards their goals because they are not pulling their weight. For example, they might say they can't do their homework, or they don't feel well. The parent, rather than empathising while looking at the reality of the situation, instead takes what their child is saying as gospel and encourages them not to succeed. They may even take over from the child and complete their homework for them. This tends to happen when the parent is more interested in their child achieving high marks at school than improving their skills through doing the homework.

They are not encouraging their child to seek success through self-motivation, instead they are encouraging them to give up.

If your child is demotivated and achieving only because you are going above and beyond with your efforts, you are not supporting them but enabling.

Of course, you can let your child down if you don't support them enough. However, you can disempower them through enabling.

It's a sticky wicket!

Codependency and enabling behaviour

Sometimes parents are very dependent on their children doing well and they enable instead of support because of that. All parents should look in the mirror and think about the parenting they received as children. We tend to either copy this style, whether it is healthy or not, or to do the absolute opposite. For example, if we had a tough upbringing ourselves, sometimes we're overly kind and generous. The key to good parenting lies in finding the balance between this kindness and generosity and teaching our children to understand and respect rules and boundaries. This will prepare them well for living in the real world. Help them to be useful and have them be part of, and contribute to, your unit, whatever that unit may look like. That could be helping you with housework chores, serving the tea for a visiting friend or making conversation with an elderly relative.

For more guidance, read:

Balanced Parenting Guide: How to Balance Between Love, Nurturing and Enabling Your Child – M. Viskovich

Kind Yet Firm: Discipline Your Toddler the Positive Parenting Way – G. Stockholm

Parenting: The Ultimate Parenting Manual. How to Promote and Support the Physical, Emotional, Social and Intellectual Development of Your Child - A. Kats

Detachment and Enabling: Seven Simple Steps - J. M. Knowlton and R.D. Chaitin

CHAPTER 9

PIVOTING IN PARENTING: PUSH-PULL

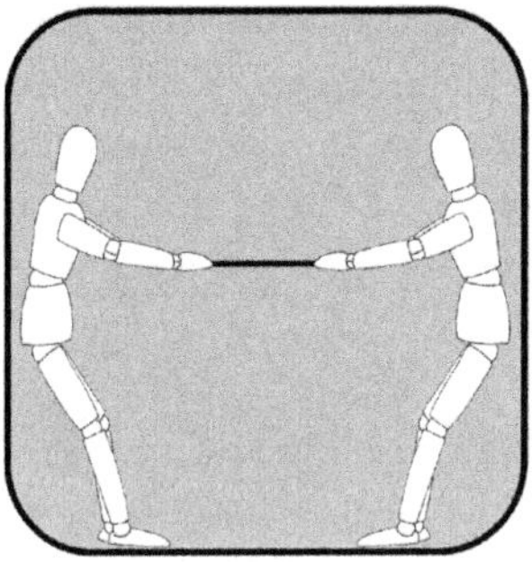

"Caring for our children's health, wellbeing and education is a legal and moral duty but it would be crazy to think we can parent our children in the same way throughout their lives."
- Michael Padraig Acton -

Parents often experience issues when their child moves to a new stage of development. They continue to parent in the same way they did before, but find this no longer works. Pivoting is about changing things up when there's clearly a corner to be turned. Parents need to see what's working, and do more of that, but change direction in areas where things are not working. This will provide immediate and future benefits for your child and your family unit.

Infants
Infants need feeding, sheltering, nurturing, observation and routine. Parents need to teach them how to accept new things because neonates are born with a fear of change.

Starting school
Young school children need help finding their voice and understanding opinion but also accepting instruction.

Parents will need to restrict their child because they will push boundaries to grow. Toddlers learn rapidly through their senses so encourage exposure to what's healthy and safe. We also need to listen to our children and share in their amazement about everyday experiences.

Parents must understand what the school is teaching including the hidden curriculum of etiquette and social intelligence. They must help with homework. If there are disabilities, a social worker, educational nurse or paediatrician can guide them through this important stage. It is every child's right to have access to these professionals.

From 11 to 18

During this challenging time, the parent is still legally responsible for their child, so it is important to understand what we have to control and what's negotiable. Health, wellbeing and education are not up for debate because they are the three mandatory areas in law for which a parent is responsible. This is the time where we help our children with their socialisation and educational choices, while helping them to overcome difficulties and social issues.

There are huge pressures on teenagers with exams, studying, sexual maturation, sexual preference and gender identity. If a child is on the autistic spectrum, this may have gone undetected until now, at a time when they are required to be more socially independent. If your child is having difficulty being with peers, even Googling 'autism spectrum' or 'ASD' can help indicate whether you need to approach Child and Adult Mental Health Services (CAMHS), a children's social worker, paediatric psychologist, psychiarist or any other local services in your area.

Many teens experience divorce and parental separation and they do have a lot of choice in court. A large number drop their parents' management at this time or decide not to see one of the parents. It's important to help the child feel safe, heard and engaged with boundaries (e.g., the non-negotiables discussed earlier). There is always mediation available through school, healthcare service, charities or the police.

Elaborated versus restrictive codes

When a child reaches secondary school, our management style needs to shift from dictatorial, using restrictive codes, to peer support, using elaborated codes.

Studies have found that in most working-class families, children communicate within restrictive codes. Everything is dictated by the parents and the child is told what to do, "Shut up; there's no discussion!"

Elaborated codes, usually used in middle- and upper-class households, involve reason, accepting different opinions, hearing the child's voice and discussing the bigger picture, "We can choose several ways forward, but this may be the best one at the moment."

Above all, realise that you are the adult, and you are helping a process; you never own the child. If you are reacting too much, you need to step back and realise you may be living through your child rather than helping them with the process. Feelings invoked in us are not always shared by our children and although they may be interested in the medal they won, their small world doesn't include our views on *how* they should have achieved. The most important thing is to encourage and be pleased when our children make mistakes because this is how they learn to become better people.

For more guidance, read:

There's No Such Thing as 'Naughty' - K. Silverton

The Young Child: Development from Prebirth Through Age Eight - M.B. Puckett and J.K. Black

Brighter Futures: A Parents' Guide to Raising Happy, Confident Children in the Primary School Years - Dr L. Dawes, N. Gorringe, Dr L. Russell, Dr K. Hodson, Dr J. Swanston and Dr S. Wimshurst

CHAPTER 10

REJECTION, WHAT'S THAT?

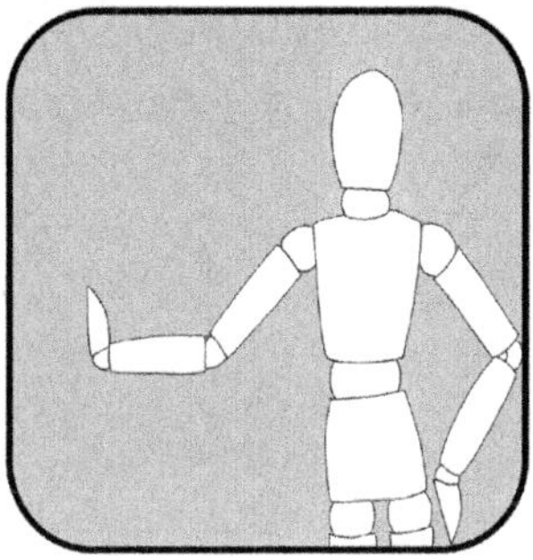

"A child rejecting their parent is healthy–to a point. However, if you, as a parent are rejecting your child then that is abandonment and is unacceptable!"
- Michael Padraig Acton -

As a parent, it is our natural position to be rejected by our kids as they grow. In fact, it is more dangerous for them to be clingy and anxious The technical term for this is attachment disorder and indicates that the child hasn't actually separated from their parent.

Some boys have been known to push their mothers through a wall. At an unpremeditated point in their development, they violently reject mother. This is normal. It's an extreme example but a child will fight for their territory.

In the post-Victorian Western world, we hold our children until 18 legally, whereas they are adults in their own right by 13 or even younger: not adults in terms of being able to survive and make important decisions in our society but they are looking for their own territory. They want their own kitchen and bathroom; they are becoming sexually mature; they want space to play their music. They want everything to be about them and rightly so. However, we need to teach them how to do that within a safe and healthy family and social environment. Yes, they want to play drums, but we need to help them think about when and where would be appropriate and how we can be thoughtful about other people.

Rejection is tough and sometimes it's very painful. How do you know when your child is abusing you though? Shock! Horror! Child abuse of parents happens and seems to be on the rise. It can happen when boundaries are not put in place; when parents are both working and the child is left on their own too much; when the child learns how to manipulate social services, the police and everything else in order to feed a bad/ unhealthy habit. How can you gauge whether it is healthy or not? If you feel you are being rejected to the point of abuse, it is always good to check this out with a paediatrician, mental health worker or even family, colleagues or somebody you trust. Just talk about what you're feeling and what's happening to see whether it's within the realms of acceptability.

Even feeling rejected to the point you just can't go on any more might be natural. It's very tough to see your child reject your handholding. It's very difficult to have a child not eat what you've slaved over to make them for dinner just because they're being individual and separate to you. But when a child healthily rejects us, they are trying to find their own centre of gravity, their own place where they can feel safe and operate.

Never reject your child! You are there to facilitate, nurture, nourish, support and guide them. If, at any time, you feel you are casting them aside or rejecting them, you are the problem!

For more guidance, read:

Safeguarding Children Exposed to Narcissistic Parenting, Coercive Control and Parental Alienation - A. Smith
Living Without a Father: Heal from Dad's Rejection - S. Tonder
Overcoming Parental Rejection and Hurts - E. Middleton

CHAPTER 11

CHILDREN WHO ATTACK PARENTS: THE HIDDEN ABUSE

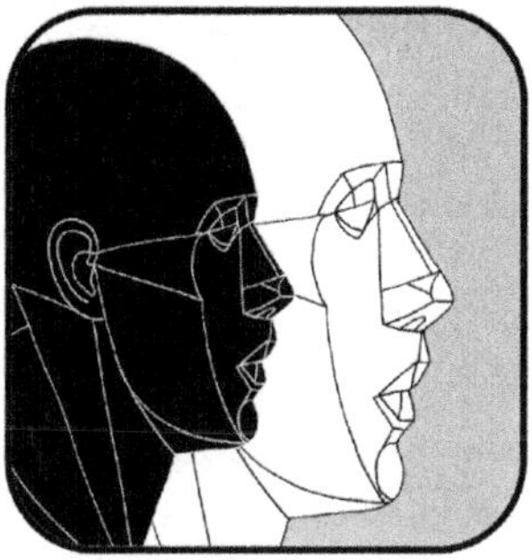

"Why isn't there a legal definition for child to parent abuse?"
- Michael Padraig Acton -

It is only in the past ten years or so that child-on-parent violence (CPV) has been recognised as a specific form of domestic abuse. And there is still far too little being said about this common issue.

As with all domestic abuse, CPV can affect any family. Parents living in caravan parks as well as those living in mansions are sometimes subjected to sustained and horrific abuse from children they are responsible for. Some child-to-parent abusers have been adopted and were themselves victims of trauma from an early age. However, most cases involve the child's natural parent. And it is not just adolescents and older children who are responsible for the abuse. In some cases, children as young as four have put parents in hospital with the ferocity of their attacks.

As with most domestic violence, statistics suggest that women–in this case mothers–are usually the prime target, although children do attack their fathers, siblings, other relatives and pets too.

The effects of child on parent abuse can be wide-ranging and severe. They include:

- Physical injury (the UK's Metropolitan Police reported 125 instances of GBH caused by children on adults in 2016).
- Sickness and absence from work.
- Emotional and mental health problems.
- Harm and disruption to siblings.
- Partner relationship breakdown.
- Isolation from friends and family.
- Lack of respite due to childcare issues.
- Disruption to education.

Some of the signs that a child is becoming abusive include:

- They are damaging property or stealing from other family members.
- They are hurting or threatening to hurt or kill you. They might bite, pinch, scratch, push, punch and kick, use weapons or throw objects.
- They attack you verbally (e.g., telling you they hate you, swearing at or humiliating you).
- They are threatening to hurt or kill themselves or are engaging in openly risky behaviour.
- They hurt or try to kill family pets.
- You worry about your own safety or that of other family members or pets.
- You change your own behaviour to avoid a scene (walking on eggshells).

In summary, any behaviour which is controlling, destructive, dangerous or intimidating is a form of abuse and needs to be dealt with before it becomes normalised.

But what is an abused parent to do? Unlike in adult domestic abuse, the victims are unable to leave the relationship, as they are also their abuser's legal protector. Parents also worry that they will criminalise their child, affecting their future.

There is also no specific legal definition for child-to-parent abuse and no one agency is responsible for dealing with it. It wasn't until 2015 that the UK government published guidance on the issue.

Family therapy can help in some cases, but the parents must contact a counsellor or therapist who is experienced and professionally qualified.

Other sources of help parents can try include:

- PEGS (https://www.pegsupport.co.uk).*
- National Domestic Abuse helpline: 0808 2000 247.*
- Family Lives: 0808 800 2222.*
- The 'Who's In Charge?' program.*
- Child on parent abuse online forums. These can provide moral support and tips from other parents going through a similar situation.

Google for your local support for child on parent abuse.

As with any emergency situation, if there is an immediate threat of harm, you must call 999, 911 or your local emergency number.

CHAPTER 12

WE ARE NOT NECESSARILY RESPONSIBLE FOR OUR CHILDREN'S OUTCOMES AND BEHAVIOURS

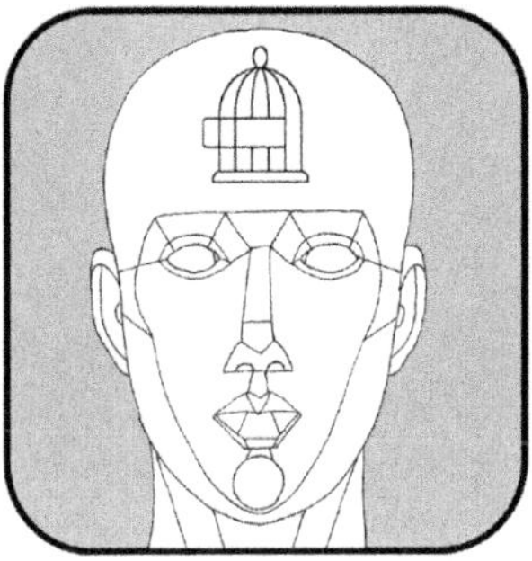

"The best parents can have poorly behaved or murderous offspring."
- Michael Padraig Acton -

How often do I hear people say of children, "Oh, look at their parents. That's why they're that way." Well, that's very untrue. Yes, as parents we influence our children; we advise them within the spectrum of our experience and context. However, we can only develop them to a certain point. After that, we can only encourage them and provide advice. We don't put drugs up our children's noses, or make them drink to excess, or put up a pole for them to dance on (of course, some people use pole dancing solely for exercise, but I am referring to the use of pole dancing in adult entertainment and the related sex industry. I have worked with many sex workers and have found them to be the most amazing, charming people who have, like us all, have hit troubled times. It depends on their reasons for working in this trade as to what kind of support or help they need). My point is that whatever our children decide to do, it is their choices at the end of the day. Influences come from everywhere: peer pressure, how their brains are wired, the balance of chemicals, the environment, etc. It could be just that they get in with the wrong crowd–or the right crowd!

So, as much as we can be proud and say, "Well done!" for their accomplishments, we can't be responsible for them. In the same way, we can't say, "I did that to you. You're uncaring, greedy, selfish or a thief because of how I brought you up." Everyone has a choice.

If we look at abused children, tortured children, children who have been brought up in poverty, many of them choose and have the opportunity to do well. Many can't. They just can't see past that abuse or deprivation. We're all individuals as humans. The one thing a parent must never say is, "I caused my child to make those choices" because at the end of the day, you can't *make* an adult child do something. You can only advise and encourage them.

Myra Hindley had a mother. Jeffrey Epstein had a father. Were they responsible for their children's actions? Mother Teresa had parents. Hitler had parents. Martin Luther King and Gandhi had parents. Who was responsible for their saintly or abhorrent behaviour? Who was responsible for them making their choices? Was there a spiritual 'soul contract' element?

If you are basking in the afterglow of your children's wellbeing, it's not because you put them there; it's because of their healthy choices. Likewise, if you are in deep, dark depression about your child's unhealthy behaviour... you did not put them there. Your children have choices.

We, as parents of adult children, are only there to guide and love and support them in the directions they choose–if they are healthy. And if they are hurting or damaging us in order to stay in their unhealthy place, we must remove ourselves.

The key is to accept you are proud or unhappy but not responsible. Even if you have been an abhorrent parent, your child can still be amazingly successful. Equally, they can be amazingly disgusting, even if you have been a wonderful, caring parent.

We have choices as humans. These may be limited by our context, but we have choices to be kind or greedy, a slave or free.

CHAPTER 13

ANXIETY: HELPFUL AND DESTRUCTIVE

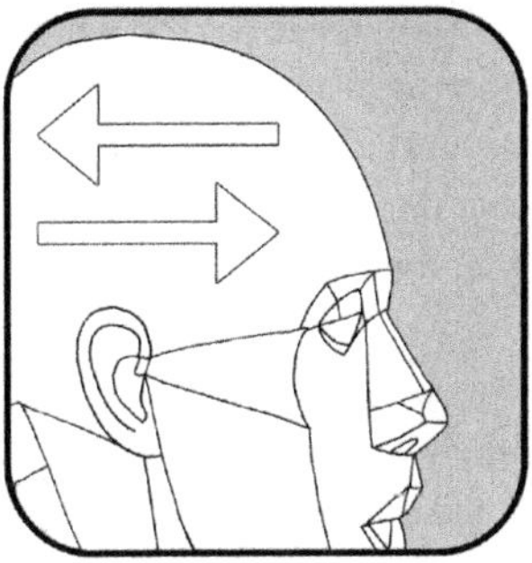

"Anxiety can lead to hopelessness and suicide! It's important we, as parents, help our children to manage it."
- Michael Padraig Acton -

Humans need anxiety to stay safe. Several hundred years ago, before Western society, our lives depended on it. When faced with a threat to survival, our bowel would empty and we would vomit, emptying our body so we could run or fight to the ultimate. Nowadays, we call this irritable bowel syndrome (IBS) induced by anxiety. Previously, we would fight or run, which would then abate the adrenaline in our body and bring the body back to relaxation.

Today, our threats are usually abstract: we rarely face being eaten by an animal or attacked by an intruder. Our threats might come from social media or from seeing the news.

Many things can induce anxiety in children: bullying, pain, feeling different, family issues, pressures from social media, exams, body image, romance and friendships.

How do we know when our child's anxiety is unhealthy and how do we manage it?

Pre-teens can usually be soothed by a nurturing parent but what happens if you can't soothe them and their anxiety gets out of control, like a runaway train?

Children rarely just open up and talk, so you need an excuse. When my daughter was growing up, we used to make meatballs together. During this activity, she would start talking to me about different things and if something was causing huge anxiety, she would tell me about it. She never knew we made meatballs because she was having problems. We just 'decided' to make meatballs and she started talking.

The most important thing a child needs is recognition, to know they can park their problems with you and that if they need assistance with something they can rely upon you to not take over but to assist them in finding a resolution and comforting them.

Things change for older teenagers and anxiety takes on many new forms. As a parent, you also have less control over what they are exposed to both through social media and in person.

Older teens also have to deal with sexual maturation and bodily development. Unfortunately, with our Western world, we're told when and how things should happen. If they don't follow that pattern, we might feel things are wrong or we're wrong, bad or different. Then there's Hollywood and media and what we are told we should look and behave like. It's really good to bring to our teenage children the idea that that celebrity photograph was taken after eight hours of make-up and three hours of personal training. . . and has been airbrushed.

So, what is our role as a parent of a child with anxiety?

- Never ridicule or make light of their worries or tell them they shouldn't be feeling that way.
- Take their worries seriously. Hear (don't just listen, hear) what your child is saying. Tell them they are not alone. Ask what you can do to help them solve the issue.
- If there is no resolution at the time, comfort them, promise you will revisit the issue tomorrow and be sure to revisit as promised.
- If the worry has been dissolved, make sure you monitor the situation. Sometimes, simply talking can solve the problem.

- If you're an anxious parent, you're going to have an anxious child. If your child acts like a cowboy sleeping with a gun under their pillow, you might want to take a good, hard look at yourself. Try some relaxation techniques or even see a mental health advisor about how you might be able to create a more peaceful, serene environment for your children to function in.

For more guidance, read:

An Introduction to Coping with Anxiety - B. Hogan and L. Brosan

Helping Your Anxious Teen: Positive Parenting Strategies to Help Your Teen Beat Anxiety, Stress, and Worry - S.A. Josephs PhD

The Opposite of Worry: The Playful Parenting Approach to Childhood Anxieties and Fears - L.J. Cohen

CHAPTER 14

WHAT'S WINNING ABOUT? ENCOURAGEMENT VERSUS CONTROL

"We have to bring the gift out of the child.
Making them perform an activity until they feel it is the only way they can gain your reward is verging on abuse!"
- Michael Padraig Acton -

When does encouragement become control and who owns the encouragement guidelines?

When we are encouraging our child to do something, we have to make sure it is safe and manageable for them, and we have to ensure it is age appropriate.

There's a healthy level of narcissism in parenting whereby we live through our children's accomplishments and are rewarded by their development. This is natural. It gets unhealthy when we start to encourage our children to do something to fulfil our ambition. This could be a realised ambition: a mum pushing their child through dance school because they were a dancer or a dad pushing a child through football coaching because that's how they felt they achieved. It could also be a frustrated one. Perhaps you were a failed chess player and want your child to be the best chess player in school or in their club.

It doesn't work that way!

We have to look at what our child's skill set is, what they feel comfortable with and what they're interested in and go with that. It could be creative, scholastic or sports-orientated but like Mr Miyagi's internal image of the completed bonsai tree from the movie *The Karate Kid*, your child's vision of accomplishment is always right. We're so busy doing with our children what society tells us we should be doing with them, even at what age and level they should be doing it, we sometimes miss the point.

Bringing the gift out of the child is your mantra for encouragement versus control.

How do we know if we are controlling our children rather than encouraging them to bring their gift out? If our child can't catch a ball, we can help them for a while but how comfortable will that child be playing tennis? Should we encourage them to try it five times and then drop it if not? Or should we control them and make them go to the court until they feel that is the only way they can please us and gain our affirmation that they are a good person? That's verging on abuse!

A large part of it is self-reflection. Ask yourself, "If I didn't take them to tennis next week would they really be bothered? Would I see relief?"

All children need to be encouraged though. They need choices. They need exposure to things. Sometimes children can seem very lazy but is this really the case? From ten years of age until their twenties, humans produce more of the hormone melatonin as part of sexual maturation. Melatonin is taken as a sleeping aid in adult life, so when your teenager is lying in bed saying, "I'm exhausted," they really are. For parents, it's about creating structure, using light, providing support and encouraging our children to do more with their life.

So, why do some children seem to suffer from this hormone and others don't?

You can fight through tiredness–you can fight through melatonin–if you have a passion. If your child has found their passion and you're encouraging them, great. If your child hasn't found their passion, your best job as a parent is to help them find one (or several); something that will get them through that tiredness barrier and get them out and enjoying life. This is encouragement and support!

Throughout this book, my main emphasis will be about putting the child in the center, hearing their voice, and bringing out their gifts and ideas. If you're controlling your child, you're damaging your relationship with them and maybe even damaging their future!

For more guidance, read:

Wonderful Ways to Love a Child: Inspired Ideas for Raising Happy, Healthy Children - J. Ford and A. Ford

Am I Yelling: 45 Highly Effective Strategies to Control and Manage Anger for Parents - T. Zaid and J. Green

Calm Parents, Happy Kids: The Secrets of Stress-Free Parenting - Dr L. Markham

CHAPTER 15

LISTEN AND LEARN: KATHY DAVIS, LICENSED PARENTING EXPERT OF 38 YEARS

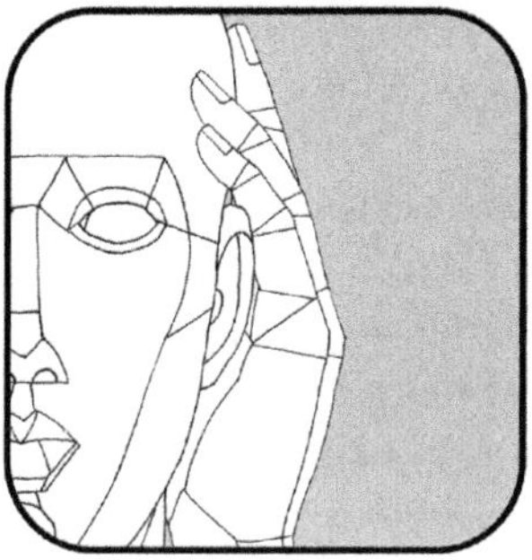

"The best education we could want is the wisdom, patience and learning of a professional mother to hundreds of children over several decades. Most humbling."
- Michael Padraig Acton -

Michael Padraig Acton (MPA): So, Kathy, for how many years have you been a saint with children?

Kathy Davis (KD): [laughing] I've been looking after children for 38 years. I first started looking for work in day care when we lived in Arizona. It was really hard because we didn't know people.

In small towns, like where we live now, you know by word of mouth who's good and who you should avoid. There, we had to look in the newspaper for want ads. I did get some names of licensed people from the state, but it was still hard to find good care. I went to a couple of licensed homes and there were actually chunks of broken glass in the back yard. Then, I found a nice lady who was really good, but I only worked part-time. You can only employ so many people when you're licensed so it was financially more economical for her to get a full-time person–she gave me my notice after a few months.

My husband, Dave, worked third shifts, so we tried letting him stay up with our son David after work, while I was working, but that didn't work out.

I thought, 'I've got to find a way to earn money from home,' as it was too hard to find good childcare–with me working only part-time especially. So, I decided to start doing childcare myself. I found some really great families and got licensed by the state soon after. The people we met in day-care were amazing and became really good friends. It worked out really well when my children were little because they had playmates. We would do zoo trips and field trips with the parents. My day-care families would keep my kids for the weekend or overnight and we would do the same for them. It was really nice, and I had an income and got to enjoy being home with my own children.

MPA: I struggled with being the father of one. How do you do it?

KD: It wasn't that bad when they were little because I was young and full of energy. Back then you didn't even have to have kids in car seats so I could put them in the car and take them to the park. I would take five children to the park. I don't transport anymore as it is too much of a liability nowadays.

MPA: My daughter is 35 and your children are grown adults. We're now in a very different era. What is it like for parents to entrust you with their kids and what struggles do you see parents having these days? What is different?

KD: Right now, with Covid, it's hard. You also hear horror stories about children being molested and beaten in day-care and you don't know what goes on in somebody else's home. Parents do feel more secure that I'm licensed because licensors (quality and policy control) just drop in, we don't know when they're coming. They're very thorough. We can't even have toothpaste in our bathroom cabinet as it could make a child ill or worse. Now, I have never heard of a child eating toothpaste but obviously there have been cases and that is why they made it a rule. There are so many rules and restrictions, and you get written up if you don't follow through with them. There are rules that seem silly and many that are very good. The object is to keep the children safe. Now, I am not saying that unlicensed day-care is not good. There are many I know personally that do an amazing job. We are just inspected regularly and put in 15 hours of class time each year as well.

MPA: If you had somebody coming to you to train to be a licensed child caregiver, what things would you absolutely make sure they could do?

KD: First and foremost, you have to love and care about children. You have to have patience and really good time management skills. If you don't, you're in trouble. I've had up to eight children, although I only have five now that I'm older. They are all usually here by seven-thirty and you've got to give them breakfast, inside play, outside play time, do your school curriculum, lunch, naps, snack and almost time to go home. Juggle that with changing diapers, feeding babies and tons of paperwork. You have to juggle a lot and if you don't keep up with it, you're not going to make it. It will overwhelm you.

MPA: How do you do it?

KD: Over the years, I have learned a lot from my own experience and with the help of mentors along the way. You have to keep a good schedule and routine. Children always do better with consistency.

MPA: What other skills would you be looking for if you were to take on someone who could uphold your reputation as a child caregiver?

KD: I'm a control freak so I wouldn't trust anybody else. That's why I've never opened a centre. My husband always wanted me to open one and have people work for me and watch the children. But I would be nervous not being the one in charge of the children to make sure things were done the way they are supposed to be. Again, I would look for someone who loves children and enjoys seeing them learn and grow, and someone who can multitask.

MPA: My biggest issue as a dad was calming down a storm. I used to try and fix stuff, but I realised that sometimes, by trying to fix it, I was fuelling it.

KD: When things start getting out of control here, I just get them involved with something else and side-track them. I will try and see if they are hungry, thirsty, need their diaper changed or are feeling ill. If everything is good and it is a younger child, sometimes they just need a little ten-minute rest or nap. Now that I have done this for so long, I can usually see it happening before it starts and head it off at the pass.

MPA: Our readers/listeners and myself will be saying, 'And how the heck do you do that?' How do you not get frazzled and what advice would you give to somebody, a parent, who is overwhelmed?

KD: We learned in our child and abuse classes that if, for instance, a baby is crying, you have tried everything and nothing works and the baby isn't ill, you put the baby in a safe place, let them cry for a while and keep checking on them. You don't want to get overwhelmed, as that is when many parents harm their child. Usually, when a toddler is upset, it is because they are tired and/or hungry. Sometimes, if they're fighting over a toy, you just redirect them. Children of three sometimes just need time out, not as a punishment but to cool down.

MPA: So, time out is important. What advice would you give a parent whose child is acting out?

KD: Depends on each situation. I still say consistency is the best. I see some parents that will get after the child for one thing and then the next time they don't. They get confused due to the lack of consistency. Try to stay calm. Sometimes that child might need more attention from Mom or Dad if they have been working all day. If it gets really bad, I suggest they seek counsel from a professional.

MPA: So, you're saying you create these really wonderful babies, toddlers and children because you give them a really strong framework and they know where they are and what they're doing? Most parents when welcoming a baby turn their whole lives upside down to accommodate their new-born... I guess this is making a rod for your own back.

KD: Yes. Structure is very important for little children. They like to know what's expected and what's coming next. It makes children feel safe to know they have boundaries. Not saying that you should not love that baby, toddler and child to pieces.

MPA: What advice would you give to a family that may have a disabled child? What about families with a destructive child or one where the parents work 12-hour shifts? What would you suggest to parents that have been dealt a really beautiful child but a difficult hand of cards and are struggling to get that routine down?

KD: I try my best to give them that routine at my house. I do feel bad for many parents. I've had families with three kids that are at my house at six in the morning and they weren't picked up until almost five at night. So, by the time they get home at five thirty, Mom's got two hours to do laundry, help with the homework, make supper and spend time with the kids before they're in bed. And they have to go to bed early because they have to get up so early. They are very good parents but just have so much on their plate. There have been a few children with anger issues who have had to go to counselling, and it has really helped.

MPA: What did you think about bringing to the table today? What kind of things do you think might help people?

KD: Parents need to take great care in choosing a good quality childcare, be it a licensed home or a non-licensed home. Children's brains develop the quickest in their first five years and getting someone to help your child develop to their potential is important. Children can be taught in many ways at this age, best through play. You can teach almost anything through play as well as a curriculum. You just need a good provider to do it. Teaching doesn't just begin when children start school, it begins at birth. I know parents really appreciate that I teach their children their numbers, shapes and letters and to learn to use scissors and write their name. It works best when parents work on this at home too, but some just don't have time. I do a regular curriculum and we learn through play, so the children also learn many good social skills such as saying 'please' and 'thank you', how to not interrupt and to take turns. If your child isn't doing some of these things by school age, most catch up very quickly. They all learn at different times and in different ways and that is OK. I do take pride in seeing the children learn and grow.

MPA: My daughter would only eat sausages, beans and chips for eight years. Back then, it was seen as horrific that she wasn't eating green vegetables. But for a quiet life, I said, "OK, it's fish finger sandwiches; sausage, beans and chips and as much ham as you can reach in the fridge and get." That was my life, I'm being very honest. I was working several jobs, studying and struggling. In psych, the first thing we were taught about was food management. Children's first power is what and whether to eat or not.

KD: When I look back, I would make my first child sit there until he ate his food; if he didn't, I would wrap it up and give it to him again later. I would never do that to a child again. I told him I'm surprised he turned out so well. I felt very pressured by certain family members to make them eat all of their food including their veggies. It made me feel like a bad parent. I will never make another child eat something they don't want again. Now, I am not saying if you don't eat anything healthy you can still have ice cream for dessert either. It is a control issue for the parents and the child; it is not healthy to force children to eat. They come around and

I have yet to see a child go hungry for very long. I also feel most of my day-care children eat exceptionally well and I think it is because I don't make a big deal out of them eating. If you pressure them each time, I feel they start to dread mealtime and that in itself causes more issues.

MPA: So, you did your parenting to please your family members?

KD: Yes, in the food issue I did, and it was wrong of me to do that. I see many of my day-care parents struggle with the same issue. But, as I got older and more confident, that changed. Family members mean well, and it was how they were raised, I am sure.

MPA: How do you manage it when a child doesn't eat all day and is just pushing your buttons?

KD: Most of them will eat eventually. I will bribe once in a while and say, "We've got these great treats if you eat some of your food," but I never push it. Because I am licensed, I belong to the Child and Adult Care Food Program. It is a group that supports healthy eating and they come unexpectedly three times a year to make sure we are serving healthy meals and snacks. The children are all served a fruit, vegetable, protein, whole grain and milk. I have never had a child not eat at least one or two of the foods served.

MPA: I think the biggest thing you're saying is that you've learnt not to react, whereas if a child sees a caregiver or a parent react to them not eating food, they've then got the power.

KD: Definitely. Eating and going potty are the only things they can control. We can guide them, but they have the final say.

MPA: In fact, the second part of this book is about how to parent adult children. It really is different because we need to be very careful. We need to be advisory, but we can't tell them what to do. It's not our place.

However, if they don't take our advice, we have to swallow it, literally, when it comes to food.

KD: That's true. Parenting adult children is something we shouldn't do. My feelings are if that adult child is living in my house, then I have the right to set up certain rules. If they are going to school or needing temporary help, I am happy to have them home. But they need to act like adults and pitch in: offer to help around the house and clean up after themselves. If kids are not in school, I think they need to pay rent or be putting money in the bank each week and not just playing video games and going out and blowing their money each weekend. My eldest son followed our guidelines and was able to purchase his first home aged 22. Our middle child didn't like our plan, so he moved out. Our youngest went to college and then to California to start his career. I would help any of my children if they needed me. But my goal was to teach them to be independent and I was blessed with all three of them.

MPA: Fantastic. I work with parents from a large variety of backgrounds. Some are so poor they live in a garage. At the other end of the spectrum are those with titles, multiple homes, staff, helpers, butlers and drivers. I have worked with these families a lot throughout my career and still do occasionally. What advice would you give them because I used to get called quite regularly with a parent saying, "My child's doing drugs," or "My child's not behaving," etc. The child could be anything from eight, nine years of age up to 21.

KD: Eight, nine years old doing drugs? That is so scary.

MPA: Yes, unfortunately. Sometimes the parents moved from house to house and if the children weren't in boarding school, they would be left in the house with a nanny or two–or even three–a driver, housekeeper, cook, etc. and they'd be taken to their friends' houses in a Rolls Royce or a Bentley. This sounds bizarre and fictional but it's actually not. The parents used to want me to fix their children and I would say, "Well, OK, but the intake has to be with the family, so both parents if that's possible, or the main caregivers and the child." I used to ask them, "When your 14-year-old goes off to their friend's, who's at that household?" And they would say, "We don't know." I would say, "OK, so you're not at home and your children are being looked after by all these people. What makes you think that the house they're going to, in the same neighbourhood, worth the same amount of money, doesn't also have no parental control there? What makes you think that the driver's going to tell you where they're taking the child, risking their job?" Because some of these children would know the social system very well, from the Internet or from peer support at school, and they would know how to twist their stories and get social services involved. Even in these gilded cages kids would say, "Parents back off or I'm going to say this about you and I'm going to say that about the driver. . ." What advice would you give parents who are in this situation and can't be with their children?

KD: Those kids did not have parents as far as I'm concerned. They had sperm donors. They weren't there for their kids. That's another reason I continue to do day-care. I used to think that when my children were all in school, I could go and do something else. Then I thought, 'Who's going to watch them in the summer? Who's going to watch them on Christmas break and spring break?' Could my eldest have watched the other two by that point? Probably. But it was more important to me to be there for them.

MPA: So, what advice would you give them?

KD: They've got to be parents. You have to be there physically and mentally for your children. You have to teach and guide them and do your best to keep them safe.

MPA: So, what you're saying, if you're a parent, is that you need to be responsible and you need to follow through with your child?

KD: Yes. It is the hardest and most rewarding job there is to be a parent.

Those kids need you, even when they are teenagers and pushing you away. That is when they need you the most.

MPA: I can see that it's affecting you and it affects me too. It used to make my blood boil. We used to call it babysitting in therapy, where parents really want you to fix their kids.

KD: It is the parents who need to be fixed.

MPA: Exactly. If somebody came to you for help and said, "It's not working. I need to do it differently." What advice would you give them? Perhaps they don't know any better because they grew up this way too?

KD: Talk to your child; know what they are doing, who their friends are. We called it Parent Patrol in our day. The parents, we all knew each other; we all knew the kids and they were at each other's houses all the time. We worked as a group to keep our kids safe and out of trouble. If any of us had any inkling they were up to no good, we would contact each other. It was like a group support system. One stupid mistake and it could ruin your child's future. You can't watch them every second and you don't want to be a helicopter parent but don't be that parent that isn't there at all either. Make sure your children know you're proud of them and also if they don't follow the rules, there are consequences.

MPA: We are writing a chapter on responsible parenting. What are your guidelines for responsible parenting?

KD: Let them know you love them unconditionally, but you have to parent along with that love. You've got to know where your kids are, who their friends are, what they're doing. And you need to make your kids accountable. If they lie about it, there must be consequences for their actions.

MPA: When is it healthy control and when would it be unhealthy control… because there's a fine line between those two?

KD: I always felt I should have some control over my children until they graduated and then, for those that did live here, the rules lightened up. They could stay at a friend's house all night, but they had to let me know so I am not worried when they aren't there in the morning. My kids were not allowed to drink alcohol in our house until they were 21. I didn't want anyone leaving our house and getting in an accident.

Our boys all started working around 15 years of age. Part-time to work around their schooling and sports. They learned a lot of valuable lessons on working with the public and what it felt like to earn your own money, budget, and save for purchases. They learned to show up to work on time and plan and ask permission if they needed time off. I think you feel differently when you buy something with the money you earn yourself rather than money that was given to you.

MPA: So, to respect and value things.

KD: I asked all three of my kids, "Was I too hard on you guys?" and they all said no, other than Justin who said the midnight curfew at high school kind of hindered him. Lol.

MPA: That's good feedback. How many children have you parented as a carer?

KD: I wish we had kept track. I still get Christmas cards from the very first two children I ever watched. We are now Facebook friends. One of them is a lieutenant colonel in the Air Force. Many of the children and parents still keep in touch. I met one of my best friends through day-care.

MPA: You've really touched these people's lives.

KD: I think so. And they've touched mine.

MPA: There's a bit of Kathy in all of these people.

KD: Yes, and them in me.

MPA: You have a wonderful, grounded, real nature to you. Where does that come from?

KD: Thank you. I think with age comes wisdom. You learn what is important and what is not so important as you get older. I feel I was blessed to grow up when the world was a different place and had wonderful parents. I have an amazing family, great friends and love my day-care families present and past. I have so much to be grateful for.

I have day-care children that have been gone for years, some college age, who stop back out of the blue. One young man was in middle school, and he stopped over and asked if he could come in. I said, "Sure." He walked through the house, gave me a hug and left! When we were at a basketball game, this same one came across the gym, up the bleachers, gave me a hug and left without a word!

MPA: What do you think that was about?

KD: I hope it was because they had good memories of being here and wanted to revisit them. I have these children ten hours a day, five days a week. I become like a second mom to them, and this is their second home. Some of the parents and I both cry when it is time to move on. It isn't easy losing a child you have had every day for sometimes eight years.

MPA: So, you give these children security, a sense of calm.

KD: I would like to think so. I am strict. They have to follow rules. I raise my voice at times, but I don't know how many times a day they give me hugs and say, "I love you, Kathy." It's nice. A lot of people think I'm crazy for still doing this, but I still enjoy it. I wish I could have watched my grandchildren. I did now and then but mostly for fun as they were lucky enough to be able to stay home with their moms. I remember my middle son asking me when he was about four, "Mom, why didn't I get to go to day-care like the other kids?"

MPA: Is there anything I haven't touched on that you would like to say right now?

KD: I think Covid is really going to change day-care. When Covid came about, schools shut down, but parents were still working. Parents were afraid to send their kids to day-care because they didn't want them to get Covid. We day-care providers were afraid to have children in our homes because we didn't want to catch Covid. The state was begging us to stay open. We usually have a limit to the children we're allowed but all of a sudden, we can have as many kids as we want because people don't have anywhere to take their children. So many places closed their doors.

MPA: What is the number one message you'd give to those parents struggling at home with their kids, especially after Covid?

KD: I try to make them feel relaxed, but it is scary. I just had a new baby that started two weeks ago, and the mom was so nervous about Covid. I said, "All I can do is the best that I can. We don't go to restaurants; we don't go to big groups. When people come to my door, I have a mask and they have a mask. I sanitise their kids right away, I take their temperature. That's the best we can do."

I send the parents pictures every day, texts of what they're doing and little cute videos. I used to tell parents they were free to drop in anytime during the day. But now, due to Covid, they are not allowed in the house. We do a child exchange outside the front door.

I would also say that if you have a bad feeling about a day-care provider, follow your instinct.

MPA: What happens if you have a bad feeling about a parent? What do you do?

KD: I have only had one in all my years and I terminated the contract. The dad didn't feel he needed to pay the weekly rate because they missed a day. I charge a flat rate per week, and they signed a contract. He was so angry he was shaking. He paid me but I called his wife and said they were not to come on Monday due to his actions. Not bad out of 38 years. Most of my parents are amazing. I got a huge bouquet of flowers from one family yesterday for no reason at all.

MPA: A lot of parents end up in my office–or in my online world–who have an unequal, non-agreed, parenting plan where one parent either doesn't respect the other, or there's a divorce or separation, and one parent is trying to do their best, while the other thinks they're doing the best, and it's just a mess. Sometimes, there's a narcissistic parent who is doing damage or there's a selfish, drunk or drug-abusing parent. What do we do with that? For example, the guy who was really nasty and angry with you and his wife are parenting the same children. What would you say a parent can do if their co-parent is not healthy?

KD: Well, I have no control over that one. If I thought that a parent was abusing their children in any way, I would call Social Services. I would be mandated to take care of that. Thankfully, I have never run across anything like that. I did not have those parents I mentioned for long, so I guess I don't know what kind of father he really was.

I have dealt with a handful of divorced families. Most have handled everything so well and I was very proud of how they put their child's needs first and not their own.

MPA: I often find that one parent is helpful and supportive of boundaries and the other just doesn't care or one is too controlling and the other one's trying to be nurturing to make up. It's this kind of balance. What would you say to a parent that's really struggling where the co-parent isn't helpful? What would you say they could do from their side to help the child?

KD: I've even offered to help myself. To those parents that have divorced and don't have family around, I've actually said, "Bring your kids over for the afternoon on a Saturday so you can have a break. You can clean the house, read a book, take a nap." I do this for married families that have no family around as well. I will tell them to go on a date night and bring me the kids. They are so tickled and grateful, and the children think it is extra special to be at our house at night.

If the children of the divorced parents are having issues, I will talk to both of the parents and ask if we can make a plan of action so we can all be on the same page. It will make such a difference in helping the child and situation. It is back to consistency every time.

When many of my parents go to have their second baby, I've kept their first child overnight at our house. The child feels safe at our house as it is their home away from home and it is a treat for me to be a part of their special event.

MPA: That's wonderful. So, you're saying your vast amounts of empathy is very important because you're empathic to the parents and the children.

KD: I could relate somewhat as my family was back in Wisconsin and we didn't have family near that would just give us a break now and then. Everyone needs a support system. It felt good to give them a break and they really appreciated it.

MPA: When I do mediation for dysfunctional parents–I call them dysfunctional but there's always good and bad and helpful and unhelpful in everybody–I ask, "So, where's the child in this family? You two are huge and this child, you can't even see it. So how do we make the child bigger?"

KD: By not being so selfish and self-absorbed. Some parents always put themselves and their interests before their children. Children are young for such a short time. I do believe how you parent depends on how you were raised. So, some don't know how to parent.

MPA: Maybe that's the difference between us. I get people coming only when there's a problem. I don't get healthy parents coming through my office door.

KD: I did have a single mom that came picking her kids up drunk one night. She wasn't happy that we wouldn't let her take her children home, but they were not going to get into that car! The children spent the night and my husband had to drive her home. I know she loved her children, but she obviously had some issues. It was positive how those children grew up to be wonderful adults.

MPA: However, you've just given me an example of how you put the child first.

KD: Yes, you've got to put the child first. If parents come to pick up and their kids aren't in car seats, I tell them they can't leave my house until there is a car seat, or I will have to report them. That has only happened one time; most parents are responsible.

MPA: Well, I would be in your day-care any day. What about adult children moving home? Do you have any tips for managing that?

KD: First of all, before they've even moved in, there would be a discussion on a plan that will help them get back on their feet and that it is important for them to pitch in and help around the house and to pick up after themselves. I love my kids and their families and would help if they ever needed it. Because they are and always have been independent, they would already know this and would not stay any longer than they had to. But communication is the key. I have seen so many kids just stay home and play video games, who don't want to work.

MPA: So, you're making a rod for your own back if you don't give them the idea that they need to take responsibility?

KD: If they want to be an adult, they have to act like one. That is being responsible, being able to plan, budget and set goals, and to work at a job you don't like until you find another one. Nobody ever said adulting was always going to be fun.

MPA: And they also need to understand there are more things than video games.

KD: Yes. And maybe that's where they've got some mental issues. Where they need a therapist like you because they have some hidden anxiety. I guess I haven't had to deal with kids like that or who are drug users and alcoholics. I can't put myself in those parents' shoes because I've never been in those shoes.

MPA: Kathy, thank you so much. Thanks for everything you did for all of those children too.

To watch a video of this interview, go to https://mpamind.com

For more guidance, read:
Parenting Isn't for Cowards - Dr J.C. Dobson
Raising Boys in the 21st Century - S. Biddulph
Parenting 101 - M. Miller and HowExpert

CHAPTER 16

DIFFERENCE IS SCARY AND COOL

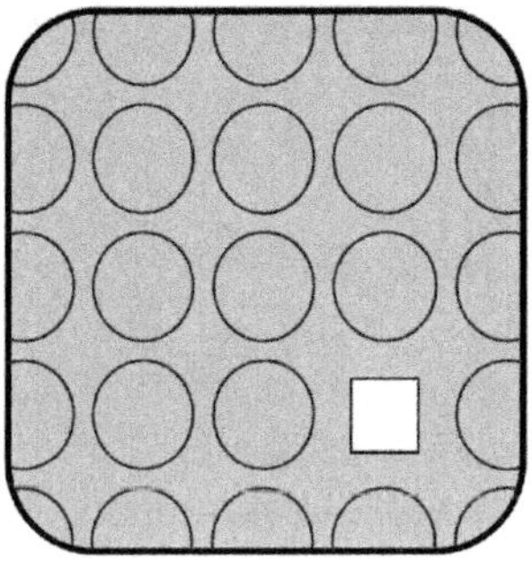

"Out of the billions of people in the world, every soul is unique and different, including your child. You have to recognise and allow that. If we embrace difference, we embrace peace."
- Michael Padraig Acton -

Embrace the new, even though it may be different to your experience growing up as a child or even different to your experience of being a parent. If your child is saying they are gay, lesbian or straight and you happen to have a different sexual preference, you have to allow your child to have their individual identity. They might decide to do a different set of courses at school. They might decide they want to play with dolls rather than trucks. They might decide to do any number of things different from the way you do or did them.

Be mindful that the way you were brought up and your experiences as a child may not necessarily be the right ones for your child. Maybe you were controlled by your parents and made to do certain things? That may not necessarily be a healthy way to bring your child up. It might be that your child needs more reason or logic in their life, and to debate or discuss things.

If your child has a disability, they might have created a unique set of coping mechanisms. As long as they are healthy and don't endanger education, wellbeing, health and safety, you need to be open to them coping in a different manner to you.

If we embrace difference, we encourage our child to go forth and gain as much opportunity as possible. If we reject difference, we are stopping our child from accessing those opportunities and choices and denying them love and peace. If we reject difference, we reject our child. If we reject difference, we abuse our child.

How do we open up to difference? Recognise that if we hate something in our child, it's probably got more to do with us than them. The adage, 'that which we hate in others, we hate more in ourselves,' is true. To be a psychologist or psychotherapist, a large part of the training is to do with accepting that we have judgement, prejudice, pretentiousness, and competitiveness in our systems because it's part of the human condition and necessary for survival. So many people like to cast that out and pretend they don't have these so-called negative traits. If we acknowledge that we can be selfish, judgemental, opinionated, etc. then that's going to help our children when we start to think about difference and our own prejudices around that.

Maybe, at times, our children can teach us more than we can teach them?

For more guidance, read:

The ABCs of Diversity: Helping Kids (and Ourselves) Embrace Our Differences - C. Helsel and Y.J. Harris-Smith

The Gender Affirmative Model: An Interdisciplinary Approach to Supporting Transgender and Gender Expansive Children - C. Keo-Meier and D. Ehrensaft

Why Are People Different Colours? Big Issues for Little People Around Identity and Diversity - E. Waddington and C. McCurry

SUCCESS MANTRA

Ralph Waldo Emerson made such an immediate impact on me at an early age that I have used his words as my success mantra for as long as I can remember:

To laugh often and much
To win the respect of intelligent people
and affection of children;
to earn the appreciation of honest critics
and endure the betrayal of false friends;
to appreciate beauty,
to find the best in others;
to leave the world a bit better,
whether by a healthy child, a garden patch
or redeemed social condition;
to know even one life has breathed easier
because you have lived.
This is to have succeeded.

-Ralph Waldo Emerson-

CHAPTER 17

WHAT IS SUCCESS?

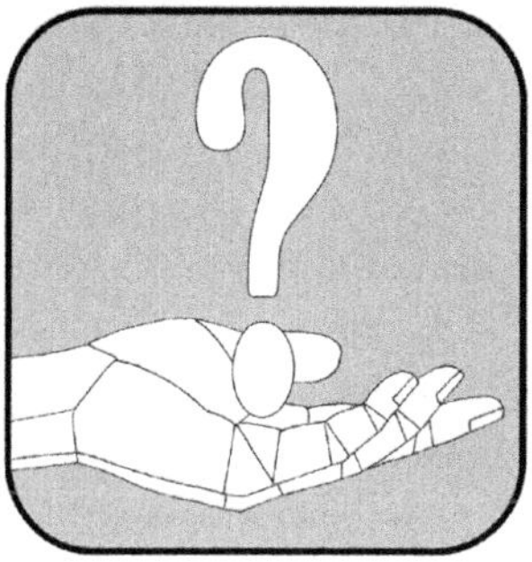

"Be mindful that children's success is usually in the moment:
in the now, this year, this month, this week, this day.
It's not until our children start to develop worldly ideas of time and achievement, progress and stages that they will come out of the now and go into the future."
- Michael Padraig Acton

Who we are, where we come from, our age, our level of development and where we are in life—our context—determines what successful means for us. As young adults we might want to own our house or to save up for a holiday. When we become more accomplished, it might be that we want our sister to return from the dead or for our unhealthiest child to be well. As Mrs. Obama once said, "I'm as happy as my most unhappy child." That's her success statement.

It's important to understand what success is to us, where we are in life, but also what success is for our children. They will develop a sense of progress and we can step back and grow ourselves through witnessing their development and ideas of success. I was once walking behind my granddaughter, and she was having a conversation with her friend about her hopes, ambitions and dreams as a 13-year-old. They were unadulterated, unpolluted, dreamy, lovely and wonderful, but not real (although for some it may happen).

Don't forget, our children's world is very small. Success might be achieved on the walk to school; it might happen in their bedroom; it might happen within a small circle of friends or within the family. Success is very, very different for every child. It could be taking their first steps. It could be winning a football game. It could be dancing like no-one's watching.

It's very important not to get our own successes and ideas of success mixed up with our children's. The only success we should demand for our children is their wellbeing, their health, their education, their options in life and for them to be peaceful and content.

It's important we grow with our children, and understand where they are at, in different stages of development. Sometimes, growth is accelerated and success of one child at nine might be that of another child of 15. It could also be reversed: a 15-year-old could all of a sudden realise they want to do childish things and enjoy the hugs they didn't have. That would be success to them.

The most important idea about success that we can give to our children is that we won't get anywhere unless we believe we can. If we believe we can be something; if we can believe we can do something; if we believe we can choose something; if we believe we can give something and get a reward for it, that's success.

Children's brains are wired differently to ours. Their emotions are wired differently. Any kind of success is OK if it doesn't harm somebody and if it generates peace and contentment. Allow our children to create their own version of success; assist, aid and support them in doing so.

For more guidance, read:

Chess for Success: Using an Old Game to Build New Strengths in Children and Teens - M.G. Ashley

The Seven Spiritual Laws of Success for Parents: Guiding Your Children to Success and Fulfilment - D. Chopra

Let Them Play: The Mindful Way to Parent Kids for Fun and Success in Sports - J. Lynch

CHAPTER 18

HOW DO WE MAKE QUALITY TIME?

"We must allocate quality time for our children and structure their lives so they can spend quality time with us. Without time, what do we have?"
- Michael Padraig Acton -

Encouraging our children to spend quality time is all about practising what you preach.

It doesn't matter if you're a family of TV couch potatoes or a family into active sports, educational trips and museum tours, we can't expect our children to ever learn how to allocate and spend quality time if we don't do it. Whatever your situation is, your children need to know they are loved, valued, respected and nurtured and that takes time. We all have our responsibilities. We all have bills to pay, accounts to do, our favourite film to watch, our dearest friends to see over a glass of wine. We must allocate quality time for our children too. We also have to structure their time so that they can spend quality time with us.

As Freud and Salvador Dali discussed many, many times over, time is both binary and fluid. Look at Salvador Dali's famous melting clocks: that's what this is all about. Time is so exact: second by second, minute by minute, hour by hour, year by year. Yet, it's so fluid and tricks the mind so completely that before you know it your children will be grown and out the door and you will be thinking, 'My gosh, that felt like a second, that felt like a minute.' There may also be parts of your child's growth where you think, 'That was difficult; that felt like a year,' but still overall time is fluid.

However, in day-to-day life, as a healthy, effective parent, we have to make sure time is allocated for human interaction: socialisation, discussion, sharing and simply double checking everything is OK because that can be swept under the carpet and missed.

Mealtime is the perfect time for this, so make sure you insist on no device time; it's healthy! You have to do the same. You can't take your child's device away and then sit there on your phone texting or talking. Unless it's a life-or-death emergency, nobody needs to interrupt a meal or social gathering. Even if it's just one parent and child, make this a regular occasion so that you and your child both know that time is allocated.

Weekends: don't fill them with things to do. Make time. Do the garden together; make some rock cakes together; put the trash out together. Make sure there's time for both chores and enjoyable things to do. It's about leading by example but also providing the firm structure children need to be healthy.

At any age, children need our time, our attention, and to feel special. Time also gives us the ability to see things, hear things, check in, discuss and resolve issues, discuss successes and plan the next day or the next year. Time is free but takes effort to manage. And in a world where we're given too many activities and not enough time, it's important to carve this out for you and your children.

For more guidance, read:

Parenting: The 7 Secrets of Spending Quality Time with Your Children - N. Ghostleaf

One Million Minutes: What My Daughter Taught Me About Time - W. Kuper

Dad Can Do: Build, Make, Do. . .The Best Way to Spend Quality Time with Your Kids - C. Barnardo

Guides for Familly Quality Time: Series 1: Indoor Sports - S. Guo and A. Guo

CHAPTER 19

FOOD IS AMMUNITION. DISARM!

"Abusing food is about control. If your child is obese or anorexic, it's your responsibility. You have to act!"
- Michael Padraig Acton -

The first power our children ever have over their world is food. They can throw it, they can make you pick it up, they can refuse to eat, they can eat too much. It's about control.

We are the only species in the world that teaches our young to eat a variety of food.

It's a misconception we need to make our children eat everything on their plate before they leave the table–that just creates a battle without serving any purpose. A child won't go hungry if there's food around. If you put three things on their plate and all they eat is mashed potatoes, that's fine. If there's a nutritional issue and you need to start them eating something else, make it a team effort, make it fun and interesting.

We've got to be very careful how we manage food in our family unit. One of the severest cases of obesity I ever worked with in the hospital was a 15-year-old-girl who was 5 foot 4 and weighed 290 pounds. I found out her older sister had anorexia and my patient grew up with her sister demanding all of the family time. She would lean over the bannister at night and watch how her parents encouraged her sister to eat, saying, "good girl," when she complied, hugging her. My patient naturally tried to please her parents by eating everything given to her and became morbidly obese as a result. Once we cracked the reason why she was inadvertently feeding herself, we broke the cycle and she lost an awful lot of weight. She went on to university and became a well-adjusted young lady.

Think carefully about your own childhood. If you've got into a situation where food is power and control, you need to find a way of changing that, so food becomes a sociable and integral part of the family. It's important to lead by example. We can't expect our children to eat all the different ingredients they need for healthy growth if we're sitting there eating biscuits, fried chicken and a packet of potato chips!

Get everyone involved. Make sure your whole family respects food and knows where it comes from. Milk comes from cows not the fridge. Bread is a process. Vegetables can be picked from a farm. Not everyone is a natural cook but let's all be involved with the preparation, delivery and consumption of food in a healthy, balanced way. Take your children shopping so they know the value of food. When they waste food make sure they realise they're wasting money and you've worked for that money.

Dealing with anything that affects the health, wellbeing or education of your children is compulsory. If you have a child who is bulimic, anorexic or obese you can't just ignore it. You are in control until that child is 18. You must act. Be careful of secret eating, purging, vomiting, diarrhoea tablets, etc. Any kind of food intake needs to be balanced with energy output.

Obesity is about passivity; anorexia is about control. Even if we're obese or a recovering anorexic ourselves, we need to lead by example.

Childhood and food are a minefield. Children will use whatever they can to manipulate a situation and be warned: food is one of those areas they have massive control over. They can shut their mouth and not eat, they can take their time over it, they can do all sorts of things, but if you react in anything other than a balanced, mindful way you're going to tell your child that their behaviour works.

For more guidance, read:
The Good Parenting Food Guide: Managing What Children Eat Without Making Food a Problem - J. Ogden
Healthy Food, Healthy Gut, Happy Child: The Real Dirt on Raising Healthy Kids in a Processed World - Dr M. Shetreat-Klein
Help Your Teenager Beat an Eating Disorder - J. Lock PhD and D. Le Grange PhD

CHAPTER 20

1, 2, 3 OR MORE: A JUGGLING ACT, FOR SURE. DAWN BIGGERS WITH MICHAEL PADRAIG ACTON

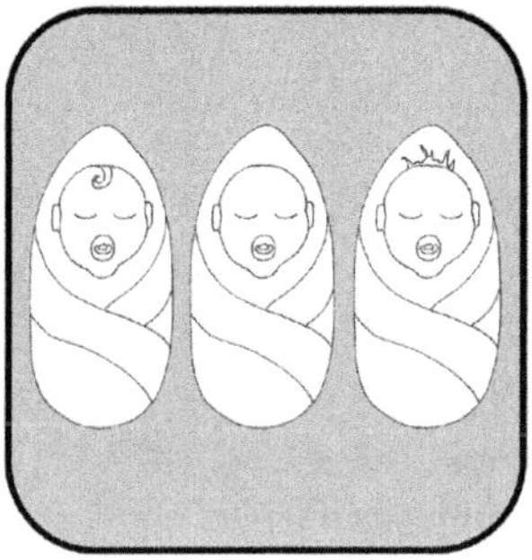

"With a healthy vision, passion creates super parenting."
- Michael Padraig Acton -

Dawn Biggers is an Early Learning Years School Inspector, foster care parent and mother of healthy triplets.

Michael Padraig Acton (MPA): This is an interview about having more than one child at the same time and any advice you can give to parents that are about to have twins, triplets, quadruplets, etc. or that already have them.

Dawn Biggers (DB): When you realise that you're having multiple births there is all the anxiety and worry that goes along with it because you don't know if they're going to be born with a disability and you wonder how you're going to manage it financially and practically.

But once they're here, you will be able to access a lot of support and help. It's a big life change and it has its highs and lows, but it's very rewarding. There's nothing that compares to that love and attachment you will feel with those children.

Looking at practicalities, seek the help of your family and friends because this is a time of adaptation and you're going to feel really tired and maybe emotional. Be aware that you might experience post-natal depression. If you're not being yourself, it's not a failure on your part because your hormones are all up in the air. My advice is to seek medical help and share your concerns with your family and close friends so that they can support and guide you through those feelings and emotions.

Remember that you're going to feel really tired because of all the practicalities of feeding, changing nappies, etc. So, get as much support as you can and don't give yourself a really hard time. Also, remember that if you are with somebody, you are both going to be tired, but it is important to build in time together, even if that is just going out for a coffee. Otherwise, you will just get so embroiled in the day-to-day routine, which can be overwhelming.

It's about realising that it's going to be a very different experience with more than one child. You are going to be pulled in so many directions because you have two, three or more children who are going to want your time and attention. But it's also such a wonderful experience because you are taking that time to get to know them. It's really fascinating watching and observing twins or triplets because they might reach their milestones differently and you are building a bond with each child. It is wonderful spending time lying with them on the floor and just giving them eye contact. You're going to have such an amazing role: a teacher and a mother [parent] all in one.

Then there are the practicalities. You're going to have to try to organise your time and make sure you've got your resources like nappies, changes of clothes and a packet of wet wipes in the car. Always make sure you have wet wipes with you (even my 11-year-olds are still using them). Other practical things include your car. Is it going to be big enough to carry more than one child? Will the buggy fit in it? And the family dog?

For me, I was always thinking ahead. I would need to purchase three cot beds, three baby gyms, etc. but you don't necessarily have to have lots of money for that because there are the buy and sells. I purchased a lot of resources through the buy and sells because they were in good condition. That might mean they don't have it new but sometimes they've got nearly new.

Look for things that are on a budget and ask family members to help (e.g., on their birthdays). When they're a lot younger, they're not going to realise you're not giving them toys but there is the ongoing expense of shoes and coats and similar basic practicalities. So, some core advice is thinking one step ahead: What do I need? How am I going to do that? What financial income have I got? With my boys I'm often thinking, 'Right, they need this and this. How?'

It might be helpful to purchase a child development book so you can be aware of any signs of delay, particularly if they were born prematurely. Build that relationship with your doctor and health visitor who will pick up on things like any sort of hearing delay. Again, you have to think ahead because if you've got an appointment, you might need help. I used to have my nephew come with me because I've only got two pair of hands and three children. So, it's just that pre-planning and thinking ahead and not giving yourself a hard time. It is a learning process–don't be afraid to ask for help.

It's an amazing journey having more than one child. You're going to form a lasting relationship with them all and you're going to do the best you can for them. Take things from your parenting that worked and change things that didn't work, for example, how you were treated or how you were spoken to. Let your children know you don't always get it right. With my boys, if I make a mistake I'll say, "I'm sorry, I didn't get it right." It helps them to learn about respect and healthy relationships.

MPA: So clear communication with them is key?

DB: Absolutely. You have that crucial unconditional love bond, but you also have to set clear boundaries and be a good role model for them.

MPA: Talking about role models, you spoke of a very intimate, lovely thing about lying on the floor and making eye contact with your children and your future as a parent and teacher. However, there is a common phenomenon with couples who have twins, triplets, quadruplets, quintuplets, etc. where there is a breakdown in relationship between the parents. This transcends all genders and sexualities. What happens to the co-parent–the person that isn't giving birth to the children? It's another known phenomenon that the mother giving birth is taken care of by the midwifes, the doctors, the hospitals, etc. leaving their partner isolated. What happens to the relationship dynamic?

DB: Obviously that changes slightly so you need to be really aware of your partner being actively involved. It's about teamworking and communication. I was on my own for a year before I moved down here so I had to rely on my wider support networks. But if you've got a partner, it's important to communicate and make them feel involved because it's not like you are just sharing your attention with one child. It's about sharing and giving your partner the opportunity to build that strong bond.

As I said earlier, you also have to ensure that you have time alone together, maybe just to have a glass of wine or squash, just to remove yourselves and remember that you are two people with needs as well.

MPA: Talking about clear communication and honesty, it's a common thing when we've got multiple children or grandchildren for people to ask, "So, which one's your favourite?" In my experience, both clinically and personally, most people don't answer that honestly. It's interesting to see their responses as sometimes people are aghast at being asked. But it's a very important question when we have multiple children so I'm wondering if you could answer that honestly.

DB: Honestly, I have a connection with all three of them. I can give you an example of a time where I felt something stronger. I had three of them in the premature unit for three months after they were born, and I remember one time when I walked into the NICU centre and saw Reuben lying in an incubator. His eyes were wide open, and he was looking at me and it just really melted my heart. I just looked at him and I thought, 'I'm going to look after you.' It was just a moment's real connection.

But my triplets are so different and there's something unique and special about each of them. I've got one that's really affectionate and really open about their feelings and emotions. Things tend to go over the heads of the other two, so you don't always know what they're thinking and feeling. But then they might just come up and give you a hug or send you a text saying, 'I love you'. So, it's like I have different connections with each of them but at the end of the day, if something upsets any of them, it really evokes so much emotion in me.

People have said to me, "Oh, you've just made a comment about Reuben, he's your favourite." And I say, "How can I possibly make that division? I can say I had this experience with Reuben, and I felt overwhelmed in that moment but actually I have a connection with all of them and I love them all."

MPA: We've touched on depression and anxiety. We've touched on the struggles of parenting multiple children. What would your advice be to parents of multiple births, irrespective of the age of the children, if they've got anxiety or depression, some trauma has happened to them or something's just not going quite right and they're rejecting their children?

DB: I can give you an example, although not involving a multiple birth. My niece had such a horrendous birth that she didn't initially connect with her son. Some people do experience that feeling of either, 'I don't want anything to do with my child' or, 'I can't connect with them,' so it's then about seeking medical help and support, someone to say, "That's a natural feeling." Give it some time and talk with your partner about these feelings and emotions. Maybe they will have to do a bit more of the care because you might be suffering from post-natal depression. As a woman, you've got all of these hormones and there are going to be difficulties thrown at you in your life. You might feel at times that you can't cope with your children and it's acknowledging and realising that life can be really tough and people do generally experience a lot of mental health issues. So, seek that support and obviously if you're feeling you might be a risk to your children, seek help immediately.

MPA: The biggest thing healthy parents carry, in my experience as a parent, a grandparent and a clinician, is guilt. We carry guilt for those fleeting moments if we are overly stern with our children, if we're too lenient or if we just want to go into our cave and hide. A healthy parent has guilt because we triple-check everything. We try and do the best by our children. What would you say is the best way of managing your own guilt bearing in mind we are speaking honestly? Every parent carries guilt because none of us are perfect, we're just OK enough.

DB: For me, having children is a learning process, isn't it? It's not about giving yourself a hard time. Sometimes you think, 'Oh, I set the boundary too hard' and you feel a little guilty but tomorrow's another day. I'm not going to hold grudges. I just start afresh and try to do it differently next time. We're not going to always get it right.

MPA: What about parents of adult twins or triplets? Whatever's going on with the children, parents tend to blame themselves. Say for instance their children are in their twenties and all of a sudden, they're having this reflective moment and start getting racked with guilt. You know, 'I could have done more. I am to blame for the drugs or the pole dancing'.

DB: Yes, they do blame themselves, but you can only be there for your children. The outside influences, you cannot control. I know that parents think, 'Oh, if I'd done this differently or I'd done that differently, maybe they wouldn't have got into the drugs or alcohol' but you can only prepare them and make them aware of potential safety risks.

With my children, thinking of sexual abuse, I just say to them very clearly things like, "What's in your pants is private. If anybody touches you there, please come and tell me." With stranger awareness, I've been really open with them and said, "You don't go in people's cars. If somebody approaches you and asks you to go in their car because they're offering you sweets or toys, you might never see me again, they might try and touch you on your private parts or they might kill you." It's not about putting the fear of God in them, but they need to know what might happen.

A lot of children give in to peer pressure, but you've just got to be there and hopefully have built a relationship where communication is open and if your child is feeling scared or worried you'll pick up on it and they can come to you.

There are going to be times when you're going to feel really guilty about how you've treated them. But it's OK if you can turn around at the end of the day and say, "Look, I've tried to do my best for my children, and I am going to be there for them no matter what. If they get into drugs or alcohol I'm going to try and still be there to get them the help and support, they need."

Your role changes when they get older because they are independent and think they know everything. They might need to go and experience something and realise for themselves. Get support from your family network and health professionals if you are picking up on things.

MPA: It's about a balance between supporting and enabling in a way. You've been a mum of triplets for 12 years (your triplets are 11 now and, of course, you carried them for almost a year). What would you say your top issues have been as a parent?

DB: My top issues have been around recognising that Romeo, one of my triplet sons, was struggling with their development and I wasn't being listened to as well as I should have been. He has got moderate learning difficulties and was more or less floating. His teacher had just come out of college and couldn't actually see his individual needs. Because of his inexperience, he didn't realise there was a problem until my son moved into the following year and the gap in his learning was significant.

If you're picking up on concerns, you need to have your voice and not be worried about standing up for yourself and saying, "I know my child. I have concerns," and then seeking out the medical help and support you need for the investigations to happen. So, stand up for yourself and challenge authority because you want the best for your child, and you know them best. At the end of the day, the teachers have them, but you can see the way your child behaves, you can see the way they interact, so be confident in expressing any concerns you have and following through and hassling the school. It wasn't until Romeo went to listening clinic and the medical professionals backed me up that we got an educational healthcare plan to help support my son into his senior education.

MPA: My word of advice to parents is always to keep everything in writing, to make sure there is a paper trail.

DB: Oh, definitely. Keep copies of everything because that always stands you in good stead if they are asking for evidence. Write down times and dates, and how they're reacting and responding, so you've got an evidence base to support your concerns.

MPA: Thank you Dawn. And lastly, what do you feel, over the years, has been your trick to staying sane?

DB: I just try to remain open-minded and to take each day as it comes. I really wanted children and I wanted to invest as much as I could in them, so I try to be as upbeat as I can. You've got to take care of the practicalities. When you have children there's no, 'I can't do this', even though you might feel like it. You've got to get on and be positive because the rewards of your relationship with your children and that unconditional love outweigh anything for me.

MPA: You've just mentioned something that parents really berate themselves for and that is the unconditional love because when we're going through parenting sometimes we don't like them. How do you get over that?

DB: Remember not to label the child. Some people say their child is 'naughty' and then that child's self-esteem gets low and you get into this cycle. If children are displaying behaviour, it's the behaviour you want to change and not the child. For me, they may have driven me crazy and I may have got really cross with them but because I have such overwhelming feelings, I move on. You have to move on otherwise you will just build up resentment and negative feelings towards your child. They're learning about the world as much as you're learning about being a parent. To me, you pick yourself up and say, "Right, I haven't really liked the behaviour much today but it's a new day and let's start again."

MPA: Dawn, thank you so much. You've given us so much valuable information and made so much sense.

To watch a video of this interview, go to https://mpamind.com

For more guidance, read:

Twins and Multiple Births: The Essential Parenting Guide from Pregnancy to Adulthood - Dr C. Cooper

The First Year is Survival: The Essential Guide to Parenting Twins and Multiples - L. Huie

OMG It's Twins! Get Your Twins to Their First Birthday Without Losing Your Mind - A. Perry

Having Twins and More: AParent's Guide to Multiple Pregnancy, Birth and Early Childhood - E. Noble, L. Sorger et al

CHAPTER 21

OWNING, APOLOGISING, LEADING BY EXAMPLE

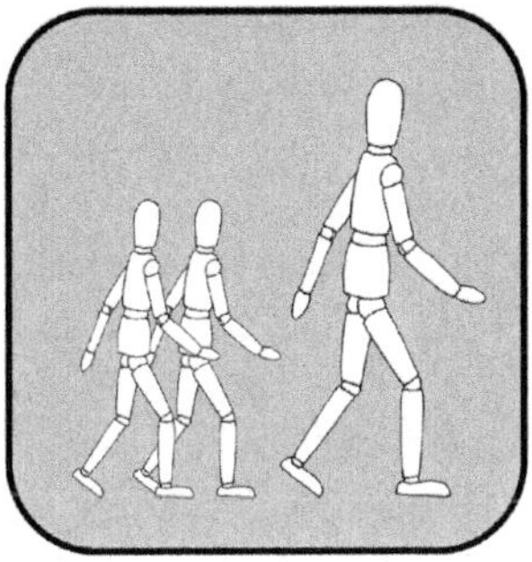

"If you're not mature enough to accept your part in a situation,
how will your children ever learn to apologise?
Sorry really doesn't have to be the hardest word."
- Michael Padraig Acton -

The act of recognising a mistake and acting upon it is an achievement given the normal tendency to defend (refusing to accept we have a problem) or deflect (i.e., give somebody else the problem).

It's very important to understand that, as parents, we're not always right and consider what part of the blame we hold for things not going right.

By giving this example to our children, they will very quickly understand that it's OK to own their part in a mistake and use clear, reasonable communication to resolve the conflict.

If this process doesn't happen within a family unit, people start treading on eggshells and the path to resolution becomes treacherous and difficult.

How do we find a formula to ask for forgiveness or apologise for something?

- First, recognise your feelings. Do you feel agitated or worried?

- Secondly, ask yourself why you are feeling worried, sad or irritated (to own our part, we have to use the word 'I').
- Thirdly, apologise and ask for forgiveness.

Not all children will be used to this openness so it might be an idea to explain that transparency and truthfulness is healthy for family relationships. When things get tough, we can then bring in this applied '1, 2, 3' of how we feel, what mistake or error of judgement is taking place, request forgiveness and commit to doing things differently.

We can all make mistakes as humans, but we have to learn from them.

For more guidance, read:

Sorry, I Forgot to Ask: My Story About Asking for Permission and Masking an Apology! - J. Cook

Ellie Jelly and the Massive Mum Meltdown - S. Naish

I'm Sorry: The Art of Apology and the Gift of Forgiveness - A. Krusinski

CHAPTER 22

SIX VITAL STYLES OF PARENTAL MANAGEMENT

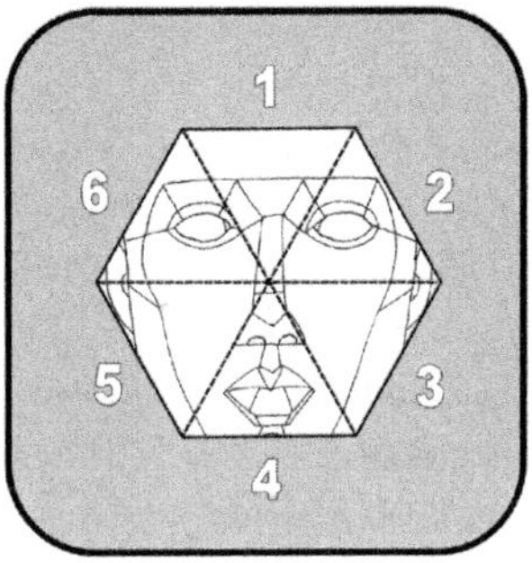

"What would you say to your 14-year-old if they came home at two in the morning smelling of alcohol and drugs? You need to choose the appropriate management style for the situation."
- Michael Padraig Acton -

Parents need a toolbox of management skills when managing their children, the family unit and each other.

Management styles move from directive to more elaborate, depending on the task at hand.

A directive, controlling management style would be saying, "No, get away from that!" if the child is putting their hand in a fire. The other end of the spectrum would be the gentle style of management: leading by example, negotiating or having a discussion about the correct outcome for the family, relationship or individual child.

It depends, of course, on the nature of the family. All demographics are different. All families are from different backgrounds and have different situations going on. There might be extra leeway needed because of a sick child. There might be some immature behaviour because of a lack of development.

We need to find the appropriate style of management at any one time.

If we're going on vacation the next day, we can prepare for this situation beforehand and allocate time for each person to pack, therefore starting off with a more elaborate code of discussion. However, if someone's not packed their case and left their things in the bathroom and you've asked them several times to pack, you might have to go up to the more directive style of management.

One thing parents must do when managing tasks is to ensure the child has downtime from devices, including mobile phones/cell phones, tablets, consoles and the TV. Everything should be turned off so that the child can focus on the task at hand.

What happens if your child comes back at two in the morning at age 14, smelling of alcohol and drugs? What kind of management happens then? We might go into directive management and say, "Take a shower, get to bed and we'll talk again in the morning."

Then we need to think about what we are going to talk about in the morning. Are we going to still be telling them, 'Do not drink, do not smoke, get home at the right time,' or will we have more of an informative discussion where we're educating them as to why there are rules and asking them to follow them otherwise there will be consequences?

So, to manage is to lead by example; to manage is to allocate time; to manage is to choose an appropriate style at any one given time.

There is no 'right way' to deal with a parenting issue because no two situations are the same, no two people are the same, no two families are the same. However, standard management models can help. In their book *Primal Leadership*, authors Goleman, Boyatzis and McKee described six effective styles of management. If they work for corporates and employees across the world, they can certainly help you to manage your family, your children and each other.

The six styles of management

1. **Affiliative.** This is the loving, positive management style where the focus is boosting your child's self-esteem and getting them on side. The aim is to get your child to want to follow your instructions because

it strengthens your bond. Potential downsides are siblings feeling neglected and a drop in standards if the parent just want a quiet life.

2. **Coaching.** This is the most impactful management style as it helps your child to develop the skills they will need to achieve their goals. Coaching takes time and patience but is the ideal way to support your child's success.

   Coaching is a more directional style than some others. You can personally work out, with your child, their objectives. Usually, the top three objectives are the most potent (e.g., the top three places they want to go or what they want to achieve at school or at a weekend club, etc.). You then look at the coaching strategies that will get them there. So, what is their motivation? What's going to keep them in that place? What is their bigger picture, and is it feasible? Not all dreams are. If your child really wants to go to Walt Disney World, that might not be immediately achievable. You could look at steps that might make this achievable in the future. For example, if they save money, work hard at school and get a good job they could then have the benefit of going to Walt Disney World.

3. **Commanding.** This is the directive, controlling method mentioned before. It is best used sparingly and for short periods, as it can affect your child's morale and create an unpleasant atmosphere. As an example, the commanding management style might be used when a child refuses to get on the school bus. The parent might say, "Please get on the bus now or you will have no allowance for a month and we will take you in to explain to the head teacher why you are late."

4. **Democratic.** As in politics, this is where every member has the chance to explain their position and a majority decision is respected. This management style might be suitable when deciding on what to eat as a family or which movie to get on Netflix. It empowers the child while instilling in them notions of fairness.

5. **Pacesetting.** This is where the parent acts as a role model and demon-strates the standards expected from the child. Used effectively, it can help your child to develop new skills. Parents should be careful not to slip into 'enabling' behaviour by taking over the task. Be mindful of your child's capabilities. Showing your six-year-old how to make a souffle is probably a rung too high for them.

6. **Visionary.** This style of management is all about inspiring your child by painting a picture of the goal and supporting them in achieving it. You many need to spend time overcoming roadblocks, but once your child really gets the end game, their own motivation will take over.

For more guidance, read:
Primal Leadership: Unleashing the Power of Emotional Intelligence - D. Coleman, R.E. Boyatzis and A. McKee
How to Win Friends and Influence People - D. Carnegie
The 7 Habits of Highly Effective People - S.R. Covey

CHAPTER 23

IT'S ALL ABOUT LANGUAGE: BRUTAL OR REASONABLE?

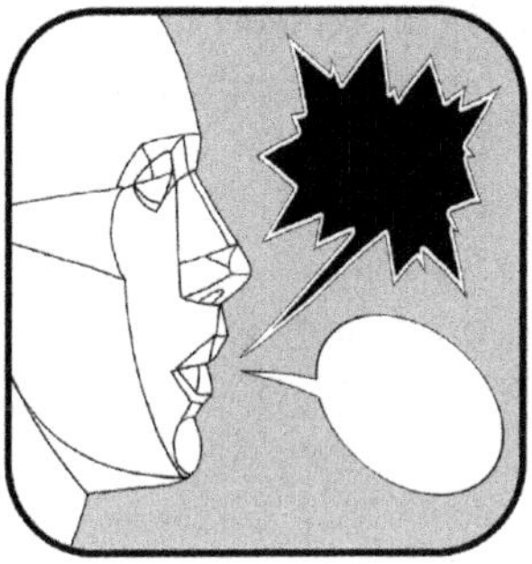

"Brutal communication is never ever effective and has no place in a healthy family. If you understand that then we have to find an alternative."
- Michael Padraig Acton -

Wouldn't it be lovely if every family was always reasonable with the language they used?

There has been much documented and researched over the past few decades on physical domestic violence but emotional violence, which is often perpetrated through brutal language, is as severe if not more damaging than physical violence.

How do we know if someone's using brutal language, whether that is the parent towards the child or the child towards the parents? According to the Cambridge Dictionary, to be brutal is to act in a way that is cruel, violent and completely without feeling.

If we use our comments as a form of attack and ignore how the person on the receiving end might be feeling, we are being brutal with our language.

Drawn from transactional analysis, reasonable language doesn't dictate or attack. We can raise our voice and still be reasonable (e.g., if we're not getting a person's attention or we want to emphasise a point) but brutal language would include taking things that the person has said, twisting them and throwing them back at them or saying something like, "Oh, you're like so-and-so" (often someone with a very bad reputation within the family).

It's been shown over and over, time and time again that this type of attack isn't useful. Nobody is like somebody else; they are choosing to be the way they are.

Parents can get scared and intimidated by children using brutal language. How do we stop the child using brutal language?

For a start, stop rewarding them for using it. Children who use brutal language often get their own way by doing so. If a child is very young, then you might need to get some outside help. There might be something else going on.

How do we stop ourselves from using brutal language? How do we know when we're using brutal language? Well, it's very easy to slip into screaming mad language with our children, especially if we tend to be reactive.

A lot of families get into a brutal way of being because they're just annoyed or haven't got the time to be reasonable. Then the child gets the better of the parent and the parent tries to get the better of the child. One feels too controlled, one feels out of control. All types of dynamic could be going on by this stage.

Brutal communication is never effective or helpful. If it worked, great, but it doesn't. In fact, if we're using foul language or any kind of cuss words, we release more testosterone (whether we're female or male). This escalates things into more of a battle-type engagement rather than moving towards a situation that's reasonable and useful.

Brutal language is never acceptable, so the key is to recognise the brutal language, sit down together when things have calmed down and say, "We used that language with each other! Is that nice? Do we want to continue doing it? How can we do it differently? What can we do as a team effort to change it?"

Think about the language you would use with your boss, some special guests or at a wedding where someone has gone to an awful lot of effort to accommodate you. That's reasonable language.

Brutal language has no place in a healthy family; has no place in life.

For more guidance, read:

The Language of Parenting: A Parenting Guide Designed to Help Parents Meet the Everyday Challenges of Parenting - S. Schumer M.A.

Fowl Language - Winging it: The Art of Imperfect Parenting – B. Gordon

Small Talk: How to Develop Your Child's Language Skills from Birth to Age Four - N. Lathey and T. Blake

CHAPTER 24

WHEN TO NEGOTIATE

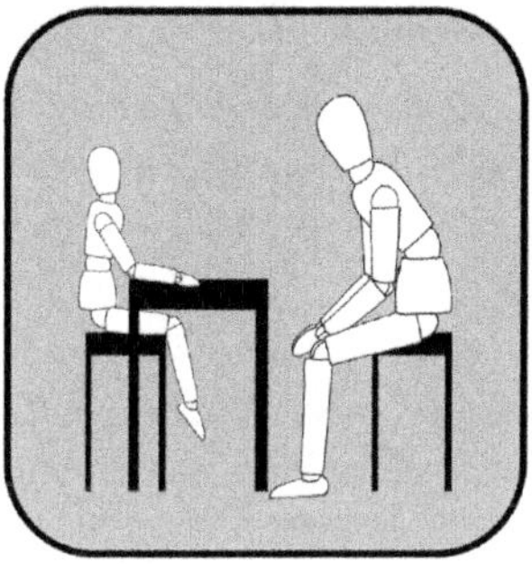

"Looking after your child's health, wellbeing and education is non-negotiable. No parent has the right to shrug that responsibility. Do this and you fail as a parent."
- Michael Padraig Acton -

There are certain principles in this book that can be applied to all situations, and this is one of them: some things are negotiable; some things aren't.

So, what is negotiable with our children? Most things are negotiable, but it does depend on their age and the family. It also depends on their context and environment: country versus urban, village versus town, beach versus bush.

However, for somebody under the legal age of 21, 18 or 16, depending upon which country you are in, certain things are non-negotiable. The most important of these are health, wellbeing and education.

Education is mandatory. Countries have different legislation regarding the age to which children must be educated. Within this, we have to do our absolute best for our children to make sure they're supported, guided, understand education and are given the time, support, equipment and facilities to do as well as they can. That is our job as parents: to set them off on a path that is going to be really helpful for them. Anything less and you are failing as a parent. It is nobody else's responsibility apart from the parents'. If the parents are disabled or unable to help for a good reason then they will need to ask for support from a family member, friend or an agency. A child should always have support through education to do well.

How long does direct parental responsibility for education last? It depends on the country again. Some countries have a requirement to 16 and some to 18; some countries even have a requirement, due to divorce laws, insurance and taxes, of 21.

Second, health is non-negotiable; a child has to be kept safe. Opposing any decision that the child is making that could impinge upon their health is your duty. From doing drugs and drinking alcohol to fighting to putting fingers in electric sockets, you have to get involved.

We also have to take care of any behavioural or mental health issues our child has. Are they being bullied or bullying or abusing others? This is never acceptable. Are they feeling depressed because of dyslexia? Do they feel alienated because of social issues (which may be the onset of Autistic Spectrum Disorder (ASD))? Whatever's going on, we have to take care of it. It's mandatory, mandatory, mandatory. There is no negotiation when it comes to mental and physical health.

Lastly, but just as importantly, is an umbrella called wellbeing.

Wellbeing is overall good health: mental, emotional, physical. It is the result of a cluster of different influences on our lives. Usually somebody who is in a wellbeing situation is peaceful, they can engage, they can interact. They have their needs and most of their wants met. Life won't be perfect but if we can hit 70 out of 100 then we're doing really well.

The most important thing for a top athlete is that their wellbeing is taken care of so they can perform to the ultimate of their personal ability and that's what we need to do for our children. We need to make sure their nutrition's good; we need to make sure their environment's supportive; we need to make sure they are challenged enough, etc.

So, mandatory non-negotiables are health, wellbeing and education. No parent has the right to shrug that responsibility. Again, if you are a parent and you're not able to support your child you can access help.

For more guidance, read:

Negotiation Parenting: Or How Not to Raise a Brat in Today's Complex World - F.K. Hean

Talks and Negotiations with My Child - Dr P. Jednaszewski

Negotiation Generation: Take Back Your Parental Authority Without Punishment - L. Reeves Griffin

CHAPTER 25

FAMILY SCAPEGOAT: UNKNOWINGLY CRUEL

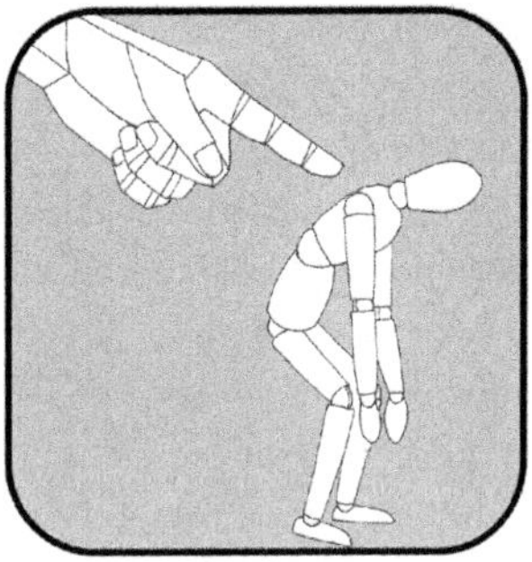

"Is one person in your family being picked on or unfairly blamed for everything? If the answer's yes, you need to act because a family with a scapegoat is a damaged family."
- Michael Padraig Acton -

What is a family scapegoat?

All groups, including families, work themselves into a hierarchy where one person is the strongest, one the weakest, etc. It's a way of creating a homeostasis: a familiar, comfortable way of being. Even if the homeostasis in a family is unhealthy (for example, with alcoholism, narcissism or domestic abuse), it's familiar and we crave familiar because it feels safe. Unless you go through therapy to adjust your unhealthy patterns, you will go back to homeostasis.

In a family, there is always a scapegoat. They are blamed for everything because all of the 'bad' in the family is split off and projected on to them. This theory is very well discussed within object relations theory and informs psychodynamic and psychoanalytic counselling.

What's meant by projection and splitting off? For psychological safety, children need to split the world into good things and bad things. As we get to be more adult, more educated, more aware of the world, we tend to go and work in the grey areas as well. But in the family unit we often slip into those rudimentary, raw patterns where we're looking at who's the best in the family and who's the bad person: the one to blame. We then 'project' all of the family's negative energy on to that person.

You might hear language like, "There you go Betsy, you're spoiling things again," or, "Oh, aren't you amazing? You're always good." These are the ways we position somebody in the family. Sometimes the scapegoat's the parent, sometimes the scapegoat's the child. And the role can even move around depending upon what's happening in the family at the time.

You will also see this play out in reality TV, the most popular and, in my mind, the most unforgiving and rude type of TV today. The producers make a lot of money out of putting people in a group situation and seeing how they fend for themselves. In all of these programmes you will see that one moment somebody's a star, the next moment someone's a scapegoat.

However, a family will try and make the original scapegoat come back because it's familiar and humans crave this familiarity, this homeostasis. They will manipulate situations as a family group until that person is the scapegoat again, the one who takes the blame, the weakest link.

Untold damage happens to a scapegoat's development, and they will tend to repeat these patterns when they're older. How many times in your life have you heard about someone who has broken up with an abusive partner and within six months is back in a relationship with another abusive person? It's because it's a familiar pattern for them. However, sometimes a scapegoat will do an absolute flip and become the bully.

If you have a scapegoat in the family, you will generally have a prince/princess too. All of this is unhealthy, not just for the scapegoat but also for those who think they're the best and invincible. What is healthy? Fairness, understanding and defence of each other. If you feel one person in the family is being picked on too much, being unfairly blamed or is generally seen as the weakest person, you need to do something about it.

Think about your family. Who generally ends up carrying the load? Who's the scapegoat? Work it out and do something about it!

For more guidance, read:

Black Sheep: This Can't Be Happening - R. Scholl
The Parent Gap: Tools to Keep Your Cool, Stay Connected and Change Unhealthy Patterns - R. Rubenstein
The Practice of Family Therapy: Key Elements Across Models - S. Midori Hanna

CHAPTER 26

SOCRATES CAN HELP UNLOCK YOUR KIDS' SECRETS

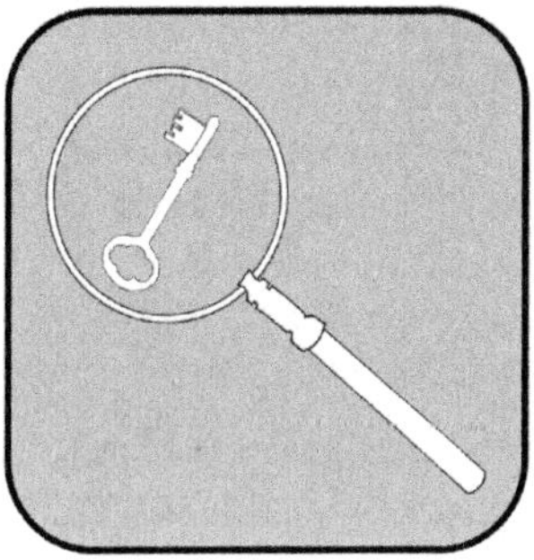

"So, when are you going to start learning about your children? By being Socratic, we also start learning a hell of a lot about ourselves."
- Michael Padraig Acton -

It's very important when we're parenting that sometimes we step back and start asking questions. Sometimes we're too close to see the wood for the trees!

Socrates was very famous for wandering around market squares and trying to solve the mysteries of the universe and life and people. Socratic questions are open-ended, inquisitive and fun—but telling!

What kind of questions could we ask? Well, apart from the obvious: "Are you OK?" "Is all going well at school?" "Have you got enough friends?" and the usual parenting things, you can ask open-ended questions.

Socrates was very famous for asking a question that would lead to somebody divulging a lot of information about the area he was interested in.

What top three questions could you ask your child in order to find out how they're doing and what they want?

Here are some examples:

- When has been your unhappiest time and why? I'll tell you mine if you tell me yours.
- I know your favourite dish but what kinds of food do you tend to like the most?
- Are we similar to families you know at school? How are we different? (That's a leading question to ask your child no matter what age as it can tell you how well you're doing, what your child would like to introduce to the family and what they would like to change.)
- We don't have any Internet next week; they're pulling it down for repairs. What would you like to do?

You might want to slip a Socratic question in during Sunday dinner, when driving to an event, during the school pick-up, or as you're making meatballs, doing the garden or sharing in another family activity. Just begin with, "Oh, I was wondering!"

By being Socratic in our parental fact-finding missions, we avoid becoming lazy. We become a more reflective parent who tries to do things better each time. We become a parent who looks at the umbrella, the overall situation, as well as specific daily things.

We can also work out what we can do to better protect our children. If we don't ask questions in our family, we will never know when there's a problem. How many times have you heard people in the news, friends or relatives saying, "We had no idea"?

Being Socratic is a positive, proactive, mindful practice. What harm can it do?

For more guidance, read:
Stop the Lecturing Start the Conversation - S.H. Sidsworth
The Socratic Parent: How to Raise a Child of Any Age by Asking the Right Questions - P. Sweetow
The Case Method Miracle - A. Jones

CHAPTER 27

BULLYING: HELP!

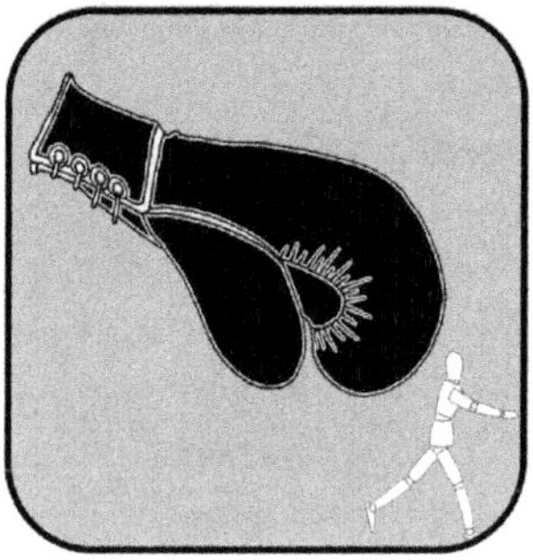

"Finding out that your child is a bully, or being bullied, is probably one of the biggest shocks a parent can have, but don't be silly. Instead of getting caught up in their drama, hear your child and assess the situation."
- Michael Padraig Acton -

What is bullying? In 2018, the UK's top dictionaries updated their definition of bullying as follows:

A person who habitually seeks to harm or intimidate those who they perceive as vulnerable.

Bullying is to persistently hurt somebody by attacking them. The intention is to project on to another that which we don't like about ourselves. For example, if someone sees femininity in somebody else and doesn't accept their own femininity. Parents often teach their children to be bullies, training them to also project that perceived weakness on to others.

Bullying is different to normal inter and intra-group rivalry where a group or individual asserts its position because we all have opinions and beliefs. Bullying is when the bully knows they are hurting somebody, and they are enjoying it. They are getting a relief from it.

Bullying can show itself in many ways. Ten top signs that a child may be being bullied are:

1. Becoming quiet and withdrawn.
2. Acting out at home by becoming violent or disruptive.
3. Avoiding school.
4. Frequent illnesses (headaches, stomach aches, etc.).
5. Unexplained injuries.
6. Seeming to lose or break a lot of their property.
7. Change in eating habits (skipping meals, binge eating, etc.).
8. Nightmares or difficulty sleeping.
9. Sudden loss of friends or avoidance of peers.
10. Slump in grades or the quality of their schoolwork.

What can we do about bullying? It depends on who's doing the bullying. Is it in the environment at school or where you live? Is it in the family? The context around bullying is very important.

As adults, we experience bullying every day in the news, whether it's somebody bullying someone else on a train or politicians bullying each other (they often call it other things but it's still bullying). We see friends of ours being bullied.

I see quite a lot of bullying in my family work. Given the safety of my sessions, all of a sudden, a person will explode, and the family had genuinely no idea that this was the black sheep, the bullied one.

What do we do with a child? How do we separate our own fears and concerns and actually help them in their environment, rather than projecting on to them what our sense or experience of bullying is, or telling them what we would do, even though we're in an adult environment and have more power at times?

What's the extent of the damage? Do you need to remove the child from danger (e.g., is your child being burnt with cigarettes or having needles stuck in them)? Are they likely to suffer emotional damage?

What do we do if our child's the bully? How do we teach our child that bullying may deliver immediate 'rewards' but it doesn't help in the long term?

And when is bullying not bullying? When is it being assertive? When is it that somebody's feeling bullied but they're actually not being bullied? Is there something they haven't told you that other children are seeing and you're not seeing? Are they gay? Do they have a big nose? Do they have smelly feet? Do they have body odour? Is there some truth in the bullying? I know that might sound really controversial but if it's something you can help them with, like etiquette or grooming, maybe you can stop them from being bullied?

The first thing you need to do is assess the situation of the child in their environment. Be Socratic and ask lots of questions and maybe again make meatballs or do the gardening together. Having some kind of stimuli makes the conversation flow easier.

Whether they're a bully or being bullied, ask questions about it:

- How is this happening?
- What do you mean, they almost kicked you in the head?
- What do you mean, you hate this person and you got everybody to gang up against them?

Assess the situation. Talk to somebody you respect and who will not take sides.

Do not get caught up in your child's drama! Don't react. Sleep on it. If they're a victim of bullying, nurture them and help them to understand it's not about them, it's about the person doing the bullying.

Ask the child what they think you can do to resolve things because they generally know the environment better than you.

If your child is the bully, explain what's right from wrong.

Depending on the severity you may need to involve teachers, the Police or a professional such as a psychologist. As parents, you may need to work on stopping bullying in the family unit. This could mean asking an exterior family member for help.

It may be dramatic; it may be benign; it might be that something needs urgent attention, or it might be something you need to monitor for a while but don't get caught up in the drama and really make sure you assess; it's the only way you can help your child.

For more guidance, read:

Bullying: Real and Lasting Ways to Stop Bullies, Stand Up for Yourself and Overcome Fear - A. Caldwell

Bully-Proof Kids - S. O'Malley

The Bullying Antidote: Superpower Your Kids for Life - L. Hart and K. Caven

CHAPTER 28

POSSIBLE SUCCESSFUL CO-PARENTING

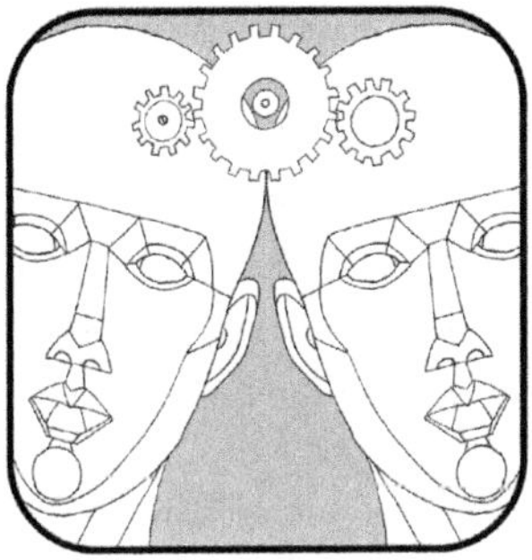

"One of the typical accusations I hear in my work with families is, 'Well, why doesn't he or she do that? What do they do with all that time?' We don't know somebody's life until we live it. It's easy to judge somebody else and avoid judging ourselves or taking responsibility!"
- Michael Padraig Acton

Whether we're living together, separated or divorced, or a family member helping a parent, or a professional such as a psychologist, counsellor or paediatrician, we have to understand the forces at work and the limits of co-parenting.

When co-parenting. we must at all times keep the welfare of the child or children at the forefront. It's very easy for us as parents and co-parents to involve our egos and for the dynamic between us to influence the children's wellbeing. A simple case of this is divorce where the child gets involved in the fight but the fight's not really about the child, the fight's about the adults (see the next chapter for a lawyer's perspective on this).

A co-parent could be a grandparent, sister, brother, family friend, partner, etc. Co-parenting is even about babysitters and after-school sitters. We have to be mindful as to what each person's agenda is.

If our co-parent is the mother or father of our child and that child is living with them part-time or full-time, we have very little power over that time. It doesn't matter how much we want to believe otherwise, unless that child is living with us full-time, that co-parent has an awful lot of influence.

What are the rules for co-parenting in a healthy way? Communication. Not accepting everything you hear as the truth.

How do we find ways to co-parent in a healthy way? How do we identify somebody as an unhealthy co-parent? If any parental management impacts our children in a negative way, we have to assume it's unhealthy.

First, we have to understand our children's co-parenting structure. Who does influence our children? Who is responsible legally for our children? Are there any agreements in the courts or social care?

We also have to understand our agreements and our children's social environment. Is there a conflict? For example, a parent might say, "It's all well and good school saying that we need to do two and a half hours of homework but I'm at work until seven, the children are with their grandparents until I'm back, so how do we do the homework?'

We need to negotiate what's the best for our children.

With co-parenting, we each have to take responsibility for the welfare of our children.

Here are five top rules for co-parenting successfully:

1. Keep the child's welfare at the centre.
2. Hear each other.
3. Make sure our stuff's not getting in the way of the child's wellbeing.
4. Understand your children's influence structure (i.e., is it just two co-parents? Is there another family member that's influencing the child? Is it a good or bad influence?).
5. Observe the child and ask them what's working for them and what's not. Take the answer with a pinch of salt but sometimes kids really do see a lot more than we give them credit for. They might feel trapped, they might feel they have to please certain co-parents. It's really good sometimes to just take a reflective pause on life and ask

them what's working and then make an adult, informed decision on what the child's saying to you.

Don't necessarily think that if something seems unhealthy or an example of bad co-parenting that it is. You have to be really self-reflective, stand back and triple-check that.

When I was training to be a teacher, the first thing I learned was the way I was taught at school wasn't necessarily the best way and I was there to learn the most effective methods. That also works for parenting: how we were parented or how we parent may not necessarily be the best way. We have to be open to healthy criticism and new ideas.

For more guidance, read:

Overcoming the Co-Parenting Trap: Essential Parenting Skills When a Child Resists a Parent - J. A. Moran PhD, T. Sullivan and Matthew Sullivan PhD

The Co-Parenting Survival Guide: Letting Go of Conflict After a Difficult Divorce - J. Zimmerman

Co-Parenting 101: Helping Your Children Thrive after Divorce - D. Philyaw

CHAPTER 29

WHY ARE PARENTS AND CHILDREN CAUGHT UP IN THE COURT SYSTEM?
BY ALYSSA D. HONICKMAN, P.A. FAMILY LAWYER

"Good parenting alongside expert family law guidance supersedes any misconception about what justice represents."
- Michael Padraig Acton -

It was such a pleasure talking with Lisa about the law and parenting. When we parent, we will undoubtedly, at some point in time, have a reason to consult a lawyer or consider doing this. Yes, there is divorce, there are mistakes, there are numerous reasons why lawyers get involved with our parenting roles. Lisa made it clear, from the very start, how parents' ideas of the role of law or a lawyer may be so different from reality. Over to Lisa's wise and detailed support.

How parents get the law wrong

The first misconception is that the lawyer knows every single answer to every single question. People ask me a question and they want a black and white answer. They want me to say, "Well if this is the scenario, this is the answer."

That's not law, that's not life, that's not reality. In my practice, I tell clients the truth: the real truth and not a cookie cutter version of what people want to hear.

I explain to people that when it comes to the law you have to take the statute, which is literally black and white text, and then you have to convert the law to the facts. The factual scenario might be the same for three different families but when you get to court, the outcome is completely different. People get upset by that. I wonder why this upsets people. Then I realise quickly that we live in a world where people want guarantees and definitive answers. If you are putting all of your parenting issues out for a stranger to decide, there are no guarantees. In fact, as lawyers we are barred from making promises of outcome to clients.

Every fact is taken into consideration and the judge's role is to marry the facts to the law and then come up with an outcome. But here's the kicker, judges have discretion. And judges are also real people with real life problems as well. Judges are often torn between keeping things neutral and also having to use their own common sense and morals to make decisions.

One of the common complaints about lawyers is that they waste time and money. It is a hard truth often said about my profession. How do you save your own time and money when meeting with a lawyer?

Common tips on how to save time when meeting with a lawyer

I like people to come in prepared when they meet with me. When I say prepared, I don't mean that they need to come in with an outline.

1. **Prepare yourself mentally and get ready to have an open mind.** If you are a parent, you need to be mentally prepared and have an open mind to listen to what the attorney is going to tell you. What's frustrating as a lawyer is when you have a client come in and say, "This is the direction I want to go" and you give them advice and preparation. Then all of a sudden, 20 minutes into the meeting, they go in a totally different direction.

   So, when I say be prepared, you need to understand, as somebody walking into the danger zone of the court system, what your goal is. What are you looking to achieve? And if you're not sure and you're literally just talking to an attorney because you need advice on what to do with A, B and C situation, you need to let them know from the beginning by telling them, "I haven't made a decision yet. I'm here to get some information. I need your help in guiding me through that process." That's what I like to see.

2. **Understand integrity.** For me it comes down to integrity. I mean be true to yourself and what your real intent is. If your intent is to merely trash the other parent and achieve nothing in the end except cause grief for the entire family and your children, then you have no integrity. If you don't know what you want but need advice and direction on how to achieve a certain result, be honest with your lawyer. A good lawyer can see from the beginning of a meeting what someone's true intent is. If you play games and hide behind grandiose versions of reality, you can't be helped by a lawyer. You have to be true to yourself and realise what is important in your case.

3. **Speak your truth.** Finding your voice in the legal system is difficult. Finding a lawyer that speaks your truth is even more difficult. You have to be able to state exactly what you believe to be true and your true intentions with a lawyer. The lawyer can't help you if you truly don't speak up or are so confused with the situation that you don't know which way to turn. Be honest with yourself and set realistic goals for your own life and your own case.

4. **Take referrals to other professionals.** When a lawyer meets with a client, we often look for certain signals. These signals dictate how the case should be handled and what direction is best for each client. The same facts can be applied differently in each case. If the person is truly lost on what to do, or needs specific help on mental health issues, or with the impact mental health issues have had on them individually, or on their family, we refer these clients to mental health professionals. I know what a legal case can do to a person's mental state. I usually refer those clients to a therapist immediately. These clients will be best

served with a lawyer and a mental health professional on their side and aiding them through the process. I can't answer mental health questions or diagnose issues. I need the client to accept referrals and get help from the correct professional.

Tips from the lawyer when meeting with a client who may be a victim of domestic violence

Domestic abuse can be in the form of emotional, verbal and/or physical abuse. Emotional and mental abuse can be in the form where the person is consistently being broken down verbally by their partner, spouse or relative.

In this case, people need to be handled differently because they're so scared, they don't know what they need for protection. I always take my time with these kinds of clients.

Oftentimes, they don't understand that they need help. Sometimes they put up a wall where they just can't accept anything. They repeat over and over, "This is what's happening, and this is what I'm doing." These clients are usually involved in the cycle of violence. They are constantly being manipulated to think they are not adequate or not smart enough or just not good enough all the way around. People who are victimised over and over again can translate this abuse to their children without even knowing it.

1. **Getting a therapist.** These clients need a therapist on board immediately. I will usually help them find a therapist to guide them with mental health issues.

2. **Listening to the client even if they do not make sense.** Meeting with them initially is really just listening and hearing what they have to say, being a soundboard for them to express themselves in a safe environment. I'm taking notes and figuring out in my head what's the best way to protect them, but I don't discuss that with them. I don't tell them what I'm going to do to protect them because they're not going to want me to do it or let me do it anyway, but I start getting myself prepared for that. What I mean specifically is that I need to

help them formulate a plan for safety. They may not think they need a plan, but the purpose of a plan is to help them feel safe and know there is a support system for them. I do not want these clients to wait until something terrible happens if the facts show a pattern that could lead to something very dangerous.

3. **Explaining about victim advocates.** I provide victim advocate information for the counties I work in: Palm Beach, Miami-Dade and Broward and I also give them details of domestic violence shelters where they can go and speak to a therapist that will usually charge a lower rate or use a sliding scale based upon their income for fees. There are also places where they can go with their children, where they're safe, there's fun stuff going on and they're out of that abusive environment. Places are popping up all over our state and I wish we had more of them.

4. **Following up with a client.** Lastly, I follow up with them, even if they don't hire me. I call them, I text them, I send emails. I want these clients to know they are supported, and it is not about hiring me as their attorney but more about letting them know another individual cares about them and their children.

How to support children going through a family breakdown

First of all, it depends on the age but what's most important to me, from observing my own kids, is to understand that they are watching, paying attention and repeating. And they're sometimes repeating things in inappropriate situations because they don't know what's appropriate and what's not.

Children have to be comfortable talking to either parent about what they're feeling and how a situation is affecting them. That comes from the parents encouraging their children by saying, "If you're upset, if you're having a bad day, if you're mad at dad or mom, you need to be able to talk about it."

An easy way to get your child to open up is by asking, "How are you feeling about (insert topic)?" For example, "How are you feeling about Dad not calling you tonight when he said he would?" or "How are you feeling about Mom forgetting to bring you the snack you asked for during the daytime?" *I am guilty of this one with the snacks all the time.*

Kids should also know, from their parents, that they will not be judged. They should not be told, "Oh, that didn't happen," or "You're wrong," or "You're misinterpreting what mom or dad said." No. The point is, they need to be able to talk to their parents and say, "I'm upset when you do that," or "Dad told me this and it made me upset and I want to talk to you about it, Mom." Or mom and mom, dad and dad, it makes no difference who the parents are.

For example, I came home from work the other day and I was angry at everyone; it had been a stressful day. I hadn't had a chance to really process what went on during the day and I started yelling at my husband over silverware on the table or something. My eldest (she's eight) comes over to me, in front of my other daughter (aged four) and my husband and asked, "Why are you yelling at Dad?" At first, I said, "No, I'm not yelling. What are you talking about?" She insisted, "No, you were yelling," so I had to stop for a minute and realise that she's watching me and she's going to start yelling at people if she thinks that's OK. So, I turned, acknowledged her feelings and told her she was right. She usually is! Yes, my eight-year-old is usually right. I don't like admitting that but it's true. I said, "You know what, you're right. I was yelling. I lost my temper. I should not have been yelling at Dad. There was no reason for that. I'm sorry. When you're angry about something you really shouldn't be yelling you should be talking to people and letting people know how you feel." And she said, "You're right, Mom. That's what I should do when I get angry too." So, it became a lesson. I think a negative reaction would have been to get mad at my daughter for telling me that I was yelling, whether I was yelling or not. I should not have questioned her because that's what she saw and that's what she believed and that was her reality in the moment.

What we see with children growing up in environments that are toxic, where mom and dad are fighting all the time–and I had a lot of this growing up myself–is that they don't know what to do. So, sometimes kids hide or act out and behave inappropriately, screaming and yelling, throwing things. Some kids just shut down completely and won't talk at home but act out in school.

They have to be able to tell their parents how they're feeling about the situation. That's hard but if children have learned, from their parents, that they can talk about the situation regardless of whose house they're at: grandma, grandpa, mom, dad, whatever, they have to speak up. Talk about it.

Honesty and being human

I had different beliefs when my kids were younger but now that they're older and we talk about everything, I think it's important to be honest with your children. You can't tell them bogus stories that they'll figure out later are a lie. You have to tell them what's going on. Your kids will resent you later if you are not honest with them. Even if it hurts and it is uncomfortable, kids need to know the truth and you as the parent have to explain it in a manner they understand without confusing them or making them scared.

Secondly, you have to let them see you get emotional. There were definitely times when I was very upset and I would just hide in my closet about all different kinds of things, not often but every now and then. I was scared for my kids to see me cry because I didn't want them to think mommy was upset. Then there came a time, probably in the pandemic last year when we were all in quarantine when I admitted, "I'm really upset right now and I'm crying and this is why I'm crying." You might not want your kids to see you upset but it shows them that you're human. You've got a pulse. It's OK.

How could the law be better to parents?

The first thing I would change is the amount of time that it takes to get a hearing in front of a judge. That is probably the biggest pitfall in the counties that I work at: Palm Beach, Miami and Broward.

It's this concept of what's considered an 'emergency.' In Florida, you can check a box on the e-portal when you file your case which says you certify–you're basically making an affidavit (sworn statement) –that your situation is considered an emergency under the law. But that is basically, for lack of a better term, life or death. If a judge does not step in, somebody's life is in danger to the point where they could potentially be killed–it's big stuff. Most emergencies don't fall in those categories because if they did, you're calling the Police and law enforcement is taking action. You're not waiting for a judge to agree to give you a hearing date in 27 days.

So, I think the concept of an emergency has to be amended. You should be able to check a box to say if there is a significant issue affecting the emotional wellbeing or mental state of a child you can get an Ex Parte hearing in front of a judge within 15 days. I'm not saying you are going to win and the judge is going to grant whatever you're asking for but you should at least get access to the system. It's literally a five-minute review by a judge who can decide if the person has properly pled that issue and whether the child is in danger because of the reasons given. Danger can be mental abuse as well as physical abuse. In fact, mental abuse is sometimes worse in my opinion.

The problem with it taking months to be heard is that parents cut back on their lawyer time because they don't want to pay the legal fees because they think they're not going to go in front of the judge for a long time. But during that time, they're sabotaging their case and ruining their chances of ever winning the petition they've filed. They're making poor choices because they're so mad and frustrated with the system and then I come in and I'm like, "Now what?"

The other thing I believe is, if you can show that one parent has not had contact with the child within a six-month timeframe and you can plead it properly and have it notarised with an affidavit submitted by the affected parent, you should immediately be given the next available court date, a 15-minute Special Set Hearing or whatever it needs to be. That should take priority over everything else on the docket: the money, the property AND the attorneys' fees. It shocks me how quickly you can file a motion to get attorneys' fees, get before a judge and be heard on your issue. Whereas I had a case where the dad was stopped from seeing his kids for 18 months because the mom had taken them out of the state and hid them and refused to allow the dad to have any contact. Unfortunately, my client's former attorney had a heart attack and was in the hospital and completely unable to work. His case sat in the system for almost 18 months. Then we had to get a Guardian Ad Litem on the case because the judge wouldn't hear anything until the Guardian had completed an investigation and spoken to the kids to see if they were safe. The dad finally came to me. I took three days and said, "No, no, no! Guardian, you've been paid, you need to talk to the kids. Second, the mom has to be in front of a judge and get a temporary time-sharing motion because she's preventing the dad from having any contact with those kids." I don't know how but I ended up getting a hearing within about 20 days but prior to that 18 months had passed since the dad had seen his kids. That sort of stuff drives me crazy. It is unfair but is a reality of the court system.

The role of therapists in the courtroom

The statute has to be amended in some way because there are so many requirements for therapists to be able to testify in the courtroom. I have always believed, even when I was a prosecutor, that if a therapist can testify to the things that they have seen, to help a family, that can save hours of trial time because the judges should be able to take the therapist's word as opposed to crazy lawyers' arguments and the 'he said, she said' battles in the courtroom. Therapists are professionals testifying as experts drawing on their experience and training. People are scared of that and judges often don't like to hear from therapists in the courtroom and so their testimony is struck.

Parent lawyers – dealing personally with tough cases

I'm still working on how to deal with personal issues within my own family and dealing with clients with difficult emotional cases. I haven't mastered it yet. It's definitely a work in progress. I've done better this year. 2020, I really worked on it to try to make myself a better human being in general: a better mom, a better wife, all of that. Part of this is SELF CARE. Not just saying you are going to take time for yourself, but actually clearing your calendar once a week and getting a massage, facial, or mani/

pedi. You have to do it. And you can't do it and feel bad about yourself. You have to embrace the time you spent out of your day to take care of yourself.

I think what's helpful is being able to talk to people that you trust. And sometimes it's not always lawyers. A lot of my friends that I became really close with before I had children were lawyers because we worked all the time and could bounce ideas off each other. But now, when I'm having those moments, I need to talk to other moms and it doesn't necessarily have to be other mom lawyers. I have a lot of friends that are mom lawyers, running their own practices, and they're in what I consider healthy marriages–who knows if that's real or not–with kids and it's nice to be able to talk to them. But I think it's even more powerful for me, when I really need to just process what happened in court, to just talk to other moms because the legal part of it is just frustrating sometimes. After I've been in court for eight hours, I don't want to talk to another lawyer when I just want mom advice. I end up having a legal argument about the statute and the case law and what the judge should have done. . . I don't care about that. I just want to vent. I just want to bounce ideas off each other, not really to understand it but just to talk about it.

I think talking about it is the first part of the process but not to people that are going to tell you what they think you should have, could have done. No, it needs to be someone that is listening with an open ear and is willing to hear what you're trying to say without criticising and judging. It's very hard to find friends and relatives that are willing to do that–like finding a needle in a haystack–but I think that's where you must start because otherwise you just bring it home and dwell on it. Understand yourself too: your thoughts, feelings, and emotions and how you deal with things.

To watch a video of this interview, go to https://mpamind.com

A note from Michael: If any lawyers are reading this, get rid of your alpha when you're dealing with a case involving children. We are all the parents of all of our children. That's my motto. They have to be heard and seen. Stop the games when people are getting hurt.

Children in the Family Courts: An English Perspective

by Alison Green, Partner and Head of the Family & Relationship Team at Mackrell.Solicitors

Becoming a parent can be one of the most joyous occasions within our lives, but raising a child is not without its challenges. You are often offered advice from friends, family, the media and online about how you should be raising your child and how to deal with the difficulties that come along the way. No two parents or children are, however, the same and so, rather than focusing on one particular strategy, parents often find it best to adopt a general approach. This is a set of values and parameters that are flexible and not necessarily rigid or applied the same way time and time again.

Having worked with many families during my 25 plus years as a lawyer, I have certainly seen my fair share of different approaches to parenting from couples and guardians. Those that find themselves in difficulties often find it is down to a lack of collaboration, both between the individual parents and/or a child and their parents. In fact, an inability to reach a consensus on how a child should be raised is a common reason for conflict within a relationship, which could eventually contribute to separation. Collaboration focuses on making the family a team, where each person is guided by the same principles, values and goals. Rather than set rigid rules, it creates a framework for communication and agreement that keeps each party involved. This imparts ownership on each individual and makes them feel like their thoughts and opinions are valued, which keeps them invested in maintaining the status quo.

This is particularly important for families where a divorce or separation has taken place, as is so common the case these days. The breakdown of a relationship is often acrimonious (to some degree the legal system has for too long been focused on blame). This, unsurprisingly, creates barriers to communication and collaboration when trying to raise a child, with the waters being muddied further where a former spouse finds a new partner and/or remarries. Failing to come to an agreement on the raising of a child can create great difficulties within a family dynamic that can have a lasting impact on the behaviour, values and upbringing of a child. Achieving consensus through collaboration, whether separated or together, is no simple task. It requires understanding and, to some degree, sacrifice for each person involved in the relationship - including step-parents. Everyone will have different views on parenting based on their own experiences, culture and thought processes. As a partner, you must be willing to give a little here and there to reach a point where all parties agree, which is no easy task. Being careful not to 'impose' rules or goals that create conflict is key - a process that requires careful negotiation and a lot of empathy.

For those already with children, it never hurts to discuss your values and aspirations for your offspring, while for those looking to grow a family it is a discussion that can really help to ensure you are on the same page. From my professional experience, this is the best way to build a healthy family dynamic. It ensures that parents truly work together in the best interests of a child, and it helps to alleviate any strain on relationships between the parents as well. It is, in fact, the same approach that our profession increasingly applies to most family law cases, as it allows parties to set a fair agenda, be transparent, prevent misunderstanding and, hopefully, reach an open-minded consensus.

This is clearly not legal advice but identifies many of the practicalities that can affect parents. Should legal advice be needed then a lawyer should of course be consulted.

A final note from Michael, who has worked with Alison and Lisa on several legal cases involving families

I am really pleased Alison and Lisa were able to contribute to this book. I truly value their professional experience and wisdom. I would also like to add that collaboration between parties is helpful only as far as it is balanced and is not putting the children or caregivers at risk. The children have to have a voice, but only to the extent that they are not using it to blackmail the caregivers or hold them to ransom. The same works the other way around. I have worked on divorces involving children that are at the 100 million plus ticket level. Even though these families have all the resources at their disposal, the children still suffer. One parent or both manipulate the children in taking sides or drip feed the children false and fake news. This damages the children and their relationship with their parents and caregivers. It is heartless and happens time and time again. It may make a parent or caregiver feel better but, really, at the cost of the children?

Don't believe in magic at your lawyer's office. There is none. No wand or secret handshake. Lawyers run businesses where they bill. They may have empathy and care too but it is a business. No freebies, no handouts. It is a place to mediate and uphold the law. The law gives us guidance about what is permitted and why.

Divorce and child protection are easy to resolve. Welfare of children at all times is key. In a divorce situation, do not use money, belongings and children as war weapons to feed your ego or to try and tame your upset or feelings of injustice. I may sound hard or unreasonable. However, the only people who win a battle in court, or between lawyers, when a familial issue becomes a war of individuals is the lawyers who will bill more because this takes up so much time. And, the people that get most hurt in the end is YOU and any CHILDREN involved. People do not realise but lawyers are severely monitored over their billing and have to only bill time used. They have to prove this too. It is the client and their positioning that runs up the bill. My best advice is to mediate issues between the family with a therapist (an experienced therapist who is trained in systemics and the law), tame your demands and agree the best way forward. Then go to your lawyer. ONLY use a FAMILY LAWYER for issues concerning FAMILY. Same as therapists. ONLY USE A TRAINED AND EXPERIENCED THERAPIST for your familial issues. I have seen so many train wrecks in my career. . . this situation can be diverted.

Always remember that lawyers take care of the law; they are not there to make decisions about your family issues and dictate to your family. You are the expert of your family and your positioning. You must first consider what you want and need from the process, and then YOU brief your lawyer. Be open and honest: ALWAYS tell your lawyer everything, otherwise they will not be able to take care of you in the name of the law. Your lawyer will keep confidentiality, but if you hold back information or lie, you could damage your opportunity of getting a good enough outcome for you and those you are concerned about.

For more guidance, read:

The Legal Adoption Guide: Safely Navigating the System - C. Alexander-Roberts
How to Annihilate a Narcissist: In the Family Court - R. Watson
Before I Do: A Legal Guide to Marriage, Gay and Otherwise - E. F. Schwartz

CHAPTER 30

FLYING SOLO: HANDLING THE TURBULENCE OF SINGLE PARENTING

"The worst thing we can do as a single parent is keep our child in chaos. If we don't teach them boundaries, they will probably fail at everything they do!"
- Michael Padraig Acton -

First, is there such a thing as a single parent?

As a parent, we'll have many influences affecting us and our children but if we have an unhealthy family or we don't have the support of our own parents or a co-parent (i.e., the co-parent abandoned the family, died, or is unhealthy and we're trying to keep them away) then we are a single parent to all intents and purposes.

How do we make decisions? How do we manage a child's challenges (which can be a thankless task, no matter what age the child)? What are the guidelines for being a successful, healthy single parent?

There is no book on single parenting. We are going to make mistakes! Therefore, it's very important to be reflective about our parenting because we don't have a co-parent to tell us when we're being too strict or too lenient. When there are two or more parents involved, we can find a way of balancing, which is healthy for the child. The child can learn how to argue and what's reasonable. A single parent hasn't got that benchmark or lever.

In an unhealthy situation, when a child challenges a parent, they will either have too firm boundaries or no boundaries at all. The worst danger is when a parent takes what their child does as personal. When we have our children, we are training them to have an independent life from us. Your child is in training for their adult life. We are part of their journey, so when a child starts doing things to annoy us, they're really just pushing the boundaries to learn what they need for their adult life in the world. Don't expect your child to be your friend all the time!

Is your child testing the boundaries too much? Are they becoming aggressive, not eating, pushing power around, not coming off the Xbox, being on their device all the time or otherwise being difficult? If it worries you then it probably is an issue and you, as a single parent, need to find a way of tackling it in a reasonable and fair way.

Sometimes, we get caught up in the drama, especially when we're under the same roof. The best way is to be in a neutral place where you can discuss things. If that doesn't work, bring in professional help: a teacher, a nun, a priest, an auntie. . . anybody who is wise, gentle and can help you manage.

Imagine a court room. It's got people arguing and it's got a judge thinking deeply before announcing, "Well, in my opinion, that seems to be the best course of action." That is the perfect example of what a single parent needs to aspire to.

To be the one and only caregiver is tiring. We need to triple check everything and it can feel a very lonely place. Sometimes, we need somebody to pull us out of that. We should avoid involving our child as a caregiver for us. This is natural if we've got nobody else but we're bringing challenges or ideas that really aren't for a child to process. When we share these with our children, we can make them insecure, defensive, worried and even aggressive. We are putting them in that position by over-sharing! A child needs to feel safe with boundaries and balance.

For more guidance, read:

Single Parenting That Works: Six Keys to Raising Happy, Healthy Children in a Single-Parent Home - K. Leman

I am the Parent Who Stayed: Joyfully Parenting Alone - N. Farr

CHAPTER 31

KINDNESS: WHAT'S ITS ROLE?

"There's a thin line, in the words of Annie Lennox, between love and hate.
We are all capable of hating our children at times.
But even kindness is dangerous. If we let our children run riot without correction, that's the worst unkindness of all."
- Michael Padraig Acton -

What is the definition of kindness in parenting because the Bible teaches us one thing and life teaches us another? How can we be kind when we're angry? When we have to set a boundary? When we have to slap our child's hand out of a fire whether that's literally or metaphorically (e.g., tackling teenage sex or drug-taking).

Is there a template of kindness we can follow? What were our own experiences of kindness when we were children?

Healthy parenting is about putting aside our own personal reactions and using a wisdom template to help guide our children through life's rights and wrongs. However, that all becomes very complicated when the child gets a voice of their own and enters the separation stage which, in my experience, seems to be getting earlier with every decade.

At that point, all the grey areas come in and our children test us with their demands, behaviours and reactions. They will also try to manipulate us because every person in this world bends the rules to get what they want. We must always understand that our children are not an extension of our narcissistic selves. They are individual souls and no two are identical.

Manipulation can be used to help others in a healthy manner, so when we see our children behave in this way, we shouldn't assume they're in the wrong. In fact, giving for the common good of all is to be kind. Let's see if an action is for the benefit and common good of all and that can be our benchmark for kindness.

Kindness is something we need to teach our children. We don't give birth to one child that's kind and another that's unkind. It's how we develop them. It's how we treat them. It's how we lead by example.

We need to remember to tell them that we can be kind while asserting boundaries. Being kind without boundaries is giving your child the understanding they can do anything they want without consequences. That's unhealthier than being strict and showing tough love because you're not preparing them for the world.

So, even though I'm taking your device from you for three weeks, I'm doing it for a good reason and I'm still kind and loving even though you might hate me.

If you take the device as an act of anger or wanting to hurt or retaliate, that's different. That's not kind.

What's a good way to keep ourselves in check? We can make an agreement with ourselves that if we're going to give in to a knee-jerk reaction, generally it's not going to be a kind thing to do–so take a pause. Some of my favourite parenting phrases were, "Let me think about it," and "That seems reasonable, let me get back to you." Anything to give me some time to go away and think. Then, if I did overreact, I was always quick to say sorry when things were calmer.

As long as we learn from our unkind reactions, we're on the path towards a better, kinder human life and soul experience. If we don't learn from our unkind reactions, then that's a big problem area.

So, it's finding a tricky balance in the grey areas between kindness, boundaries, healthy discipline and non-negotiables such as education, health and wellbeing. Sometimes, as the saying goes, we have to be unkind to be kind.

For more guidance, read:

Parenting Forward: How to Raise Children with Justice, Mercy and Kindness - C. Wang Brandt and R. Held Evans

A New Alphabet for Humanity - L. McGregor

CHAPTER 32

MICHAEL'S 1, 2, 3
REALLY DOES RESOLVE CONFLICT

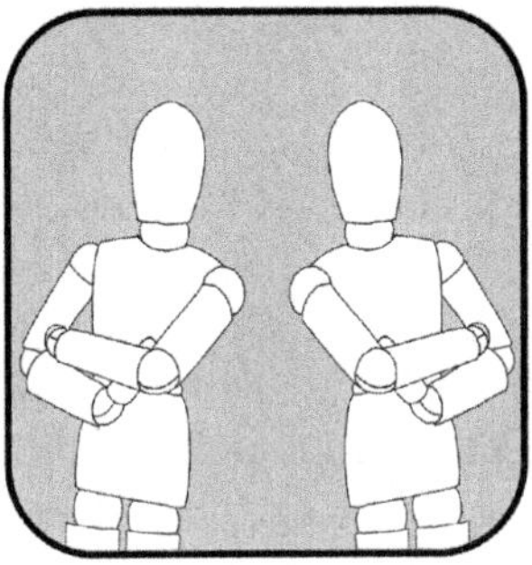

"I adapted the 1, 2, 3 in adult communication from evidence-based transactional analysis. Using it with children and adults alike has been a godsend to me, leading to earth-shattering shifts and transformations in families."
- Michael Padraig Acton -

It's a very honest and real way of exposing how people are feeling—and why—without projecting on to them what we feel they're feeling (or somehow getting inside their heads using ESP).

So how does it work? It's very simple but each of the three stages do take a lot of work.

When responding to the three questions below (and it's best to write them down), you really have to triple-check that you feel the honesty of what you're saying in your gut:

1. **How do I feel?** This has to be an emotion. You can feel angry, cheated, violated, misunderstood, hurt, happy, relieved. . . Whatever they are, we have to write down a list of feelings and pick the top three of what really sits in our gut as true. So, an example would be, 'I feel angry, sad and upset.'

2. **Because. . .** We've already done the feeling. Next is the truth, the evidence. So, for instance, 'I feel angry, sad and upset because when I came to dinner you all started without me and then called me names as a family. I sat there not wanting to be with you and you didn't give me any opportunity to tell you why I was late again.'

3. **To resolve this. . .** Continuing the example, this could be, 'To resolve this, I propose that if I'm late for dinner you wait for me or ask me if everything's OK. I can then give you an answer rather than sitting through dinner with nobody talking to me and making me out to be the bad person.'

That's a very simple example but it gets the truth out there of how I'm feeling rather than me continuing to pretend that the situation's not happening. I'm sitting quietly because I feel really hurt and misunderstood and if you had enquired, you would realise that I'm struggling with an eating disorder. I've been purging myself and I'm scared of coming to the table because I had to eat, and it puts me in an awkward situation.

Another example would be, 'I feel dismayed and hurt because you made decisions about where we were going to have my birthday meal and didn't include me. You chose your favourite restaurant that doesn't really cater for vegetarians. To resolve this in future, I suggest we discuss what kind of restaurant or experience would suit all of us.'

The 1 ,2, 3 in adult communication is the opening gambit for truth, consideration and care. Now, unfortunately, what we do by being honest and truthful is we become vulnerable because we're telling people how we really feel and why and what the problem is. That can be met with defence, agitation or even support; we don't know. However, if we really, hand on stomach, feel that these are our truths we won't really care what comes back.

When I was training with aboriginal shamans in Australia, they taught me this, 'If you fire out a boomerang that has the truth in it, when it comes back, you're OK with it.' That's exactly what they meant: the 1, 2, 3 in transactional analysis. If we divulge our truth, we can sit comfortably with it and it's up to others to then understand what our truth and experience is, and what we need, and then they can choose to act upon it or not.

For more guidance, read:
Three Pearls: Transactional Analysis Fairy World - M. Naubert
TA for Kids: Powerful Techniques for Developing Self-Esteem - A.M. Freed

CHAPTER 33

CAUTION: EVERYTHING IS SO DANGEROUS THAT NOTHING IS TRULY FRIGHTENING

"If you are an anxious parent, have depressive issues or feel hopeless or that the world's unfair, be mindful to get help because there are no ifs or buts–you are terribly damaging your children."
- Michael Padraig Acton -

The worst thing we can do as parents is to catastrophise or overly dramatise things because if we do this often enough, the child will sit there and think, 'Well, that's just another one. . .'. They won't know what to really be concerned about or what the benchmark is for something that truly is threatening or damaging.

And there's more. . .

In an experiment into depression, carried out several decades ago (fortunately one which would never be conducted today), dogs were put into individual caged kennels. Researchers were trying to work out what depression was, why it seemed to persist and what hopelessness did to a person in the long-term.

Each dog had a platform they could get to that represented safety. The bottom of the cage was then electrified to give the dogs a shock. The shocks weren't very strong, let me just say that right now, but nevertheless, I would never condone that kind of experiment personally.

Researchers did learn a lot about depression, human behaviour and the human psyche.

After each shock, the dogs jumped to safety on the platform. Next, in half of the cages, the platform was taken away and the floors were shocked again. What do you think the dogs without a platform to safety did?

The dogs had no safety, they had no hope, they had nowhere to go. So, they just lay down on the floor of their kennels and took the shocks. Very sad but it did explain a lot about depression and the human condition.

If everything is a catastrophe, if everything's wrong, if everything's a drama, you can create a no hope, no safety environment for your child. They will not only fail to realise what is dangerous and what's not, due to being on heightened alert all the time, but they can also learn to give up. They will become lethargic, hopeless and ultimately depressed because their parents or caregivers are telling them that there is no safe place, there is no hope; everything is a disaster.

To summarise, we have to be very careful what messages we give our children. With anxiety overkill, we give our children no template for understanding which situations are truly dangerous or when they need to be alert. At the same time, we leave them in a hopeless situation that leads to depression. They will give up even striving for a safe environment.

For more guidance, read:

Parenting Out of Control: Anxious Parents in Uncertain Times - M. K. Nelson

Anxious Kids, Anxious Parents: 7 Ways to Stop the Worry Cycle and Raise Courageous and Independent Children - R. Wilson PhD and L Lyons

CHAPTER 34

SEPARATING OUT IS NATURAL. DON'T FIGHT IT

"From the moment of birth, each of us, including our children, are born to die. We have to learn to let them go."
- Michael Padraig Acton -

John Bowlby, the founder of attachment theory, talked about the four phases of attachment which begin when the baby separates from the womb (maternal deprivation). He also talked about styles of attachment: secure, anxious-resistant, avoidant and disorganised. The research that followed these theories discovered that if we don't separate out from our children and allow them to separate out from us in a healthy way, we can cause myriad problems for ourselves as parents and for our children.

Unfortunately, we are never taught about this unless we study it as a psychologist, sociologist or therapist. Isn't it funny that Jo Bloggs public doesn't have a clue about this, yet parenthood is the most common occupation?

There is an unusual but well-documented phenomenon whereby boys who have had a very good relationship with their mothers, all of a sudden one day, without warning, turn around and literally throw their mothers through the kitchen wall. It's an extreme example of the fact that a child has to, at some point, separate out from its parents or caregivers.

Girls tend to separate out earlier and much more rapidly than boys. At this time, they start to express their own identity, fight for territory at home and give those dirty looks!

So, what do we do as parents when our child, all of a sudden, says, "Don't hold my hand, you're embarrassing me," or "I'm not going out with you"? It's tough. Heart breaking. We're wondering what we did wrong. Who is this monster who used to be my child? But this is all natural and healthy.

To start with, it's important to understand that we're not designed to live in boxes. Whether you live in a mansion with 17 wings and room for a pony or a one-bedroom flat with five children, separation still occurs. The process is guided by socialisation and by the templates we follow from how we were brought up. It centres around claiming territory: territory over the kitchen, over food, over bedrooms, over the way we look, over who we are in love with. . .

Different cultures have different ways of separating out. For example, Middle Eastern people tend to separate out from their children much later than Western people. This comes from the Bedouins where the strength is in the tribe.

So how do we best manage separation? When do we draw a line and say, "Yes, this is acceptable. That's just you separating out," and when do we say, "You're pushing the boundaries," or "This is unhealthy"?

Again, what's not negotiable with our children are education, wellbeing and health. If their separating out from us affects any of those areas, it's time to act.

- If your 11-year-old child is separating out from you by making dinner, unsupervised, using a hot stove, there's a problem with that!
- If your 13-year-old child is separating out by going topless in a club and taking drugs, that's not OK; that's bad for their health.
- If your child is not doing homework and saying, "Screw you, you can't tell me what to do anymore," that is a problem you need to manage and solve.

How do we give our children a feeling of healthy separation but also get them through to that 18-year mark so that they're free and have their own identity but also have a moral compass and values?

Again, the most important thing is to hear your child and ask questions. The most powerful thing we can do with our kids going through this difficult time of separation is to be interested (but not overly interested so that they feel they don't own what they're doing and saying).

Try this five-step plan to healthy separation:

1. **Acknowledge our child's level of maturity and individuality.** If we have several children, we might find that one's more mature and makes more reasoned decisions than another. We have to treat them accordingly. If somebody is being unreasonable and making mistakes, we need to get to know them better so that we can help them. Not to micro-manage them, because that's unhealthy too, but to manage them effectively.

2. **Lead by example.** If you're anxious and holding on to your husband, wife or partner and not managing things very well with your children, they will learn that everything is a catastrophe, that they are also going to have to hang on to people really tightly. That might actually stop their healthy separation, which can cause them to make all sorts of bad decisions. I know one child who got accepted to Cambridge University with a full scholarship but couldn't take the place because she didn't feel able to leave home. It all worked out for her but that's an idea of unhealthy attachment. As a child, she hadn't gone through the stages to the point where she could let go of her parents. The mother of that child had unfortunately lost her own mother at a young age because she had left the family unit and took her sister. Her father then dropped down dead in front of her two years later so she clearly had some attachment issues and passed those over to her child.

3. **Observe and understand what's <u>really</u> going on with behaviour, separation and attachment.** Remember when your child first started to toddle, when they were literally 'finding their feet'? As they take

their first steps you have to, with your heart in your mouth, let go of them so that they can waddle over to that next piece of furniture. When they make it, everyone jumps and screams and cries, "My child's walking." That's a healthy part of separation. As is refusing food. Your child is saying, "No, I'm not going to eat that; I'm going to throw it on the floor. I'm going to exert my power. This is my independence." And this is all before the child is really thinking or remembering. It's called 'operant conditioning' because the child is learning through 'operating' on their environment.

So, what happens when we take our child to school? Some children seem fine while others are screaming and crying. Similarly, if the child goes into hospital, some seem to take it very well and others scream and are absolute monsters. Again, this is part of separation. In fact, researchers recently discovered that it is the children who are quieter and seem to cope well with these situations that are actually doing ten times worse than those who are screaming. This is because they are usually dissociating and going into themselves. They often have extreme issues later on with attachment in both their families and personal relationships. So, if your child seems to cope with any circumstance, you need to dig beneath the quietness to see if something else is going on. On the other hand, if our child is very disruptive and 'acting out', it means they want something but don't have the language to express it. I once secured a job in a hospital working with young people because I told the interviewer that my real role was understanding what a child means when they say, "This is shit." It's really important to delve down layer after layer to discover what the 'shit' actually is. We may know what mechanical problems and life stresses they are dealing with, but we also have to understand how the child is interpreting things. Whether they are quietly coping or screaming the house down, if we can help our children to understand and accept their feelings, they won't grow up with an unhealthy attachment to us.

4. **Play with them.** What I mean by play is say, "Sure. You know how to cook a chicken better than me? Cook it!" You have to supervise them

but let them experiment with their independence. It's a win-win. If they cook the chicken perfectly and you all congratulate them, that's an amazing thing for your child because it's the same as a toddler walking from one piece of furniture to another. It is allowing them the grace to prove themselves. However, if that child doesn't cook the chicken as well as you (which is more likely since there are so few budding child chefs), then the child will understand their dependence upon mum, dad or caregivers for nutrition and food safety reasons. But you can still give them an opportunity to separate out by asking, "What would you like to try next? Would you like to try doing something in the garden? What can you do to show yourself you've got a role in this family?" It's part of healthy separation for a child to take on responsibility.

5. **Let them go.** Even though it's painful, we have to let go of our children. When we give birth to a child, we start to let them go immediately. That's a constant across cultures and situations. In some circumstances, your teenager or adult child might need us again and we will lap that up. That's normal because we all feel the need for more nurturing at different times. But we also have to understand that this is temporary, and our job is to get them back on their feet and not keep them in that vulnerable state. Our job is to be mindful that we are always letting go of our children.

For more guidance, read:

Dibs in Search of Self: Personality Development in Play Therapy - V. M. Axline

The Simple Guide to Attachment Difficulties in Children: What They Are and How to Help - B. de Thierry

CHAPTER 35

REAL FORGIVENESS REQUIRES UNDERSTANDING

"We as parents are human. And the most difficult thing to do at times when you're human is to truly, genuinely forgive. If we don't forgive, it builds into resentment. Resentment is toxic. It destroys us, it destroys relationships and it destroys the future."
- Michael Padraig Acton -

It's worth bearing in mind that even if you think you had a wonderful childhood, how you were brought up wasn't necessarily the best way. It really depends on how the family managed anger. A really good read would be the first chapter of *Families and How to Survive Them by John Cleese and Robyn Skinner.*

We can easily understand forgiveness when somebody has deliberately wronged us. But what happens if they haven't? For example, a child may be just fluffing their own feathers and actually being pretty reasonable when they say, "I don't want to do it that way," or "I would like to eat in quarter of an hour."

If you feel that you need to forgive your child, the best point is to write down 'forgiveness' and then do a mind map of why you feel your child should apologise and seek your forgiveness. Is it because you're angry, disappointed, shocked, sad? Once you've nailed the one that feels right in your stomach, for example anger, do another mind map of that anger, asking yourself, 'What am I angry about? What did my child do to cause this anger? Why has this anger not left me yet? Is this something that's mammoth and really needs to be attended to or is it something that maybe I need to change my viewpoint on?'

As long as their behaviour didn't cross the mandatory boundaries of health, wellbeing or education, we might want to consider not resenting our child and instead think about how we can negotiate in future (e.g., "We'll do it your way this one time," or "OK, but make sure you are on time for dinner next time.").

What about forgiving our children when they are doing something wrong?

There are different levels of forgiveness that our children may require, and they fall along a spectrum. At one end would be the child who, for the second time, has come home after your nine o'clock curfew asking, "What are you going to do about it?"

How do you practise forgiveness in this mild situation?

Where the issue is severe and involves criminal activity, this really requires mediation. Support may not automatically be given to you, so speak to whoever your child's case worker is and ask them to put you in touch with a support group.

What about if we need our child to forgive us?

It depends on what have we done to our child that requires us to say sorry and again there is a spectrum. At one end, it could be that we snapped at them, or we broke something and didn't really apologise because they had left it on the stairs for the tenth time. It could be that despite knowing they didn't like shepherd's pie, we cooked it twice in a row (because we were busy, grandma was sick, etc.).

To seek forgiveness in this mild situation, I would suggest time out to talk. I always encourage families to have meals together and to not sit in front of the TV or social media all the time. So, if you feel that a child is resenting you for some reason or is holding back anger, make time to talk, either at mealtime or while walking by the river or in the local park. If it's a mild thing, they might have even forgotten what it was but generally children don't forget and it's very helpful to have these periodic 'fishing trips'. Fishing with your child means finding time to talk. Making meatballs with your child is a great activity. Not because you need help cooking but because you can make space to talk about things.

At the other end of the spectrum, perhaps we took out our frustrations on our children by beating them? Maybe we walked out on them and they ended up in care? Or we knew that a family member was abusing them but we turned a blind eye? Or we were on drugs and sold our children for sex? Tragically this all happens.

At that end, it is easy to get caught up in the emotion and say or do things that don't give our children what they need. A social worker, care worker, psychologist or family therapist should mediate so that we actually ask the children whether they are willing and able to forgive and what they hope this will do for them. These are very important questions for a child who has been badly treated and suffered horrors. We really need to understand what forgiveness looks like to them and what they need to bring peace into their lives.

So, the message and key to the title of this chapter is that forgiving our children and being forgiven by them must be assessed. What do we require forgiveness for? What was the crime and does the punishment fit? We need to be able to step back and look at whether we are chastising and needing forgiveness from our child because they're not doing something our way or because they're doing something that really has been shameful, challenging, rude, dangerous or disrespectful. These are all very good words to explore. It's very difficult to step back– that's what therapy is for!

What is forgiveness for? Forgiveness is about letting go, forgiveness is about peace and forgiveness is about moving on.

For more guidance, read:

Families and How to Survive Them - Dr R Skynner and J Cleese

Finding Forgiveness: A 7-Step Program for Letting Go of Anger and Bitterness - E. Borris-Dunchunstang

CHAPTER 36

MONEY, MONEY, MONEY

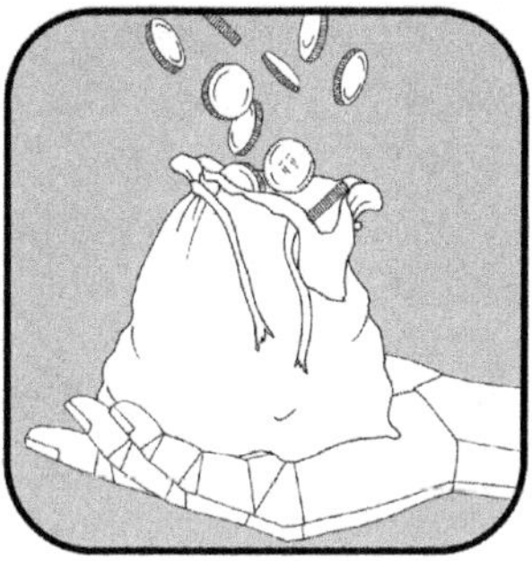

"Every child steals. Don't kid yourself. Everybody steals in their childhood."
- Michael Padraig Acton -

How do we groom our children about the importance and unimportance of money? And make no mistake. It is about grooming because we are manipulating, educating and enticing them to get their co-operation.

There is so much exposure, throughout their growing years about money, value, extortion, waste, etc. but primarily, how we as a family manage money is going to impact our children the most. If we never discuss money in the family, we're never going to teach our children about value, the need to work for a living or how to manage money. They're going to be clueless. How will they ever understand the value of things if they're simply told whether they can have something they want or not?

Recently, I spoke with a gentleman in his senior years. He explained that his family never celebrated birthdays or Christmas because they were very wealthy and just got what they wanted when they wanted it. That child grew up without an understanding of the value of money or Christmas or gifts or kindness because they were given things all the time. How prepared for life was that person?

At the other scale, how can a child learn to manage money within a family that catastrophises financial issues, constantly complaining about not having enough and worrying about paying the bills? That child is always going to approach money with fear, scared of not having enough. They're not going to think about future possibilities or take part in solution-focused discussions. They're going to think, 'Oh gosh! Money causes pain. Money is a stressor.'

The most important thing we can do with our children is discuss money. Take them to the food shop and when you're shopping explain, "That meat for tonight's dinner is the same price as your whole allowance for a week." Your child might be less likely to take it for granted and waste it. They will start to understand the value of food and realise that you don't just open the fridge and it's there. It has to be thought about.

If you're presented with three different types of cheese and your favourite is the most expensive, show your children how one week you might treat yourself to it but on another week, you might decide to go without. All the time you are giving your children little messages about value, judgement and the need to balance moderation with enjoyment.

Why buy a brand like Heinz baked beans when the supermarket own brand has exactly the same ingredients? There's another life lesson. On the other hand, maybe Heinz spaghetti has nutritious, organic ingredients that are better for your child than the Sainsbury's, Marks and Spencer or Walmart spaghetti. This lesson is about value, branding and the way companies target people.

What about the sweets/candy aisle? How do we best manage that without tears and tantrums or caving in? You should start by giving your children an allowance. It doesn't matter how destitute you are, all children should get one.

Then, rather than buying sweets for your child once a week, let them use their allowance to manage their sweet intake. Tell them, "OK, just choose whatever you can afford and whatever makes sense to you." Now, they might come to you and say, "I really want that, but I haven't got enough." Well, then you can say, "I'm more than happy to give you whatever amount will make it up and we'll take that off your allowance next week. How's that?" So, you're still giving them the responsibility while also teaching them about value and modelling negotiation skills.

There might be another time when you think, 'Do you know what? You've been so helpful, don't worry about the allowance. I'm going to buy this for you.' Now, because they normally buy their sweets/candy with their allowance, they understand the value of you treating them. It's an act of kindness and not an entitlement, so again you're getting an important and powerful message over to them.

How to handle stealing and help children to grow up honest

All children steal. Now it might be something mild: taking 10p from the purse or picking up 50p from the floor and not telling anyone they've found it. Or it could be that the child takes something from the store. They might sneak something from the fridge that they're not supposed to have. Or they might eat all the biscuits from the cupboard when they know they're supposed to share with their sibling. That's punishable. You have to punish them!

You have to explain that it's not kind, it's not polite. Explain to them why it doesn't work and then there needs to be consequences to that theft. However, make the punishment fit the crime and make sure the crime is understood before you deliver the punishment.

As well as deterring theft, we need to encourage honest behaviour and effort through rewards, and this includes praise and affection as well as money and gifts.

What happens when children grow up not understanding money?

If we don't understand value and how money works, we don't really understand the world at all. This can have a serious impact on our personal and work relationships and worse of all, we might fail to see our mistakes.

I once had a newly qualified member of my team come to me in my private clinic and ask, "Why am I only getting paid this much when patients are being charged this much?" I couldn't believe it because this person was top of their class, an overachiever who had written an excellent thesis but clearly hadn't got a clue about life.

I asked her to explain further and she said, "Well, I do the same amount of work as you, but I only get this much?" I asked her, "Who pays for the building you're sitting in? Who paid for that chair you're sitting in? Who pays for the Internet and phone calls? Who pays for the bookkeeper, secretary and receptionist? Who pays for the advertising and marketing? When you think about all these things and considering you're new to this business, it's a fair salary." She left shortly after.

So, we do need to teach our children value. They could be a scholastic genius but if they're not smart in the world and don't know about value they will always be at a disadvantage. And money is only one source of value. Value also exists in love and acts of kindness. Anything that is negotiated or exchanged between humans needs to be valued and understood.

For more guidance, read:

Money-Savvy Kids: Parenting Penny-Wise Kids in a Money-Hungry World - J. Raymond Albrektson

The Wisest Investment: Teaching Your Kids to be Responsible, Independent and Money-Smart for Life - R. Taub

CHAPTER 37

WHEN OUR CHILDREN ATTACK THEMSELVES

"Don't be stupid. Act immediately!"
- Michael Padraig Acton -

Suicide and self-harm are probably the worst experiences a healthy, caring and loving parent will need to manage in their lifetime.

Self-harm can be broken down into several categories:

Eating disorders, starving yourself, that's self-harm. It's acting out. It's getting control. But unfortunately, the disease starts when the child becomes hooked on starving themselves because of the endorphins released into the brain. It's very kind of Mother Nature to provide this euphoria before you die of starvation, but people can become addicted to it. They continue until they are out of control then their organs start to fail, their saliva glands become blocked, their teeth rot, their faces become deformed, etc. For females, the reproductive system will stop working, sometimes permanently.

In other forms of self-harm there is an instinct to turn pain into reality using knives or razor blades, usually on the inside of the legs or arms. We don't fully understand why but these seem to be the most popular parts of the body to choose. Usually, with this kind of self-harm, the person is imploding with anger, rage, fear, upset or disappointment., The only way they can manage this is to feel an anxiety release by making it real. They need to see blood being drawn by a blade or a bottle being broken and run up the legs. It's almost like they are releasing an energy from the body which then releases anxiety and stops them feeling like they're going to absolutely explode or implode.

What about suicide? There are several layers to suicide. Many of us think, 'Oh, I just want to die.' That's suicidal ideation but it's not necessarily a precursor to anything of concern. However, if you're hearing it said over and over again, the situation could get more serious.

If the person talks about how they plan to kill themselves, that should ring alarm bells because that's high-risk behaviour and needs intervention.

What is our role as parents of children who are harming themselves? What do we do with people who are crying out for help and acting out by showing us their scars and their cuts, the visual demonstration of their pain? What do we do with a child who is contemplating, planning, or attempting suicide? What about completed suicide (where the person has successfully terminated their life)? What do we do with survivors, that is the people left behind, after someone's taken their life?

In my experience of working with families, I have found that the child often seems not to be understood either by themselves or by their family. Assumptions are dangerous when someone is in so much pain.

Even physical pain can be hard to bear without the understanding of other people. I was recently having an injection in my knee and as I was quietly screaming inside, having an awful time, the person injecting me was telling a third person in the room that it doesn't really hurt that much. This put me on high alert, and I thought I can't manage the pain of the injection in my other knee because no one understands how painful this is. I screamed the roof down and I still wonder whether that knee injection was only worse because I didn't have the empathy in the room and I felt alone. It turned out afterwards that the person injecting my joint had meant to say that it only hurts whilst they are performing the injection and not for long afterwards. The point is that this misunderstanding caused me huge amounts of pain and it's a similar kind of miscommunication that can happen between parents and children.

If the children don't feel heard, if they're laughed at, if they're not recognised or comforted, if they feel their pain is not being seen, they will start doing things in order to show or terminate that pain–seen pain means cutting etc. Terminated pain means suicide!

Unfortunately, eating disorders, and the associated disruption to the body, is more of an addiction process. To understand the recovery process, read the chapter on substance abuse because we use the same cycle of change with eating disorders as we do with drug, alcohol and all other kinds of addiction.

Once we're listening to and trying to understand our child's pain, we're still left with how to manage it. What do we do if our child is scratching themselves with a pin and leaving marks that disappear? What do we do if they are using a lethal blade and making deep cuts, leaving scars? And what do we do with a child that is talking about planning how they are going to kill themselves and have the means to do so (access to a rope, a weapon, pills, etc.)

Don't think. Act immediately!

Whether it's a thin scratch, a deep cut or a planned suicide, it's not about aesthetics–how things appear on the surface. It's not about whether you believe this is happening or not. It is about getting appropriate help immediately. Go to your primary care physician/GP, make an urgent appointment, and explain to them what's going on. If you don't want to take your child with you, go on your own first. Ask them, "What's the best way to manage this? What avenues are open to me in my context, in my local area?" Make sure those avenues are open for you so you can get help.

What are we left with as parents? We're getting the child help, but we will have plenty more questions for ourselves. How much have we enabled this situation? What have we done to contribute to it? What didn't we do? These are all questions you really need to work through in your own therapy. Therapy is very important with self-harm and destruction. It doesn't matter who we are, even if we're a psychologist, psychiatrist, mental health nurse. . . we cannot begin to cope with our own children destroying themselves, in whatever way they're doing it, without professional help. The journey starts when you find out about the self-harm. You've then got to walk side by side with your child to help them reduce the risk of reoccurrence. Because unfortunately, whether we like it or not, once our child has used self-harm as a coping mechanism to reduce anxiety; once our child has attempted suicide or thought about planning it, then every time they are stressed or challenged, they will go to that coping mechanism because it does reduce anxiety. It gives the person back control.

So, we have to manage that child through all the future disappointments, all the future challenges to help keep our child alive and safe.

My biggest message is: don't be stupid. Act immediately! Go to your GP/primary care physician, and get appropriate, immediate, localised help.

Finally, don't go to a mobile app unless it's been recommended by your primary care provider because many of these apps are born out of money-making mechanisms. These apps don't know your child's medical history, don't know your family history, don't know the town your child lives in or the school they go to.

Self-harm and suicide are not about fixing something with an app. It's about finding what is causing the pain and getting professional support to manage the whole situation.

For more guidance, read:
The Parent's Guide to Self-Harm: What Parents Need to Know - J. Smith
Self-Harm: Why Teens Do It and What Parents Can Do to Help - M. Mitchell
The Mindfulness Workbook for Teen Self-Harm: Skills to Help You Overcome Cutting and Self-Harming Behaviors, Thoughts, and Feelings - G. M. Biegel MA LMFT and S. Cooper PsyD

CHAPTER 38

NARCISSISM + OVERDEPENDENCE = AN UNHEALTHY ACTIVITY BALANCE

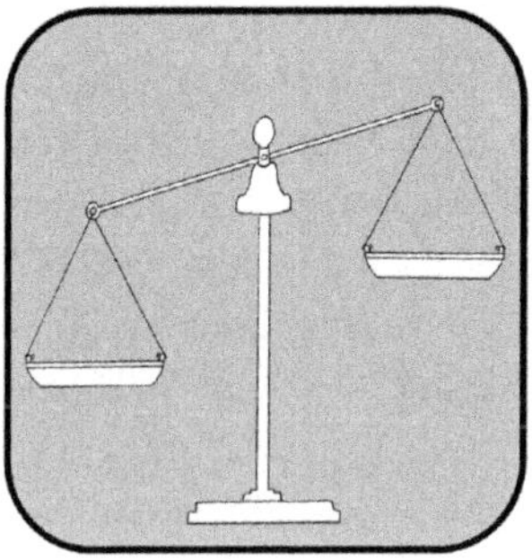

"Burnout for a child can lead to suicide.
Who is pushing the agenda–and why?"
- Michael Padraig Acton -

Modern day life is nothing like how I remember my childhood. My children and grandchildren are run ragged with getting to this, getting to that. What did we do before cars? Before clubs, after school activities and gyms? Why do we need to be part of all these things? Why is this happening now?

If you feel that getting your kids to A, B and C every week is too much then it probably really is. You need to listen to that feeling.

Most children over 11 are now expected to do one to two hours of homework per evening. This is required by law and is healthy. That being said, children can get over-stretched. If your children are also wanting to be part of every single club, that's not practical.

It might be that peer pressure is making them over-commit. It might be that they're unable to give voice to something that's bothering them at home so they're piling on outside activities to avoid their worries. It might be that they perform very well in clubs and feel they need to continue to overperform or become a nobody. There can be an awful lot of different value systems going on inside a child's head.

Whatever the reason, our children can get over-stressed, over-pushed and over-burdened with too many commitments.

So, two activities a week is more than enough for any child and family to manage.

If the desire to do too many activities is child-driven, you can manage that pretty well by creating a limit and saying, "No! You can choose two things you really want to be part of. We'll discuss anything else."

But what happens if it's not child-driven? What happens if it's us pushing our child? Maybe we're compensating for something in our past. Perhaps we were in a highly competitive school and excelling in every activity was expected.

To counter the urge, ask yourself, "What are we missing out on as a family by our children engaging in every activity? What isn't happening?"

There could be a narcissistic element at play (or codependency, if you are enabling a partner or spouse to unreasonably drive your child). As I explain in the first book of this *Power Of You* series, *Learning How To Leave*, narcissists draw their self-esteem from others, set goals based on their need for approval, have impossibly high standards and have limited awareness of the effect this has on others. If this is an area that's causing you issues, reading my book will help clarify any narcissistic and codependent patterns in yourself or your family unit.

You might be wondering what the fuss is. What damage can a busy schedule do? Why should we be concerned at us pushing an unrealistic, overachiever schedule with our children–or our children driving an overachieving schedule, for whatever reasons, with us? Why is it unhealthy?

It's unsustainable. It's going to cost money, time and energy. A natural part of socialisation is to have boring times, to have nurturing times, to have interactions with family. A normal part of the world is to have down time, to have free time. It's that old adage: everything needs to be in balance.

What happens if our child doesn't get enough of this down time? For all intents and purposes, we're developing a performing robot not a human soul. How can we nurture a soul if we don't give it our time? What is the point of a child overperforming in multiple activities if they never get to experience the simple joy of relaxing in a bubble bath and listening to soft music?

What happens to a child who, all of a sudden, has burnout at 15 because they can't keep up this momentum.Now they're doing GCSEs, or A Levels or Finals and they can't manage it all. Something's got to give.

As parents we have to predict whether something's sustainable or not and how much down time a child needs to re-energise their batteries. We need to be human and to be real. If we push our children (or we allow our children to push themselves) into an unsustainable activity schedule, it's only a matter of time before they burn out. But unlike adults, they won't have the language or the wisdom to really engage with that burnout. They might start self-harming, resorting to drugs and alcohol or they might even kill themselves. That's what burnout does.

Let's always be mindful and aware of what is a manageable, healthy and achievable schedule for our children and ourselves.

Again, if narcissism and codependency is something in your arena that you want to work with, read *Learning How To Leave* ASAP. I go into much more detail about these relationship patterns, and provide helpful ways to work them out. Be mindful that narcissists can be parents, children, brothers, sisters, lovers, etc.

For more guidance, read:
Hot Mess to Mindful Mom: 40 Ways to Find Balance and Joy in Your Every Day - A. Katz
My Cape is at the Cleaners: Choosing Happy Over Perfect - W. Elover

CHAPTER 39

OLD SOUL OR FIRST TIME ROUND: GROWING PAINS

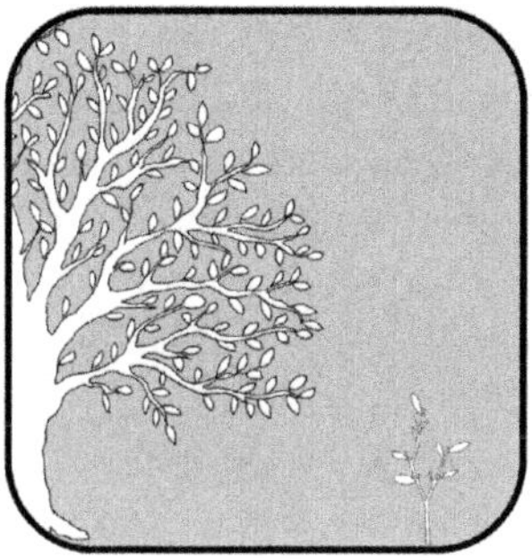

"Just because your child is well-behaved, it doesn't mean they're not screaming inside."
- Michael Padraig Acton -

We've all spoken about or heard people say of one child, "That one's an old soul," and of another, "Gosh, that one's a real handful." The old soul might seem to speak wisdoms way ahead of their time or may be truly loyal, caring or very kind. The 'handful' might behave in an immature way, show 'attitude' or act out a lot.

Sometimes kids do overachieve. Sometimes kids are wise beyond their years. And others do take a little more time to catch up, or to find that they do have a voice, so don't always need to act out. Some previously difficult children suddenly start to grow up, almost overnight.

We all have different paces. We're all individual souls.

Yet, because we see our children developing over time, sometimes we are too close to see that maybe they need our support or help.

A child that's unusually well-behaved in adult company could have ASD and may not 'get' their peer group. Or they may have experienced some trauma you don't know about, and it's actually knocked them into being a thinking person at a very young age. It might be that a disability in the family has moulded them into being an overly thoughtful caregiver.

No parent should be overly concerned if their child seems like an old soul. But if their behaviour seems bizarre, if they seem unhappy or if they don't seem to be developing in a healthy way, it won't hurt to check that out with a GP, your local psych department or your paediatrician and find out if there is something going on. Be mindful that not every child reaches the same milestones at the same times as their peers.

What about if our child is not achieving as quickly as they might? They might be doing well in school and in most other ways, but their behaviour might seem very immature. Perhaps they're not eating as well as they could. They might be overly clumsy or have a poor attention span. This is all normal too. Yes, you can read all about the stages which a child should have reached by a certain age, but these are not hard and fast rules because we all have different growth spurts–emotionally and physically.

But whether you are parenting an old soul or a young, vulnerable, acting out soul, if the situation becomes dysfunctional, it's a good idea to check it out. What's dysfunctional? If you can't take your child somewhere public. If you can't take them to a party. If they're not doing very well at school because of disruptive behaviour. If you find your old soul sitting in the corner crying because they don't want to go somewhere because they're embarrassed or insecure. That's dysfunctional.

If things are getting to the stage where the situation is affecting your old soul or young imp's education, health or wellbeing–or the health and wellbeing of the family unit–it's time to seek help.

I can't tell you what you might or might not find. It could just be that you're overly concerned, and somebody can put your mind at rest, but it could be that your child has dyspraxia. There could be HF (High Functioning) Autism. There could be a plethora of things that are mild but need to be managed well for the child to have more choices and enjoy a more comfortable life.

For example, we now know that we don't put people with ASD

into certain situations that are going to aggravate anxiety. It's also well-documented that people with ASD get on with their older peers better than their own age group and will need support with understanding social cues.

If you're computer literate, start by Googling what you're experiencing. You don't immediately want to label your child but if an idea seems to fit then you might want to see what kind of specialists you can take them to see to explore what's going on with them.

Check it out with a couple of professionals because this is not an exact science. There are clusters of symptoms and behaviours which can instruct us in the best way to manage a certain soul but there is no injection or pill that can fix things for us. It's really about us adapting the child's world exposure and our own approach to facilitate the child's development: to push them as much as we can (but also to hold them as much as we can).

People make the assumption that GPs primary care physicians and other professionals are there to make decisions for us, but they can't. They can only use their training and experience to suggest a way forward based on the information you take to them. So, you have to get it straight in your own head first. Ask yourself, "What am I seeing?" "What am I experiencing?" "What are other people seeing?" "What are other people experiencing?"

Without enough information, GPs primary care physicians may medicalise the situation. As you will read in the next chapter, there is a very real danger of relying too much on expert opinion and medication when we are lacking in experience as parents.

We often don't know where the origin of a problem lies. It could be mechanical. I could be chemical. It could be emotional. It could be neurological.

It might be that your child has ASD. It might be that they have dyspraxia. An apparently old, wise soul could actually have an undetected hearing problem that has made them more of an observer than an actor in the world. They therefore come out with profound statements.

If no one seems to be able to put a label on the issue, then find someone who can give you guidance on how to manage things. How can you bring the gift out of the child and create a supportive environment in which that child can excel?

That's your job as a parent.

For more guidance, read:

Parenting a Child with Asperger Syndrome: 200 Tips and Strategies - B. Boyd
Parenting a Child with Emotional and Behavioural Difficulties - D. Hughes

CHAPTER 40

FAMILY LOST: IT IS MORE THAN OK TO ASK QUESTIONS AS WE ARE THE EXPERTS OF OUR CHILDREN

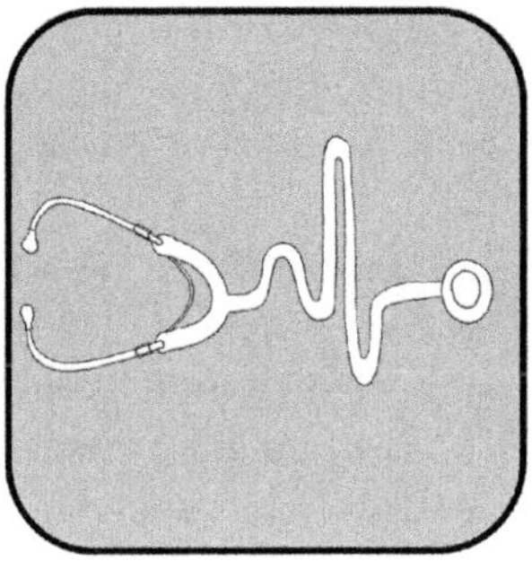

"Tragic victims of our education and health systems can become superheroes."
- Michael Padraig Acton -

Often the most poignant insights come directly from the mouths of those who have been through it all and emerged at the other side, determined to help others avoid the pain they themselves have endured.

Billy and his mother Sharon didn't have to speak out. They could have kept their frustrations secret and become another disguised, faceless case study for the experts to toss about.

The bravery they demonstrate to frankly speak out about their tragic ordeal reminds us all that we are talking about real people, not characters from a play or movie set. It should also humble any professional involved in the care of families to reflect on their own practice and how they might ensure that lessons are learned. In this particular case, a catalogue of misjudgements by those whose job it is to care for the vulnerable has literally stolen precious time from Billy and his family. They won't get that time back, but they hope that they can save families in similar situations from the pain they suffered.

It all started so brightly. Billy, Sharon's first child, was described by his kindergarten teacher (who now teaches Sharon's youngest) as a popular, considerate child. Naturally, when her son moved up to first grade, she was expecting a similar report. But Sharon was to get the shock of her life, as she explains: "I went to a teacher conference; Billy's first grade teacher had all negative things to say about him. I started crying; I was afraid. She said that the School Board could give me these forms to fill out to find out if he has ADHD. I thought, 'she's an educator and I'm not.' I told my friend I was worried that he was going to be delayed; I didn't want him to fail."

Any parent can sympathise with Sharon, can't they? Don't we all want our children to be at least as successful as the rest of their classmates? The thought that they might fall behind strikes at the heart of our deepest fears. We panic and, in reaching out to those with expert knowledge and experience, we place our fragile family in the care of others.

So here we have a frightened mother, desperate to do whatever she needed to ensure her child didn't fall through the educational net. She was also carrying a lot of guilt over the possible effects of medical procedures, such as X-rays she had been given while unknowingly pregnant. Enter psychiatric drug sales with the expert-backed solution in a bottle. Adderall was the first drug Billy, at the mere age of six, would be given, a medication that is meant to be prescribed to treat attention deficit hyperactivity disorder (ADHD) as part of a total programme that includes psychological, educational and social components.

Yet Sharon says that Billy never saw a therapist, never saw a psychologist and never saw a social worker. What's more, the paediatrician told Sharon that, while her son appeared to have attention deficit, he did not seem to be hyperactive.

Drugs like Adderall are not to be taken–or prescribed–lightly; because they affect the overall chemical balance of the brain. Any doctor prescribing these powerful drugs–especially to a child–needs to be absolutely convinced there is no other way. While Sharon was diligent enough to read the side effects, she nevertheless placed her trust in the judgment of her paediatrician. She believed that Billy would be OK.

Let's stop for a minute, and have a look at some of those possible side-effects: seizure; changes in blood pressure; irregular heart rate; shortness of breath; problems with urination; confusion; extreme sedation, excitation or mania; increased skin sensitivity to sunlight; constipation; yellow skin or eyes; lip puckering; lip smacking; uncontrolled movements of the tongue; uncontrolled movements of the hands, arms or legs; difficulty walking; rigid or stiff muscles; fever; dizziness; dry mouth; changes in appetite; weight gain; tremor of the hands; persistent sore throat. . . Can I remind you–Billy was six years old.

He remembers going to the bathroom a lot and losing his appetite so much that he barely ate. A couple of weeks into his 'treatment', Sharon recalls coming home from a nightshift one morning to find a note waiting for her. "He had never before written me a note longer than, 'I love you mom'," she told me. "But this was two paragraphs of, 'I love you so much mom; sorry sometimes if I mess up.' He hadn't been to bed all night. Then, after the meds wore off, it was crash. I don't think he went to school the next day; he was so tired he couldn't get up."

While most children of his age would have been enjoying the fullness of life, Billy's days descended into a living Hell, "I wasn't doing anything. I wouldn't even talk to anyone at school," said Billy. "I would just do work, go home, use the restroom because I had diarrhoea and go to bed." Then things began to reach crisis point, as Sharon recounts, "We were fighting one day about taking the meds and eating, and he said, 'I don't feel like eating; I'm not going to eat. I just want to kill myself; I just want to die'."

As you can imagine, this was a wake-up call and prompted Sharon to call the paediatrician and announce she would refuse to give Billy the drugs anymore. This was enough to end his association with Adderall, but sadly the drugs companies' involvement in his management had only just begun. When I asked whether her son's anguish had made her afraid, Sharon's guilt-ridden response was heart-breaking to hear, "Not afraid enough, I guess, because they prescribed him another drug that I let him take."

Did this development stimulate a concerted effort by those involved in

Billy's care to monitor him more closely, perhaps to finally offer him the psychological and social components of the programme that the drugs were supposed to only be a part of? Not exactly.

"I don't even think we saw the doctor," said Sharon. "I think he prescribed the new medication over the phone–Concerta®. Billy took that for a couple of months, but it had the same kind of effect."

"It was just the same," explained Billy. "I was talking to people, but I still got bad stomach aches and I wouldn't want to eat." Worried about his nutritional intake, Sharon thought she might have found the answer when another mom recommended a drug that could be applied to the skin; the Daytrona patch. Would Billy's nightmare finally come to an end?

"It was even worse," said Billy. "I started not talking to people again, not even to my parents or sister. I would just do the same thing over and over again; I had really bad upset stomachs, even worse than the first time; I was really depressed; I really felt like killing myself."

The strain on the family became ever more intense, as Billy's parents argued over the patch. "We fought about that for about a year," explained Sharon. "We tried to not give him as much dosage." Billy sought his father's help in ending his torment. "I begged him to tell mom to take it off me because I didn't feel right," Billy explains, his voice close to tears. "It wasn't mum's fault, I know. She didn't know."

Billy, then nine years old, had finally reached the end of the line. In his own words he knew that he couldn't live another day under the control of his medication. Mercifully, he didn't have to. The next conversation between Billy's parents ended his ordeal, as Sharon agreed with Billy's father that there would be no more Daytrona patch. After more than two years of drug-induced separation, the real Billy was on his way back to his family. Love had reunited a family that Sharon admits had 'lost its way for a little while.'

So, can we work out what had gone wrong in the first place? Billy's story reminded me about the critical psychiatry classes I attended in my training. We were asked who in the room had ever had ADD. We all put up our hands, and we all said, "Right now, because this is boring."

Billy is a smart young man and the more I dwell upon the disparity between his performance at school and his obvious intelligence, the more I suspect that he was simply bored. Perhaps he also struggled with symbolic representation (i.e., reading letters). I will never know for sure, but after taking him off the patches, Sharon got Billy a tutor. Guess what? He is excelling in his reading and has no problem with writing.

Doesn't it seem to you that this is what Billy needed all along? What he got was rejection from his class teacher and over two years of psychiatric drugs from his paediatrician, which distanced him further from his peers and came close to destroying his family. When a boy of nine years old tells his family he will kill himself if he isn't taken off the drugs, it's time to wake up; something is going very wrong. Shockingly, Billy was given drugs but neither he nor his family was offered any type of psychological or social support. He wasn't carefully monitored. His medication wasn't even reviewed. In fact, when Billy was nearly fifteen years old, getting a physical examination for school, his paediatrician asked him whether he was still on the patch!

What more can I say?

If any good has come out of this sorry situation, it is that Billy and his parents have learned from their ordeal and are in a position to advise others in a similar situation.

"Research!" Sharon says. "Don't just take the opinion of your doctors; there are second opinions. Listen to your kid!"

Billy understands that his mom was just doing what she thought was in his best interests. But still, he looks back at the fights and it makes him want to cry.

I told Billy that I hope in time he won't hold himself responsible for his behaviour over those few awful years because it wasn't him; it was the drugs. Billy is aware that he is lucky that he has a supportive family who love him, but he worries about those kids who don't have that bedrock.

So do I.

At the end of this interview, I asked Billy, because he had been so brave and helpful, if he would like to give a title to this chapter. Billy said, without even hesitating, "Family Lost. Because we were lost."

For more guidance, read:

Parenting ADHD: What ADHD Child Wants from You – G.P. Clifford

Mindful Parenting for ADHD: A Guide to Cultivating Calm, Reducing Stress, and Helping Children Thrive – M. Bertin M.D.

Mental Health in America: Misdiagnosis of ADHD in Young Children - I. Azirayah (presentation)

ADHD: Not Overdiagnosed, Misdiagnosed - K. Graham (presentation)

ADHD: Current Concepts and Treatments in Children and Adolescent - Various (2)

CHAPTER 41

RESPONSIBLE PARENTING

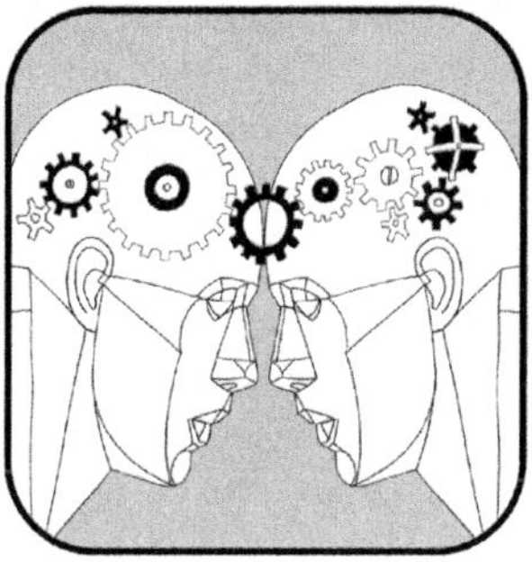

"In healthy parenting, there is no space for assuming. We need to govern."
- Michael Padraig Acton -

There are government legal guidelines, which set out what all people with parental responsibility must do for the children in their care. These are:

1. Provide a home for the child.
2. Protect and maintain the child.

You're also responsible for:

- Disciplining the child.
- Choosing and providing for the child's education.
- Agreeing to the child's medical treatment.
- Naming the child and agreeing to any change of name.
- Looking after the child's property.

So, you can't expect everyone else, including the government, to take care of your children for you. It is your job! People need to be educated that this is required before deciding not to use a condom or ever thinking about having a child.

You absolutely must make sure your child is safe emotionally, physically and in all other ways. Also, be aware that you may sometimes need to protect your children from other family members or an unhealthy co-parent. It is your duty to give the child a voice because their world is small. You must have a healthy moral compass and if you fear that you do not then GET ONE! Social services, a friend or any healthy source of counsel can help you help your child. I would add that whilst protecting your child from danger you must not stifle them.

When disciplining your child, do so within reason and effectively. By effectively, I mean by guiding them, giving them a good understanding of what is OK and what is not. Preparing them for the world is YOUR duty!

Providing for your child's education includes supporting and nurturing them through school and beyond. You must consider getting the best opportunities for your child. It is YOUR duty that they have choices. Education on all levels does that!

In terms of health. medical professionals almost always know best, but it is your duty to make informed decisions in the best interest of your child, even if these are against your personal beliefs or ideas. It is all about your child and again, you are their voice.

This also applies when naming your child or agreeing to any change of name. You need to advocate for what is in their best interests.

Finally, remember that these are the western world's legal bare minimums for parenting. This is what you absolutely have to do by law. But parenting is much more than that. It includes nurturing, loving and caring for your child. Leading by example is our biggest parenting role even though that's not legally required.

CHAPTER 42

BALANCING BLAME: GIVING OUR CHILDREN A WIDER PERSPECTIVE

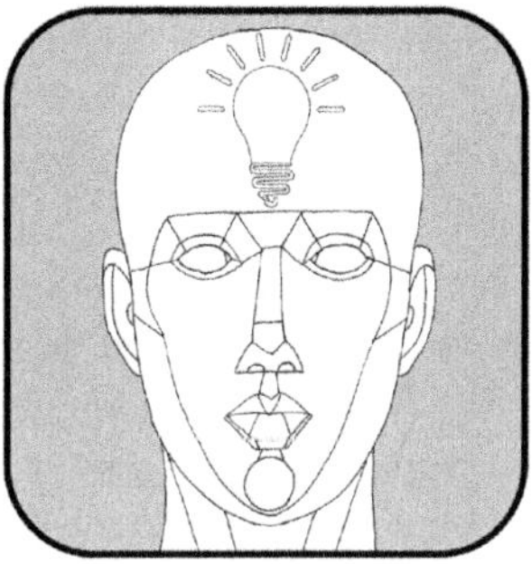

"Is there such a thing as justice?"
- Michael Padraig Acton -

It doesn't matter what your child's level of exposure is or whether you live in a mansion, a tent or a caravan, a young child's world is very small. Within that world, they learn how to make things happen. This is known in behavioural psychology as operant learning–they're operating on their environment and learning from it. One of the lessons they soon learn is the interplay of cause and effect. This can lead to problems when they use this belief in causation to explain why they're being treated a certain way.

For instance, they might think, 'I'm ugly or gay, therefore I'm being bullied.'

Several academic studies have shown that in very young children, this belief is tied in with notions of goodness and badness. For example, in 1992, Heyman, Dweck and Cain devised a study to examine the result of criticism on the motivation of five to six-year-old children. One part of the study looked at whether the children linked performance on a task to global ideas about how good or bad people were. The results showed that this was indeed the case, with successful students seen as good and nice and unsuccessful ones as bad and not nice.

Children given the task of role-playing a student failing on a task were particularly likely to rate themselves as bad and not nice, even when the role play explained that they were trying to do something nice for the teacher. As children get older, studies show that they are more able to split their traits into compartments. Even a self-critical 11-year-old who fails a task is more likely to class themselves as 'not smart' rather than bad.

Interestingly, the children most sensitive to criticism were more likely to seek to repair the relationship with the teacher rather than improve upon the task. We can see here the root of the 'people-pleasing' trait.

If the person lives in a 'vanilla' kind of world, they will understand that if they work hard they will get good grades at school. If they grow a plant and they feed and water it, the plant will be healthy and grow. Unfortunately, it's the same when a child is abused or bullied. They will believe that they are getting the negative reaction because of who they are.

For sure, we have to encourage our children that there's always a consequence to their actions and that their good actions will often lead to good outcomes and their bad actions will deliver bad outcomes. But we must also teach them that there is an exception to this rule and that is when someone is just being horrible, vindictive, or racist, etc. That's not about them, that's about the other person.

As parents, we need to help our children to balance the need for them to take responsibility for their behaviour and achievements and to defend themselves against unfair criticisms and downright nasty attacks.

For more guidance, read:

How to Teach Your Child Responsibility: Nurture Self-esteem - Kidbizu
Blame the Child - It's Easier: Learning Difficultties Can Be Solved - H. Blumenthal
Parenting with Love and Logic: Teaching Children Responsibility - F. Cline

CHAPTER 43

COMPROMISE

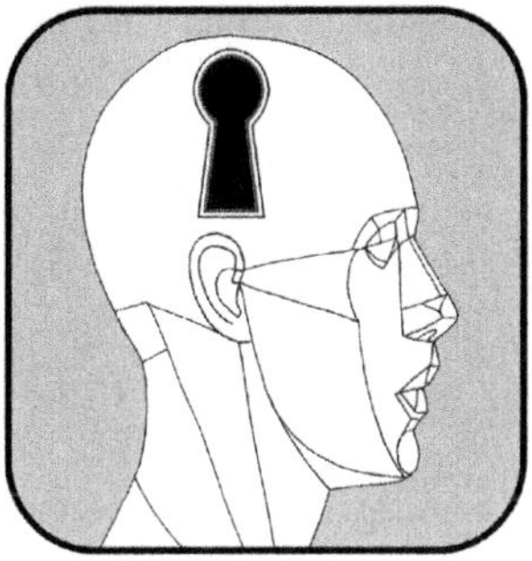

"Wisdom is to compromise."
- Michael Padraig Acton -

I've often been at weddings, anniversaries and funerals with older people in the family who have been married for 50 or 60 years. I ask them, "What's the secret to being together for so long." The answer is always, "Compromise."

It's ridiculous to think that two people will always want the same thing so we have to compromise to think about, understand and act on what both parties need. We need to learn to give and take in a healthy manner.

It's the same with our relationship with our children. They are not a mirror of us; they are their own beings. We have to encourage them to do well within the norms of what's healthy, but we shouldn't expect that they will always do what we wish for them. With the exception of the three non-negotiable areas of health, education and wellbeing, we have to be willing to compromise.

How does compromise play a part in healthy family relationships???
How is it that the ability to compromise promotes healthy families? Here

are five ways on learning how to balance our needs with those of our children that benefit the family unit:

1. **Increased self-worth and better mental health.** When our children feel that they are receiving what they need from us, they feel better about themselves, are more optimistic about the future and generally feel happier.

2. **Protection from stress.** When compromise is not reached, children feel stressed. Evidence shows that family conflict has a powerfully negative effect on physical and mental health.

3. **Social control.** If we continually refuse to meet our children halfway, they will often rebel or find hidden ways to fulfil their needs. This can, in some circumstances, lead to trouble at school, with neighbours or even with the police. If we come to sensible compromises (e.g., allowing them to play loud music for a short period as long as it's before 9pm), they are more likely to toe the line.

4. **Access to resources.** Parents who can compromise tend to stay together (as my quizzing of family members revealed). This provides additional financial and practical security for children.

5. **Long-term family support.** A lack of compromise can lead to alienation with adult children using their independence to put distance between themselves and their overbearing parents. Parents who compromise with their children are more likely to maintain strong relationships into the future. This is a win-win situation with parents supporting adult children with childcare and practical help in middle age and then drawing on support from their children in their later years.

Compromise is part of the so-called 'elaborated' or 'unrestricted' codes in language. This is where we teach the child to listen to and understand different points of view and then use reason to determine what's best for them–with your guidance. Children are not robots–they all need a voice.

For more guidance, read:

The Day No One Played Together: A Story about Compromise - D. Helsley and S. Harkey

Why Can't You See it My Way? Resolving Values Conflicts at Work and Home - A. Estes

Mastering Confrontation: Become an Expert at Effective Communication. Master the Art of Dealing with Conflict - R. Hunt

CHAPTER 44

PARENTING A NARCISSISTIC CHILD

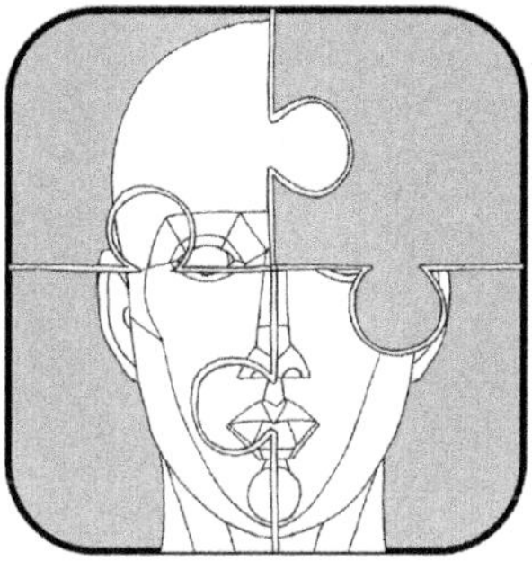

"No warm blood runneth here."
- Michael Padraig Acton -

Reflecting upon the first book in this *Power of You* series: *Learning How To Leave*, probably one of the saddest, depressing, awful, awkward, draining, painful relationships we can have in the world is when our child has narcissistic personality disorder (NPD) or many of those traits.

We yearn as parents to be in a warm and loving relationship with our children. However, if our child is NPD or thereabouts, that's impossible because they have no empathy and they don't learn from their mistakes. They are lost and all they will do is turn up when they need something and repeatedly drain you. They will offer you something in order to hook you over and over again, but they won't know how to genuinely give or how to feel–they will just look out for themselves. They will also project on to you all their bad habits and ideas while using you to build their image.

It's very important to put boundaries in to protect yourself otherwise you will have a miserable life trying to parent something that's not parentable. And I say 'something' because there is very little soul in an NPD. It's very difficult to put boundaries in with our children but it is a good idea to close your cheque book while reassuring your children that you love them and will always advise them.

Read *Power of You: Learning How To Leave* for more information on NPD and how to discover the keys to safely escape toxic relationships.

CHAPTER 45

WHAT DOES YOUR CHILD BEING ABUSED LOOK LIKE?

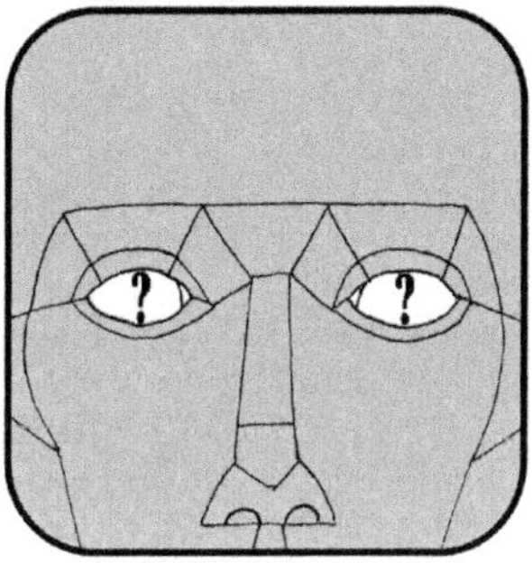

"You never know."
- Michael Padraig Acton -

When we think of child abuse, we often picture a young person being beaten senseless by a parent or exploited by a sexual predator. Of course, these examples are abusive, but child abuse has many faces. For example, routinely humiliating a child, refusing to let them have any friends or sending them out in freezing weather without warm clothing are all examples of abuse (emotional abuse and neglect).

Before we can know whether our child is being abused or not–including by us– we need to understand what child abuse looks like.

The National Society for the Prevention of Cruelty to Children (NSPCC) define child abuse as:

When a child is intentionally harmed by an adult or another child–it can be over a period of time but can also be a one-off action. It can be physical, sexual or emotional and it can happen in person or online. It can also be a lack of love, care and attention–this is neglect.

The four types of child abuse

The NSPCC splits child abuse into four subtypes: physical abuse, sexual abuse, psychological/emotional abuse and neglect. Let's look at each of these in turn.

Physical abuse

Physical child abuse is deliberate actions designed to hurt or injure a young person. Here are some examples:

- Punching.
- Hitting with an object.
- Slapping.
- Kicking.
- Shaking.
- Throwing.
- Burning or scalding.
- Biting.
- Scratching.
- Poisoning.
- Attempting to suffocate or drown.
- Causing a child to become unwell.
- Making up medical ailments (leading to unnecessary physical treatment).

Sexual abuse

Sexual child abuse happens when a person under the age of 16 is forced or tricked into taking part in sexual activities. Sexual abuse can be further divided into contact and non-contact abuse.

Examples of contact sexual abuse include:

- Rape.
- Penetration with an object.
- Kissing.
- Sexually touching a child (whether clothing is worn or not).

- Causing a child to participate in sexual activities, including touching someone else sexually.
- Making or tricking a child into taking their clothes off.

Examples of non-contact sexual abuse include:

- Flashing.
- Showing children pornography or exposing them to sexual activity.
- Making children take part in sexual activity, including masturbation.
- Creating, viewing and/or sharing of child sexual abuse videos or images (CSAM).
- Making children take part in the creating, viewing and/or sharing of CSAM.
- Making children engage in online or mobile sexual activity (e.g., sexting, using sexualised language in conversations, etc.).

Psychological or emotional abuse
While physical and sexual abuse cause psychological harm, some forms of abuse are targeted specifically at the psychological or emotional level. Here are some examples:

- Constant criticism or blaming.
- Humiliation.
- Shouting, threatening or calling names.
- Making the child the butt of jokes or using sarcasm to hurt them.
- Blaming for everything.
- Making the child perform degrading acts.
- Being overly controlling or refusing to accept the child as their own person.
- Pushing children past their capabilities.
- Exposing children to harmful situations (e.g., drug or alcohol abuse, domestic violence, shoplifting).
- Restricting a child's social development, including refusing to allow them to make friends.

- Being absent or persistently ignoring a child.
- Manipulating a child.
- Never showing kindness, congratulating or being positive towards a child.
- Never connecting emotionally with a child (emotional neglect).

Neglect

Finally, we have neglect. The NSPCC breaks down neglect into four categories: physical, emotional, medical, and educational neglect. Examples of physical neglect include:

- Under or over feeding.
- Not providing appropriate clothing.
- Not providing shelter.
- Not keeping a child safe from harm.

Emotional neglect is a form of psychological abuse and includes:

- Not nurturing a child.
- Not providing a child with stimulation (activities, toys, games, etc.).
- Persistently ignoring a child.
- ·Humiliating or intimidating a child.
- Keeping a child away from friends and other social activity (isolation).

With medical neglect, a parent or caregiver might not attend to a child's health needs (including dental checks, vaccinations, etc.) They might also refuse to follow medical guidance in keeping children healthy. Remember: health is one of the three non-negotiables of parenting.

Finally, educational neglect is when a parent or caregiver refuses to support a child's education. This might include allowing a child to skip school or even encouraging this. Of course, education is another of the three non-negotiables of parenting.

Recognising the signs of abuse

Now that I have clarified the four types of child abuse and their subtypes, it's time to focus on being alert to the signs of abuse. These are not always easy to spot since some might overlap with the signs of natural developmental changes (e.g., puberty). However, if a child is displaying multiple worrying signs, then it is vital that action is taken.

Signs of physical abuse

As children explore their world, they will pick up bumps, bruises and scratches, so no single physical injury should be taken as proof of abuse without supporting evidence. Repeated injuries, especially those that seem to follow a pattern, are of more concern as are cases where the explanation of an injury doesn't fit. Certain injuries should definitely ring warning bells including broken bones, widespread scarring, burns (including cigarette burns) and bite marks. Where children have been deliberately poisoned, choked or suffocated they might appear drowsy, start vomiting, have seizures or experience breathing problems.

Signs of physical abuse in babies include bruising, swelling, fractures, unusual behaviour, unconsciousness (or extreme sleepiness), vomiting, difficulty feeding and breathing problems.

Signs of sexual abuse

Children rarely talk about sexual abuse but may drop hints or show clues in their behaviours.

Does a child show fear around a specific person or do they avoid being alone with them? Do they fear and avoid people in general? These are both signs of possible sexual abuse.

Other psychological signs include self-harm, eating disorders (or a change in eating habits), mood changes, nightmares, bed-wetting and using sexualised language or behaviours that are not age appropriate. Older children may become addicted to drugs and/or alcohol to escape their experiences.

Where children are being exploited or groomed online, they might spend longer periods on their devices, become secretive about who they're communicating with or seem angry or upset after online activity.

Parents and caregivers should look out for an increase in the number of calls from unknown numbers, especially if these are stored as contacts.

Physical signs of contact sexual abuse might include bruising, bleeding, soreness or discharge around the genital area or anus. A sexually abused child may contract a sexually transmitted infection (STI) or become pregnant.

Signs of psychological/emotional abuse

Psychological abuse can be more difficult to spot than other forms of abuse due to the overlap with common childhood behaviours, especially around puberty. It can take a crisis before a child will admit they are being mistreated.

Here are some red flags to be aware of:

- Lack of confidence.
- Emotional outbursts.
- Difficulty in starting or maintaining relationships.
- Immature behaviour or, conversely, acting older than their years.
- Having few (or no) friends.
- Having knowledge and experience of situations you wouldn't normally expect of a child (e.g., criminal activity, domestic violence, etc.).

Psychologically abused babies and toddlers may seem to lack a bond with their parents and form unusually close attachments to other adults such as nursery or playgroup staff. They may come across as anxious and lacking in confidence or be aggressive or nasty towards other children or animals.

Signs of neglect

As with other forms of child abuse, some of the signs associated with neglect can sometimes be seen in well looked-after children. A child who comes into school one morning with muddy shoes or having got up too late for breakfast is not necessarily being neglected.

However, if there are multiple such occasions or you see a combination of these signs, neglect could be a problem. Examples include:

- Unhealthy appearance.
- Poor hygiene (the child smells or is scruffy).
- Child is hungry and/or underweight.
- Child is obese.
- Clothing fits poorly or is not suitable for the conditions.
- Frequent bouts of illness or infections (sores, flea bites, scabies, ringworm, etc.).
- Poor muscle tone.
- Thin body with swollen stomach.
- Poor dental health.
- History of missed healthcare appointments, vaccinations, etc.
- Untreated injuries.
- Regular accidents due to poor supervision.
- Child is often tired and seems sleep deprived.
- Poor social skills.
- Limited vocabulary.
- Low school attendance.
- Parents/caregivers frequently absent.
- Child often left to care for other family members.
- Trouble with the police.
- Unsuitable home environment (e.g., no heating; no toys, games or books, bare cupboards, damp or dirty conditions).
- Frequent untreated nappy rash (in babies).

Neglect can also lead to behaviour changes over time with children becoming withdrawn and depressed, clingy and anxious or aggressive. Parents and caregivers also should look out for changes in eating habits, obsessive behaviours, poor concentration levels, evidence of self-harm and signs of drug and alcohol use.

What can we do if we suspect abuse?

However a child is being abused; it is never their fault. It is very important that parents and caregivers drum that message home early and reinforce it.

In the UK, The NSPCC and Childline have plenty of advice for adults and children respectively. At the time of writing, the NSPCC had an agreement with Internet service providers that visits to their website would incur no data usage.

If anyone suspects child abuse is occurring they should report it either to their local council's children's social care team or to the police. Hard evidence is not required. If there is immediate risk of harm or an ongoing emergency, they should call their local emergency services number.

Important note: While your local children's social care team will ask you for your personal details, you can refuse to supply them.

For more guidance, read:

Helping Your Child Recover from Sexual Abuse - C. Adams and J.J. Fay
Freedom's Flowers: The Effects of Domestic Abuse on Children - P. Craven

CHAPTER 46

CHILDREN WITH DISABILITY: THE ROLLERCOASTER

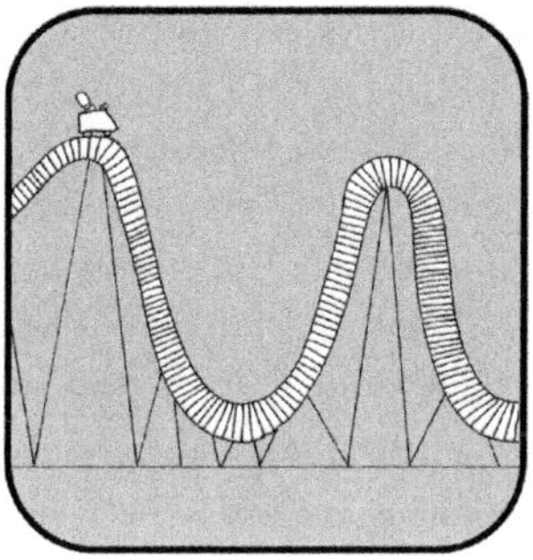

"Parenting a disabled child is one of the toughest challenges anyone can be presented with. Yet despite the hardship and pain, there are unique rewards to be found along the way."
- Michael Padraig Acton -

Much of the information in this chapter has been gathered from the amazing work and insight of therapist Joanna Griffin who herself is the parent of a disabled child.

A cocktail of emotions

Parenting developing human souls is always an emotional rollercoaster ride. However, if you are the parent of a disabled child, you will face ups and downs that other parents will never have to experience and may barely understand.

Grief is common. Although the disabled child is still alive, the parents will understandably mourn for the life their child could have had, the adult they might have become. This can manifest both as chronic sorrow and as waves of acute feelings triggered by certain events, such as family celebrations, leading to both emotional and physical symptoms of distress.

Some parents will experience the existential crisis described by Ronnie Janoff-Bulman as 'shattered assumptions'. I will cover that in the next section.

Stress levels are often high with parents feeling anxious about daily challenges, the knock-on impact on their other children and the future. Some might show signs of pre-traumatic stress whereby they are hyper-alert, fearing the worst is going to happen (to both the disabled child and the rest of their children). Griffin surveyed over 30 parents of disabled children about their emotions and 60% said they felt down or depressed, 52% experienced helplessness and half said they felt guilty. It is common for parents to wonder if something they did or didn't do contributed to their child's situation. 22% of parents had looked to escape into denial.

Then there are those moments of calm acceptance, overwhelming love and even joy. Even the smallest of their child's achievements can lead to elation as the parent recognises the effort needed to get there. Every step forward also opens up hope for additional progress. In fact, the majority of parents interviewed by Griffin (74%) felt proud of their disabled child.

Even anger, a common emotion felt by two thirds of Griffin's interviewees, could sometimes be channelled into a positive direction with parents developing a defiant attitude. 60% of Griffin's respondents said they had developed an inner strength with over half adopting a fighting spirit. Some had found a new purpose in life, advocating not only for their own children but for all children facing similar challenges. While some parents had managed to move mountains by shouting the loudest, others had experienced the opposite effect with service providers closing ranks and withdrawing support. Some parents admitted they had been worn down by the constant battles.

In short, the disability journey is different for everybody.

Shattered dreams

In 1992, Ronnie Janoff-Bulman published her social theory on understanding trauma. In her book *Shattered Assumptions: Towards a New Psychology of Trauma*, Janoff-Bulman proposed that we each construct a psychological world view for ourselves based on three assumptions about 'our' world and ourselves. These form the foundation stones of what Janoff-Bulman termed our 'assumptive world'.

These three truths are:

- The world is good (benevolent).
- The world is meaningful.
- We are worthy.

These truths are subtly kneaded into our consciousness as we grow up, giving us an inner feeling of invulnerability–like a suit of armour but one we forget we are wearing.

Trauma, including finding out that our child is disabled, tears away these truths, leaving us bare and exposed–adrift in a hostile world we no longer recognise. Our world no longer looks after or has a purpose for us. Our belief that 'bad things happen because I am bad and good things happen because I am good' is destroyed because we now know that bad things can happen to good people too. 'I never thought it could happen to me,' is the sorrowful phrase therapists are all too familiar with.

Reconstructing our world after trauma can take a lot of hard work but it is possible to find meaning in life again and develop a new sense of self.

Relationship difficulties

Parenting a disabled child places profound strain on relationships with partners, other children and friends.

Some parents of disabled children told Griffin that they felt other parents didn't understand their situation. This would clearly lead to feelings of frustration and loneliness. Many make the decision to avoid social parent-child gatherings, such as playgroups, because they don't want to have to answer questions about their child's issues or because they are anxious or embarrassed about their child's behaviour. This rips them away from a vital support network that other parents take for granted.

This lack of social contact can lead to parents feeling isolated and placing additional pressure on partners and family members to provide support.

Unsurprisingly, the pressures often become so great that relationships break down, with divorce common. Powerless to control the situation, other children in the family suffer the fallout from all of this. Griffin's research found that 80% of parents with disabled children experienced a negative effect on their intimate relationships and 70% confirmed a negative impact on their other children. 50% of those interviewed admitted to an overall negative experience although they did explain that they had both good days and bad days.

The need for better access – therapy included

Is disability a problem with the individual or a problem with society?

The medical model of disability looks at the person as an individual with a problem that needs to be fixed or managed. This has the effect of normalising a society that doesn't cater for the additional needs of a disabled person. This perspective is reflected in the language used. To talk of a person with disabilities is to put all of the focus on the individual rather than society.

The social model of disability looks at society as a whole and how it does or does not provide equal opportunities for all. If a person is disabled, it is because society is disabling them by not providing for their needs.

When the lens is shifted on to society, it is easier to see where accessibility and support services are lacking. From public spaces that are unsuitable for wheelchair access to a lack of early morning physiotherapy services, there are many areas of improvement to be made.

Therapy and counselling are included in this mix. As Griffin, a fellow therapist, points out, the parents of disabled children may need additional support, both practically and in terms of the therapy they receive. A therapist will need to be able to work with the parents on all of the areas covered above: grief, anger, denial, anxiety, couples' relationships, family dynamics, etc. At the same time, they may need to be flexible with times and fees, fitting both around the family's circumstances as much as possible.

Over time, and with the right support, parents of disabled children can learn to cope with their heartbreak and adapt emotionally to their situation. The family can not only learn to manage their child's disability but can understand it as a positive expression of difference. By building their child's self-esteem and helping them to understand and fight for their own needs and rights, parents will be playing their part in changing society. Siblings can grow into wonderfully tolerant human beings who celebrate difference. The shattered world can be rebuilt. Happiness, hope and meaning can return.

For more guidance, read:
Day by Day: Emotional Wellbeing in Parents of Disabled Children - J. Griffen
Shattered Assumptions: Towards a New Psychology of Trauma - R. Janoff-Bulman

PLEASE LEAVE A REVIEW AND GIVE US YOUR FEEDBACK

Thank you for reading this second book in the Power of You series.

- What did you like?
- What additions would you like to see?
- What topics would you like me to write about next?

I want this to continue to be the most helpful and informative book of its kind on this subject.

Please contribute to helping others by leaving a review and feedback via my contact page on my website, on Amazon, on Goodreads, and share on social media. Tell us what you feel needs to be included. We read all feedback and, where needed, will make changes to future editions of this book.

Connect with me online:

- Twitter: www.twitter.com/mpamind_com
- Facebook: www.facebook.com/mpamind
- Instagram: www.instagram.com/mpamind_com
- YouTube: www.youtube.com/channel/UCHGfUjqfS2ERjjKtPaQcQ5w
- LinkedIn: www.linkedin.com/in/michael-padraig-acton-1045562b/
- Website: www.mpamind.com
- Email: office@mpamind.com

PART 2

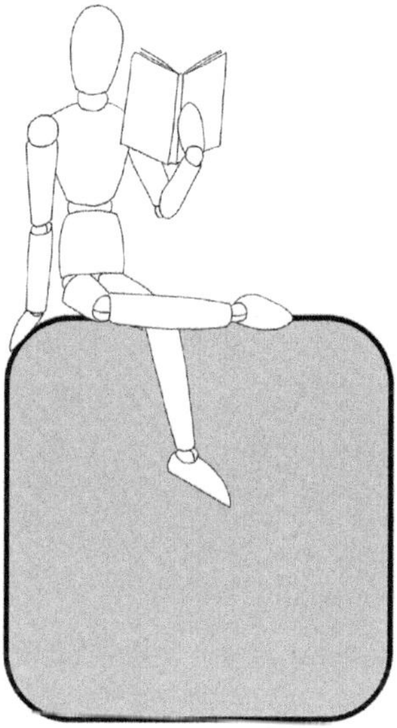

WHAT IS PARENTING ADULT CHILDREN? WHAT THOUSANDS OF PARENTS HAVE REVEALED

PART 2 FOREWORD

We have known Michael for many years, and were delighted to be asked to write this foreword.

As parents and grandparents in a blended family scenario, dealing with a wide range of challenges, *Raw Facts from Real Parents* immediately appealed to us. In fact, we were absolutely enthralled.

Michael's messages resonate powerfully. Here are a few that particularly stood out:

"We always care and love our children. When things aren't going right, we need to challenge them. Do not suffer in silence." (Chapter 61)

"(Your children) are the CEO of their lives. By all means, advise, object and suggest but never go as far as taking control of the situation." (Chapter 48)

"If you're a human and a parent, you made mistakes bringing up your child." (Chapter 57)

Michael is a parent and grandparent himself, so this is not a book that distances the reader from the 'expert'. In fact, as parents, we felt validated, because Michael takes the guilt away. The reader will quickly move from dwelling on, 'Oh, I made so many mistakes, I did it all wrong,' to, 'Well, that's just what life is.'

Michael has distilled his decades of experience into a concise and comprehensible 'maintenance manual' of applicable advice. He shares his insights in a humble and empathetic manner that invites the reader to explore their own circumstances, giving them the tools to move forward constructively. He is the consummate professional and yet writes as a compassionate fellow parent. With his refreshing humor, Michael permits the reader to look at matters from the lighter side.

For example, we loved the quote: *"If an emergency room doctor can be without their phone for an hour for a meal, so can any of your adult children."*

The crisp, readable chapters have a very interesting 'scannable' format, as each title is combined with a quote from Michael that sums up the main message. This is ideal for those readers with limited time. For those who want to delve deeper, there is generous cross referencing.

Due to its consumer-friendly language, *Raw Facts from Real Parents* will help to educate parents from all walks of life. From our own path of continuous exploration, we fully concur with Michael's note that, *"Education and knowledge really will drive you towards a more peaceful place."* This book is a significant step in that process, and we both wish it had existed before we became parents.
Dietlinde Turban Maazel and Tony Wood

CHAPTER 47

STAGES OF LIFE: AN AMAZINGLY HELPFUL INDIAN PERSPECTIVE

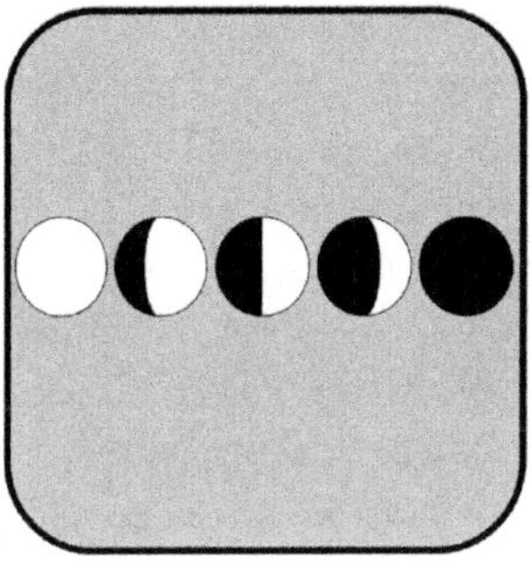

"Ancient wisdom has a place, especially in the chaos of our modern world."
- Michael Padraig Acton -

As we move into the second part of this book, on parenting adult children, it is a good opportunity to remind ourselves that the understanding of life stages changes depending on time and place. After all, there are no undisputed edges that separate babies from children, children from teenagers, teens from adults and adults from the elderly.

For a non-western perspective on life stages, let's look at the Ashrama system from Hinduism.

At first, the ashrama system was not related to age or life development and simply described four ways of being that could be applied to both individuals and social systems.

Over time, the four ashramas morphed into stages on a development pathway that led from childhood to old age. These ashramas are:

- Brahmacharya (student), from early childhood until the age of 25.
- Grihastha (householder), from 25 to 48 years.
- Vanaprastha (forest walker/dweller), from 48 to 72 years.

- Sannyasa (renunciate), from 72 years onwards.

Far from a simple way of dividing a human lifespan, the ashramas provide a way of focusing human priorities based on the concept of the four purusarthas: Dharma, Artha, Kama and Moksha.

During the brahmacharya stage, the young person's life is devoted to learning about the world and acting ethically within it. In classical times, the youth would live with a guru and learn about science, logic, philosophy and the Hindu scriptures. They would follow the path of Dharma, which is somewhat like a moral compass that shows them the conduct and duties expected of them. According to the Kama Sutra, the brahmacharya stage also teaches the student to understand Artha. As with Dharma, Artha has multiple meanings which are difficult to fully explain in English. It encompasses concepts such as the pursuit of wealth and material security in order to enjoy a meaningful life. In short, the child learns to be a decent, well-adjusted adult who can provide for their family.

The grihastha stage corresponds to that of married life. The young person fulfils their duties of maintaining a home, raising a family and making their mark on society. While the ethical foundation stone of Dharma is still very much the driving force, there is a stronger focus on Artha and Kama, the enjoyment of material pleasures.

At the vanaprastha stage, the person begins their withdrawal from the physical world of career, wealth and security and prepares to embrace the spiritual life. They pass their material duties on to the next generation and play a more advisory role in the family. Artha and Kama give way to Moksha, the pursuit of spiritual liberation.

The final stage, Sannyasa, is where the person renounces the material world and takes up the simple, peaceful devotional life of an ascetic. It is worth pointing out that while Moksha is now the primary focus of living, Dharma still plays an important role. The person may be preparing to leave the material world, but they will still be striving to live an ethical life.

How we approach different stages of life has a profound effect on society.

Consider how applying the ashramas to western society would work today. Young people would be encouraged to focus only on learning, putting relationships and worldly ambitions on hold until the age of 25. They would then use all they had learned to raise a family and enjoy the fruits of their labour in the present, rather than putting this off until retirement. Middle and old age would then be a peaceful time of gradually letting go of our material attachments as we prepare to enter the great mystery.

In most western societies, we have decided that 18 is a suitable age to mark the boundary between childhood and adulthood. Of course, our children still need our support and care, and this second part of the book looks at the many challenges and rewards that come with parenting adult children.

For more guidance, read:

Virtue, Success, Pleasure and Liberation: Four Aims of Life in the Tradition of Ancient India - A. Danielou

Raising Children: Surprising Insights from Other Cultures - D.F. Lancy

"Reasonability has to be understood and needs to be recognised and inform our laws to avoid abuse and promote support. Beware!"

- Michael Padraig Acton -

INTRODUCTION

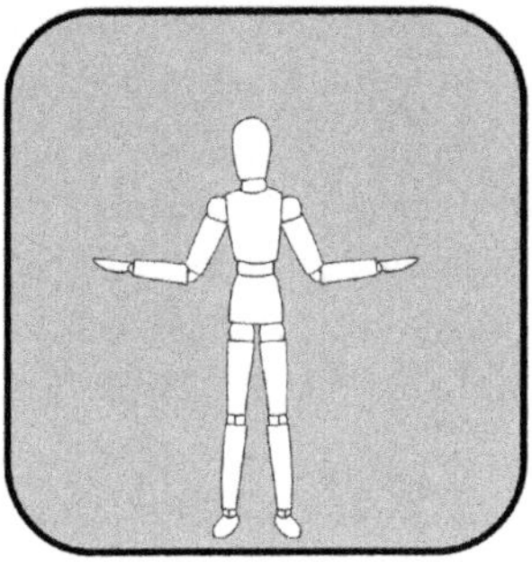

"At last, a voice for struggling adult children and their parents.
A better practise for grown-ups."
- Michael Padraig Acton -

Most parenting books are focused on children and school-going teenagers, but parenting doesn't stop at the age of 18 and there is no psychological dividing line between an adolescent and a fully-fledged adult.

There is a legal dividing line, and this means parenting adult children needs to be done differently. Adult children often need varying amounts of support throughout their lives and this second part of my book provides some much-needed guidance in that area.

Life stages in the western world

Before this chapter, we looked at the Ashrama concept in India and how age is tied in with roles and ambitions in life. How about adults living outside of that culture?

Although there is a lot of variation, it is possible to identify some age-related themes that can help when parenting our adult children. Just as with younger children, there is no precise 'mapping' of age on to achievement, but we can at least have an idea whether our adult children are 'on track' or being held back, whether by themselves or by our enabling behaviour. More on that later in the book!

Twenties: Adults at this stage are still exploring their identities and yet to fully define what success means for them. They are likely to be embarking on their careers, either working, looking for jobs or applying for post-graduate training. Many will be dating as they seek a life partner.

Thirties: A more settled identity is emerging at this stage. Many adults will be committed to following a defined career path. Relationships may have progressed to marriage or co-habiting. Where desired, concrete plans for buying a home and raising a family are likely to be in place.

Forties: Some adults will be fully established in their careers while others will be looking for a change and even returning to education. Those who have had children of their own will be raising them (often with their parents' help!). At this stage, thoughts turn towards retirement planning and caring for elderly parents or even grandparents.

Again, I must stress that these stages are generic and by no means apply to all adult children. For example, there are many adult children in their twenties who already provide care for their parents or grandparents.

Navigating this section

As with Part One, this second part of the book is split into chapters focusing on specific challenges faced by the parents of adult children. It is designed to make it easy for you to dip into the book whenever you are facing a specific issue.

Are you finding it tough to accept your adult child's life choices? Read the chapter on handling conflict and diversity. Are you looking to spend quality time with an adult child who has become distant? I have written a chapter on adult children who ignore their parents and how you can get back in touch.

Or are you so close to your adult children that they are planning to move back in with you—partner in tow? My chapter on adult children who move back home will help you negotiate a solution that works for all.

If there is one overarching message that spans this part of the book, it's to understand that adult children have executive control over their lives. They are the CEOs. Your role is as a consultant who draws on your lifetime of wisdom and insight to inform their decision-making.

The trick is to pass on this information without shutting down the conversation–something that can easily happen if advice is delivered as criticism. Empathy and sensitivity are imperative. Learn your child's preferred communication style and match it. Do they like to weigh up the pros and cons like logical machines or is it all about how they feel about a situation in their gut?

Being a non-judgemental sounding board can be tough (and you might find yourself blushing and biting your tongue in equal measures!) but the effort will be worth it as you will develop a closer bond founded on trust and mutual respect.

Setting boundaries is another common theme that runs through the rest of this book. Whether your adult children are physically distant from you or moving back home, you still need to have boundaries in place. Both parents and adult children need to have their own protected space where they can make the rules, relax and be themselves.

Don't be afraid to convene a family meeting to bash all this out. It can seem awkward to tell your adult child that you expect them to put their mobile phone away at the dinner table–or to be told that you are not to enter their bedroom without permission–but these ground rules will make life better for everyone in the long term.

Finally, don't be embarrassed about your relationship with your adult children. Every parent needs help sometimes and those who seem to have it all under control may be hiding more than you realise.

Your only goal is to be a 'good enough' parent. Perfection is the cruellest of illusions.

CHAPTER 48

THE TOP CHALLENGES OF PARENTING ADULT CHILDREN

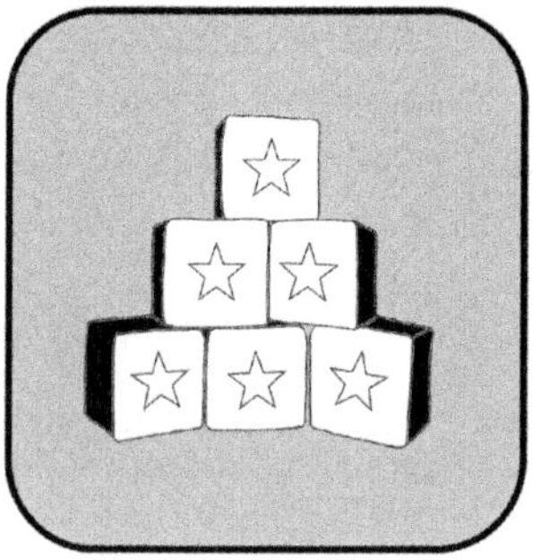

"This is one of the most inhumane times for humans to live. It's barbaric."
- Michael Padraig Acton -

As I pointed out in the introduction to this section, there are very few resources aimed at helping us to parent our adult children. With newly emerging issues such as mammoth amounts of college debt, plummeting mental health and soaring technology, the need for support and advice is greater than ever.

I thought it would be helpful to summarise some of the main challenges that parents face in the 21st century once their children have turned 18.

What should we be most concerned about?

The top concerns we should have when parenting adult children is anything to do with their education, career, wellbeing, their attitude to the wellbeing of others and their sustainability.

The world is tough now. There's no getting away from that. It doesn't matter what demographic you are part of. It doesn't matter whether you come from wealth or poverty, or somewhere in-between, or what career you're in. This is one of the most inhumane times to live. We live in concrete or wooden boxes and there's very little community–at least in the western world.

It does take a village to bring up a child and we're missing that village element. Our children are no longer as accountable for their actions. It used to be that if we made a mistake, it would get back to somebody. Nowadays there seems to be this anonymity where people can do things and just walk away. So, I think safety for our adult children is a big concern for most parents. I don't know whether it's just me, or it's because of the field I work in, or the news or social media but they seem to face more, and more complicated, dangers nowadays.

Here are some of the other top concerns parents of adult children have. With each area of concern, I have recommended the chapter/s in this section you should refer to for quick tips and powerful advice.

When do we push our adult children? When do we pull back?

Once we understand that we are responsible for our child's education, health and wellbeing, it becomes that bit easier to make decisions on their behalf. But when they legally become adults, we suddenly have to relinquish that power and responsibility. So, what will your new role be?

Are you a helicopter parent, always on hand to provide advice? Or are you a remote disciplinarian who believes children need to learn from their mistakes?

Chances are you, like most of us, are somewhere between the two extremes.

So, when is it OK to intervene in our adult children's lives and push them forwards and when is it best to hold back and let them work things out for themselves?

Difficult as it may be to read, you should only ever act on behalf of your adult children if they are at serious risk of harming themselves or somebody else. You might want your child to pivot–to change direction–but they are the CEO of their lives. By all means, advise, object and suggest but never go as far as taking control of the situation.

We haven't got any control over our adult children, but we can be concerned for them, for sure. It can be tough and painful to hold back when we know we could push a few buttons or make a call but it's time to cut the apron strings.

I cover this topic next in the chapter *Caring By letting go: supporting versus enabling revisited.* If your child is living with a mental or physical illness or disability, read the chapter When your adult child has mental health issues or other special needs for more guidance.

How do we help our adult children sort out their finances?

We need to balance the healthy desire to support our adult children with their finances with the overall goal of supporting them to achieve financial independence. This is not always easy to do, especially if we can see our children are struggling to get by.

But be mindful. If we allow our adult children to rely on handouts, we can slip into an unhealthy pattern of dependence that affects the whole family. Some adult children will take advantage of their parents' financial support. If you are concerned about this, refer to the chapter *When to call it a day: stopping adult children taking advantage of parents* for more guidance.

How can we support our anxious son or daughter to cope with life?

It is terrible to see our children struggle to progress in life because of mental illness. Anxiety is a common issue and the best way forward for them–and you–will depend upon the severity of the problem. You and your child may need to talk with a professional or, if the anxiety is mild, you may need to help them to develop better coping skills. Refer to the chapter *When your adult child has mental health issues or other special needs*

Should my child and their grandchild move back to the family home following a breakup?

If an adult child wants to return to live with you (or you want to invite them back), always take time to think and talk things through with everyone involved. Be prepared for some disruption, even without the added complication of grandchildren and partners.

I recommend reading through the chapter *Oh no! How to navigate adult children who move back home.* If you have become part of the extended, modern-day family, you should also refer to the chapter *Adult children in the modern-day family.*

How on Earth can I balance being a good parent, spouse and grandparent with caring for my own needs?
Setting clear boundaries and committing to honest communication is vital when we have conflicting responsibilities. If you feel your adult children are trampling on you, take a look at the chapter *When to call it a day: stopping adult children taking advantage of parents.*

Whatever your concerns, it will help if you have someone you can talk to about them. Friends with their own adult children may have experienced something similar and can give you tips and strategies that have worked for them.

You will see that many of the issues we face with managing our adult children boil down to setting and protecting boundaries. Sometimes there are wounds from the past that must be healed before you can enjoy a healthy, grounded relationship with your adult child. *Mistakes: owning and resolving the past* is a chapter worth consulting for this situation.

If you need additional help with any of this or are struggling to cope, seek professional help from a suitably qualified therapist with proven experience in working with families. You don't have to do this on your own.

CHAPTER 49

CARING BY LETTING GO: SUPPORTING VERSUS ENABLING REVISITED

"Growth cannot happen within a vacuum.
Be mindful of responsibilities."
- Michael Padraig Acton -

Childhood is a magical time, and it is easy to slip into nostalgia. But as I explained in the first part of this book, the journey to adulthood is a process of gaining independence from the childhood family unit. We have to let our children go.

This is easier when our adult children are secure and independent but what if they are demanding and needy? We must overcome our urge to remove all their obstacles and fight all their battles for them.

At some point, most adult children will struggle. They will have issues. They will face problems. When should we give them a listening ear and when should we spring into action and fix things for them? Well, we don't ever do the latter. We never fix our adult children.

At this stage, all we can do is offer a consultation. Ask them what they're looking to get out of your conversation and then maybe offer some suggested resolutions, ideas that they can run with or not.

Unless their wellbeing, i.e., their life or the life of a third person, is in danger, you cannot direct them, you cannot take control, you cannot take over.

That's very difficult for a parent to accept because we love our children. We want to fix things. We used to get such a reward by comforting our children. By saying, "Oh, there, there. Let's mend the wendy house," or "Let's repair that bike tyre." But now they're adult children we've got to take on a new role. They are the CEO of the company, and we are a wise and experienced sounding board, ready to offer ideas and scenarios that our child can listen to, learn from and perhaps act on.

This doesn't mean we should never provide any practical or emotional support for our adult children. If they ask us for help, we should consider how best we can support them. It may be that we refuse what they've asked for but come up with another solution. For example, your adult child might be running late for work and ask you for a lift that would mean you missing your Yoga class. However, it might be possible for you to drop them down to the train station instead.

It can be difficult to know when we are supporting our children and when we are enabling them. Ask yourself the question: by helping them, am I moving them closer to their goal of independence? Or am I disempowering them by acting in their place?

Make sure you are firm with your boundaries, or you could find yourself being taken advantage of. This is a common thread that runs throughout this part of the book.

One dilemma which is particularly common in these times is whether to offer or agree to your adult child moving back in with you. That's the subject of the next chapter *Oh no! How to navigate adult children who move back home.*

For more guidance, read:

Setting Boundaries with your Adult Children: Six Steps to Hope and Healing for Struggling Parents - A. Bottke

25 Ways to Stop Enabling Your Adult Child and How to Set Boundaries - E.S. Addington

CHAPTER 50

OH NO! HOW TO NAVIGATE ADULT CHILDREN WHO MOVE BACK HOME

"What would you do if you wake up one morning and there's a stranger in your kitchen? However pleased we are that our children are returning, it's going to be a drain. It's going to be complicated."
- Michael Padraig Acton -

Deciding whether to allow your adult children to move back home always presents a quandary. First of all, you need to be absolutely sure that having them back with you is the best solution for everybody. It can be hard to say "No," especially when the thought of having them back makes you happy, but you need to think about their future development and also about the health of the family unit as a whole. If they are returning to the fold because of a strong attachment to you as a mother or father, welcoming them back could be a step backwards for them.

So first ask why they want to move back home. What is it for? It could be that your children have finished university/college and need to save for a home. It could be that they are in between jobs or have just left a relationship. They might be down on their luck for some reason and need a safe place to go.

Even more importantly, work out how long they will be coming back for. If possible, clarify this before agreeing to them moving back. Will it be for three months? Six months? A year?

A good strategy I suggest is to do a three-month trial and then review it. This might seem very stiff and formalised, when you're excited that your kids are coming back, but it's very important to set boundaries and have rules in place. A time limit is a great first step. We can manage so many things with a time limit on them much better than when we're thinking, 'Is this going to be forever?'

Complications to be mindful of

What if your adult child is moving back home because they're unwell or they have some serious issue? Perhaps they've been in prison or are recovering from drug addiction. You are not qualified to manage that. Always remember that. You weren't even qualified to be a parent, you learnt that as you went along–as we all do!

If your child's coming back and there's a serious issue, you need to get professional help in that area to help manage them. It's paramount that you do not think that you can manage the situation on your own. Even if you're an oncology specialist, you are not qualified to look after your child with cancer. You need somebody to be professional and one step removed.

It's also very easy to 'enable' and disempower a disabled or sick adult child with certain issues. I cover this in more detail in the chapter *When your adult child has mental health issues or other special needs.*

What if it's not just your adult child but also their partner wanting to move in? This is complicated because they will have their own lives, careers, issues and arguments. How do you manage having what literally comes to two families in one home?

In short, whatever the situation, living arrangements need to be planned very carefully before you agree to your adult children moving in with you.

Ground rules and expectations

The comfort and routine of home can have a strong regressive effect on adult children, so if you decide to accept them living with you again, you must set ground rules to avoid them slipping back into old habits of dependence.

It's a bit complicated to set rules for adult children living at home. The main problem is that they are now their own executive management team. They are of an age where they are legally responsible for themselves, and they will have also developed a navigation system of their own.

You need to respect them as adults by setting out your expectations just as you would any other long-term visitor to your home. Make sure they know that you expect them to share the load. How can they best contribute to the smooth running of the home? Even if they're down on their luck, your adult child might be able to wash the windows, pick the dog's poo up from the garden, feed the cats or something. Tell them that they must make their bed every morning and bring their own laundry down. Because however we look at it, however pleased we are that our children are returning, it's going to be a drain. It's going to be complicated. Communicating your expectations from day one will help avoid arguments or awkward misunderstandings further down the line.

Anticipate potential future issues and come up with solutions. For example, what would you do if you wake up one morning and there's a stranger in your kitchen? How would that happen, you may ask. Well, adult children start dating. They have sex.

You are likely to find that old parent-child patterns of relating are hard to break. Conflicts may play out differently, but they are likely to still happen without a clear plan to resolve them. Reading the chapter *Unhealthy family habits exist in all families: how to overcome them* can help you to do things differently. The next chapter, *Succeeding conflict and diversity with our adult children* also has some useful management tips.

The key is working towards open and honest communication–a more mature relationship.

Fairness and equality

When an adult child moves into your home, it needs to be a fair and equitable arrangement. You are all grownups now.

You may have been living without kids at home for a while, owning your space and enjoying your independence but having them back is going to change the routine. It's going to be work. However, if you have to give up an activity you enjoy to accommodate your adult child, something is wrong. Apart from sacrificing a pleasure, you are likely to harbour resentment towards your child which will build over time, eating away at your relationship.

Money is often a tricky issue when it comes to adult children moving back home. It could be that they moved back because of university/college debt or to help them save for a deposit on a house. While it is nice to be able to support your children towards financial independence, your offer of accommodation shouldn't be an invitation to spend recklessly on shopping and going out. They still need to take responsibility for budgeting. Not only is this fair for everybody in the family but it will also ensure they can cope in the real world when they eventually leave the nest for the second time.

For more guidance, read:

The Hands-On Guide to Surviving Adult Children Living at Home - C. Newberry

The Crowded Nest Syndrome - K. Shaputis

CHAPTER 51

SUCCEEDING CONFLICT AND DIVERSITY WITH OUR ADULT CHILDREN

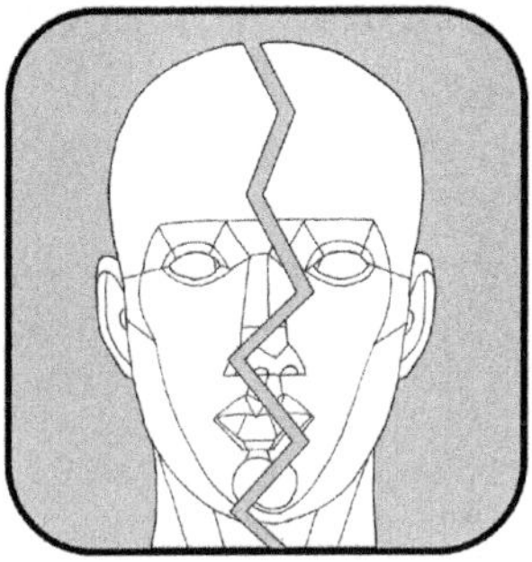

"If an adult child is coming back and flaunting something they know you have an issue with, in a way that's disrespectful to you, then that needs a conversation."
- Michael Padraig Acton -

This is a major hurdle at times. If our fundamental belief systems regarding sexuality, gender, work roles, education or anything else are challenged by our adult children, it is going to be tough for us.

It may be that we're already very liberal and we're OK with our lesbian daughter or our gay son or our transsexual adult child, etc. However, sometimes things do touch us, and we have to work that out. Ask yourself why it's getting under your skin. How do you manage that?

Conflict over belief systems can get super-heated because of territorial issues. In our own home, we have every right to act and behave and believe what we want. As long as we're not harming a third party, we can do what we wish in our own home. Anything consensual and legal is OK.

However, if someone, especially an adult child, is coming back and flaunting something they know you have an issue with, in a way that's disrespectful to you, then that needs a conversation. We look more closely at the issue of respect in the next chapter.

If there is a big conflict, the best thing to do is to talk it out with someone. Work it out with your adult child. Sometimes we're brought up in a very strict or a very controlled way and we may not feel safe with diversity or difference or change. If you love your adult child, try and love them by understanding where they're at and what their wishes are. And then talk with them about how you can, as a family, manage this in a way that's good for them and OK enough for you. Because you matter too.

There's an old adage saying, 'Our children bring us up very well' and they do because they challenge us. I can't emphasise enough how much education and knowledge really will drive you towards a more peaceful place.

Good luck!

For more guidance, read:

How To Really Love Your Adult Child: Building a Healthy Relationship in a Changing World - G. Chapman and R. Campbell M.D.

Doing Life With Your Adult Children: Keep Your Mouth Shut and the Welcome Mat Out - J. Burns

CHAPTER 52

STOP ADULT CHILDREN WHO WRONGLY DISRESPECT YOU

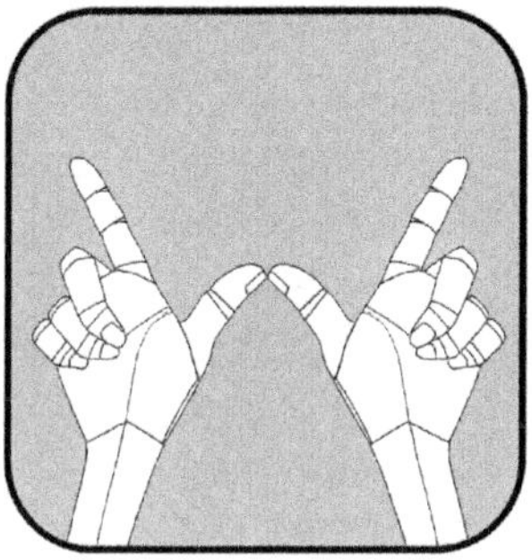

"Disrespect is a very heavy word.
If we have earned respect in life and our adult child is disrespecting us, we need to think about protecting ourselves because that's quite abusive."
- Michael Padraig Acton -

By the time your child becomes an adult, you might expect the rebelling and acting out to be over. Unfortunately, this is not always the case.

Disrespect can become a serious problem if your adult children are still living with you or have moved back. It can be incredibly stressful for everyone in the family if they are not prepared to follow the ground rules in your home.

Adult children who disrespect their parents need a boundary put in place. Of course, it depends on what that disrespect is. Disrespect can mean anything that deviates from etiquette, social norms or socially accepted behaviour and our ideas on that can differ (e.g., see the next chapter *A short note on tech devices*).

Adult children living with mental or physical illness should not be given carte blanche to disrespect you and other members of the family. This means they should still follow the same rules as everybody else and act responsibly if they are unable to stick to an arrangement because of their situation (e.g., calling to say they are too anxious to meet up for a coffee).

I have provided some practical ways for managing this tricky issue in the chapter *When your adult child has mental health issues or other special needs.*

The roots of disrespect

Why is your adult child disrespecting you? Is it something about them? Is it something about what you or the family unit has done–or not done? Or is it a combination of those things?

When adult children disrespect their parents, it's often a sign that there are still problems from the past to work through. The chapter *Mistakes: owning and resolving the past* provides practical ways to achieve this.

Disrespect really comes from a lack of communicating, a lack of understanding or a lack of education. If we commit the time to it, we are all capable of improving the way we communicate.

Sometimes we're not honest with our adult children or they're not honest with us. We might be holding back to protect them, or they are doing so to protect us. How can we behave appropriately or make corrections if we don't tell the truth?

Again, a favourite tool of mine to get things unstuck is the 1, 2, 3:

1. Be really honest about how you're feeling right now. "I feel disrespected, upset and attacked."
2. Provide evidence that supports your feelings. "You've been to dinner seven times in the last month and you haven't helped wash up, you haven't contributed in any way, you haven't even said thank you before you leave and there's been some kind of argument at the table. It's been unpleasant."
3. This is the most important step. Find a real way to resolve the issue. "I would like you to think before coming to dinner about how you may contribute. Make some napkins to bring, help put the plates away or wash the dishes. Contribute in some way. Let's also find a way to make dinner a pleasant experience for everyone.

> If you've got some issues, let's talk them out beforehand so we can have a nice meal."

If you are not making any headway, you need to start protecting yourself by putting in healthy boundaries and maybe having some time out from the relationship. Nobody should be disrespected, especially where it's not deserved.

Whatever your relationship is with your children, nephews, nieces, etc., adult or young, ask yourself, 'Are they speaking to me in a reasonable way? Is our relationship healthy?' And be mindful, you can't change them, they have to change themselves. You can only change yourself, and there is no reason why you should be a punching bag, or always the one to blame.

One category of disrespectful behaviour that is being normalised in society today is the inappropriate use of tech devices and I've devoted a short chapter to this next.

For more guidance, read:

Setting Boundaries with Your Adult Children: Six Steps to Hope and Healing for Struggling Parents - A. Bottke

When Parents Hurt: Compassionate Strategies When You and Your Grown Child Don't Get Along - J. Coleman PhD

CHAPTER 53

A SHORT NOTE ON TECH DEVICES

"If an emergency room doctor can be without their phone for an hour for a meal so can any of your adult children."
- Michael Padraig Acton -

Mobile phones, iPads, laptops, watches that talk to you. . . it seems these days, there are so many distractions. But I have one rule in my home. When we sit down for our meal, devices are not at the table. That's because somebody has gone to great lengths to provide a meal and it's a healthy thing to actually sit together, enjoy each other's company, catch up on the day and break bread.

If your adult child, their partner or their children come into your home for a meal and they refuse to come off their devices–even though they know it isn't acceptable in your home–then you need to set a boundary and say, "Look. You're welcome to come back for dinner at any time. However, no devices at the table. It's something we just don't like and don't want in our own home."

It needs discussion. If an emergency room doctor can be without their phone for an hour for a meal so can any of your adult children, their offspring and their partners. It's about respect and accepting that you require socialisation and appreciation of the meal in your home.

Devices have their place but not all the time.

The Narcissist's Mantra

"That didn't happen.
And, if it did, it wasn't that bad. And, if it was, that's not a big deal. And, if it is, that's not my fault. And, if it was, I didn't mean it. And, if I did, you deserved it."

- Michael Padraig Acton -

CHAPTER 54

WHEN TO CALL IT A DAY: STOPPING ADULT CHILDREN TAKING ADVANTAGE OF PARENTS

"I have worked at drug dependency units. Many parents had remortgaged their houses, used their life savings or cashed in their retirement funds to pay for their children's drug habits."
- Michael Padraig Acton -

Taking advantage of a parent's generosity is a special form of disrespect but how do we know when our adult child is taking advantage of us?

We must define what we mean by taking advantage and how serious the claim is. It's not always an easy call but if they're having an easier ride through life than you, ask yourself why. For example, if your adult child lives with you and you're scrimping and saving to make ends meet while they're out all night spending money on parties and having fun, that's not on!

Being a parent is a thankless task at times. Your adult children may have busy lives, with caring for children and the demands of work, etc. But if they are taking advantage of us, then a big question is: what is it about us that's allowing that?

It is important to look at what we can control and what we can't in any situation involving our adult children. We may not be able to tell them where they can or can't go anymore or what to spend their money on, but we can certainly withdraw access to the family car and increase the rent on their room.

Some areas are not so clear-cut and need negotiation. For example, when should an unemployed adult child be up and out of the house by? What is a fair exchange of contributions (e.g., is it OK for your son or daughter to never do the ironing if they cook for the family five nights a week?)

Once again, it's about setting expectations, drawing up boundaries and supporting, not enabling, your adult child. Driving them to a job interview because they haven't got a car, sitting with them as they work through their resume/CV or looking after their children while they attend an evening class is supportive. Just make sure there is a fair exchange–either now or further down the line. Driving them to work every day or writing their resume/CV for them is not supporting them, it's enabling them. When you're asked to look after the grandchildren three days a week on a regular basis, that's not you being a grandparent. That's you being taken advantage of, especially if you can't do it one day and it causes friction. Of course, it's different if you are being paid or otherwise compensated to look after the grandkids.

I worked for quite some time at drug dependency (DDU) units, not only with the service users but also with the families of the service users. Many parents had remortgaged their houses, used their life savings or cashed in their retirement funds to pay for their children's drug habits. They didn't realise they were enabling rather than supporting until we did some serious work together.

Changing the pattern

If you're being taken advantage of, think about why that is happening to you. What is it that you're doing? What inside you is allowing that and how can you send a clear message that you won't let it happen anymore?

You can't change your child, but you can change your own behaviour. It's tough to change things and you may need a professional's help in making that change happen.

It's very important you:

- Assess how severely you are being taken advantage of,
- Work out what part you're responsible for in that, and
- Find somebody you trust to talk about it in confidence.

If you haven't got somebody you can trust and to talk to in confidence, then find a systemic-trained therapist who works with families and ask them for some support and guidance on the way forward.

Even yours truly, me, when I was having difficulty with my daughter at one time, spoke about this in clinical supervision. My supervisor asked me one question that changed my life. She asked, "Michael, do you think you may be overcompensating for your own childhood?" That changed so much in my life because I was realising I was trying to right and amend my own history by helping my daughter.

Handling narcissistic adult children

If your adult child really doesn't seem to care about your feelings and is blatantly ripping you off, consider that they may have narcissistic personality disorder (NPD).

There is only one way to handle a narcissistic adult child–you don't. Or at least you hold them at arm's length so as to minimise your exposure to their games and manipulations.

NPD is a terrible disorder which rips families and relationships apart and you will need to put protective measures in place. If they are living with you right now, they will have to move out–sooner rather than later.

Narcissists only know how to take, and you cannot 'fix' them. Oh, and you might want to consider getting a copy of the first book in my *Power Of You* series: *Learning How To Leave.*

For more guidance, read:

Learning How To Leave: A Practical Guide to Stepping Away from Toxic and Narcissistic Relationships - M. Padraig Acton

When Your Adult Child Breaks Your Heart: Coping With Mental Illness, Substance Abuse, and the Problems That Tear Families Apart - J. Young and C. Adamec

CHAPTER 55

UNHEALTHY FAMILY HABITS EXIST IN ALL FAMILIES: HOW TO OVERCOME THEM

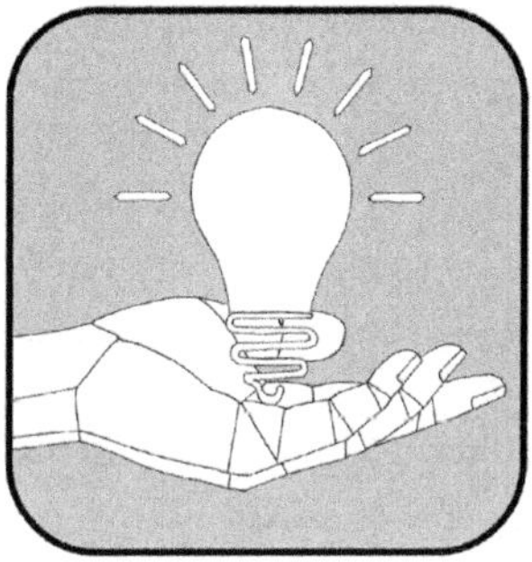

"The whole family system will knock and kick and punch and scream to get a person to not change, to return to the familiar."
- Michael Padraig Acton -

Our children may have reached adulthood but that doesn't mean that long-standing family habits magically disappear. It can be very disappointing to realise that the same toxic patterns of relating continue.

Why is this the case? It's down to homeostasis.

Homeostasis describes the way that any system, including a family, keeps a certain balance going whether it's healthy or not. Homeostasis is maintained through the roles played by individual family members and the behaviour patterns between them.

This homeostasis is so familiar, even though it might be unhealthy, that each segment of that family plays their role to perfection in order to keep to that same pattern going like clockwork. The biggest challenge we have in therapy is when we are only working with one member of a family. After we help them make positive changes, this whole family system will start to challenge the new patterns. They will knock and kick and punch and scream to get this person to not change, to return to the familiar.

It could be that one person in the family is always targeted as a black sheep and can never do any right. No matter what they do, they never improve in the eyes of the family. Or it could be that someone's an alcoholic and that this is being enabled in some way rather than the person being supported to change it. There could be all different types of unhealthy patterns being protected by the drive for homeostasis.

Homeostasis also operates in couples. How many times have you heard of somebody leaving, for example, somebody with alcohol dependency issues? Then, a year later, there's somebody new and lo and behold, they have alcohol dependency issues too! We tend to follow these unhealthy patterns in life unless we get some work completed on us (e.g., by seeing a therapist).

The only way a family can start to do things differently is if it owns up to the system not working. My advice to a family following an unhealthy system and carrying out unhealthy behaviours is to change up the routine. First find the motivation and then work out a practical way to change it.

What is the motivation? Perhaps we do not want to go to Uncle Harry's at Christmas because he's always drunk and he's very inappropriate in the way he touches us. And now we're 40, we don't want to go to Uncle Harry's anymore.

How can we do it differently? Well, we could do something without Uncle Harry on that day. Maybe we see Uncle Harry the day before or the day after, but we can't reward bad behaviour. That's what we're doing when we say, "We do it every year like this so it's OK to do it again this year."

Here's another example. Perhaps your adult child is constantly taking from you and then when it's your birthday or Christmas, etc. they don't bother with you. You may get a card from Moonpig they ordered by clicking three buttons. Yet everybody else seems to get their attention and their time investment. Why not you? What's happening? That system's broken. How can you do it differently?

So really look at yourself in the mirror. Think about the patterns that are not working for you–not only as an individual but also collectively as a family. What doesn't work anymore? What do we keep doing that leaves us feeling really low or deflated or in a bad place? How do we change that and why would we want to change it?

And if certain components of this system don't want to change, what do we do with that because the one thing you have to understand is we cannot change another human being. They have to see the need to change and change for themselves. We can change ourselves though. We can change our expectations. We can change our behaviour. And we can certainly change where we invest. It's your call at the end of the day.

If some of this is ringing true–it could relate to your immediate family or your extended family–then think about what doesn't work. Why doesn't it work? And what would be the benefit of change? So many people fear the conflict or worry about what might happen. Think also about what good would come of changing. You'll be surprised by the strength you have if you keep those motivations in mind.

For more guidance, read:

Walking on Eggshells: Navigating the Delicate Relationship Between Adult Children and Their Parents - J. Isay

The Parallel Process: Growing Alongside Your Adolescent or Young Adult Child in Treatment - K. Pozatec

CHAPTER 56

ESTRANGED ADULT CHILDREN: WHAT TO DO

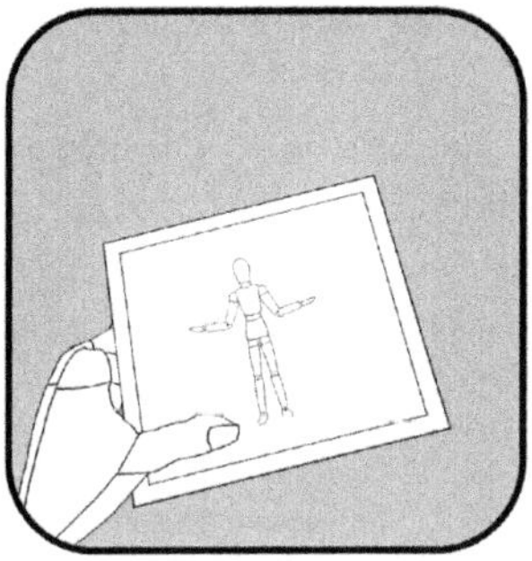

"Sometimes the weight of the past is too heavy to be shaken off. If your adult child is protecting themselves from historic abuse, they need to work out when and if it's OK for them to come back."

- Michael Padraig Acton -

Adult children can ignore their parents, sometimes for a very long time. There can be a plethora of reasons for this.

Sometimes our adult children will cut us off because they are angry with us and are holding a grudge. We might not even understand why they're so angry. In any case, talk to them about it. If they don't respond at first, persist. They may need time and space to think through things and decide whether they are ready to move on from what's been upsetting them. Try not to take it personally and keep expressing your wish to connect.

Are your adult children really ignoring you or is this about different personalities and communication styles?

There needs to be some natural separation, but you may have a greater need for family socialisation than your children. They may be comfortable with minimal contact whereas you want to see them all of the time. It doesn't mean they love you any less than you love them. You might just need to have a talk about expectations around communication. Perhaps you can compromise on a weekly catch-up call.

My advice to parents of adult children where the children aren't in contact is to simply reach out to them. Everyone's findable nowadays. No one can disappear completely unless they really are living off the grid so find out their address, their email or their phone number and get in touch.

Just drop a message once every few weeks at first. A simple and benign touch-base, like, 'Wondering what you're doing, hope you're OK. It's nice to see some warmer weather now, isn't it? Love mum/dad.' Let them see that it doesn't matter how angry they are or what difficulties they're having, there's a door open for them to walk through if they should want to.

Once you have made a re-connection, a good way to build on it is to find a shared interest or hobby and commit time to enjoying it together. Arrange an activity and a schedule that suits you both. Meet up for a fortnightly hill walk, have a monthly action movie night or get together to cook a nice meal for the extended family once a week.

When wounds run too deep

Sometimes the weight of the past is too heavy to be shaken off with a few family chats. If your adult child is protecting themselves from some historic abuse or a serious ongoing conflict, they need to work out when and if it's OK for them to come back. In this case, consider booking in with an experienced therapist for some family therapy sessions. You might also find some useful advice in the next chapter *Mistakes: owning and resolving the past.*

It can be especially difficult if you are being kept apart from the grandchildren because your adult child is bearing a grudge. However, you do have legal grandparents' rights in Europe and some parts of America. Wherever you are in the world, it's easy to Google 'grandparents' rights'. There are courts that will look after the grandparents and help them to maintain a healthy relationship with the grandchildren.

Grudges, frustration and anger do ebb over time so just make sure your adult child knows that you want to stay in touch, that you care and that your door is always open.

For more guidance, read:

Rules of Estrangement: Why Adult Children Cut Ties and How to Heal the Conflict - J. Coleman

Reconnecting with Your Estranged Adult Child: Practical Tips and Tools to Heal your Relationship - T. Gilbertson

CHAPTER 57

MISTAKES: OWNING AND RESOLVING THE PAST

"Stop playing games with your adult child.
Sometimes your mistakes really are a big deal!"
- Michael Padraig Acton -

If you're a human and a parent, you made mistakes bringing up your child.

No one gets through parenting without making mistakes unless they're a narcissist (but that's a whole different story). Perhaps you decided the wrong school for your child, slapped them out of frustration, put them in detention at home for a week. While there's no excuse for such mistakes, you can acknowledge you made them. You need to be honest with your adult child and explain to them, "This was going on at the time. I know that's not an excuse, but I acknowledge the mistake, I learnt from it, and I regret it. I apologise." It's never too late to say those words.

What you've done is owned the mistake and let your adult child know that you are not challenging their feelings or interpretation. The worst thing you can do is keep on avoiding the issue by denying or downplaying it. It won't work to say, "Oh, that's fine, stop making a big deal of it," because it might be a big deal to them. When your child was growing up, they were powerless, and you were their example of how to be in the world.

It's vital that you both speak honestly and without any game-playing. Games may have worked when your children were young, and you needed to manipulate them into getting up and getting dressed for school on time or whatever but playing games won't work with an adult child. You need straight talking. Again, as I said earlier in this book, indigenous Australians once told me, "If you send out the truth on a boomerang, you don't care what comes back."

If you made a mistake and you believe it's impacting your adult child, talk to them about it. It might be that the child says, "What are you talking about? That was nothing to me," or they might say, "Well yes, that really caused me some problems." Talk through it. Manage it. Find a resolution and move on.

And if you have owned the mistake, apologised for it and talked through it, there's not much else you can do. It's up to your adult child to work that out. Just let them know that the doors open to discuss it further.

For more guidance, read:
Restoring Family Connections: Helping Targeted Parents and Adult Alienated Children Work Through Conflict, Improve Communication, and Enhance Relationships - A. Baker, P. Fine and A. Lacheen-Baker
Mending Fences Healing Hearts: The Top 10 Keys to a Better Relationship with Your Adult Children - Dr C. Lynch

CHAPTER 58

WHEN YOUR ADULT CHILD HAS MENTAL HEALTH ISSUES OR OTHER SPECIAL NEEDS

"It's tough when our children struggle.
Don't encourage them down the dark hole of enabling."
- Michael Padraig Acton -

At the start of this section of the book, we laid out some of the general stages that an adult child can be expected to reach in their twenties, thirties and forties. If you are the parent of an adult child with special needs, particularly a mental disability or illness, you should be prepared for the journey through these stages to take a lot longer or to play out differently.

As a parent, your goal should be to support your adult child to live their best life and be as independent as possible. Without firm boundaries, it is easy to slip into enabling our disabled child, especially if they use their condition as an excuse to act irresponsibly. Deliberately using a disability to gain an unfair advantage is known as 'reverse discrimination'. This could be as simple as your child parking in a disabled car parking spot when they don't need it that day or it could be something more worrying such as spending all of their benefits on booze or not feeding their children. If you dive in to rescue mode every time, they've probably already hooked you in to being an enabler.

If our adult children aren't very well or they are disabled, we need to fully understand their illness or disability and the background to it. If we only relate to their issues on a surface level, perhaps because we are afraid of what we will find if we delve too deep, then we won't ever know what our child is and is not capable of.

Every individual is different, so you need to know the specific ways in which your child's illness presents itself. Do they experience mood swings? Do they become aggressive or have tantrums? Do they lack resilience due to depression? Is their thinking disrupted or do they lose touch with reality?

You should be aware of any events or behaviours that might trigger your adult child. You also need to know their medication regime and what the effects of taking or missing their meds are. Are they receiving therapy or counselling?

Find out what factors increase their ability or disability and how well they can function in the world. What options do they have available to them? Are they getting sufficient support and care? Are they accessing that support and care? Are they compliant with the systems set up to help them?

Many people with mental illness respond well to having a predictable routine so taking part in regular shared activities and being clear with our adult child about their responsibilities (e.g., taking the bins out every Tuesday, washing the car on the first Sunday of the month, etc.) can often help with parenting them. Living in chaos rarely works for anyone, let alone somebody with special needs.

With boundaries and a routine firmly in place, we can start to focus on what our adult child can do and how we can empower them in society.

As explained in an earlier chapter, parents of children with special needs face many unique challenges. If your child has a physical or mental illness, make sure you don't burn yourself out. Attend to your own needs as well as your child's. If you find yourself frustrated by your adult child's behaviour or lack of development, remind yourself that they are not their illness and that underneath it all is a soul that needs love and care.

Seek help from professionals. There are also many support groups out there now. All you have to do is Google whatever's going on with your adult child and ask for helplines or support groups or professional care. Other sources of help include the BACP (UK, 01455 883300), BPS (UK, 0116 254 9568), APA (US, 800 374 2721) or your country's provider of professional licensed therapists and psychological services.

Grandparenting responsibilities

It is very common now to have a situation where an adult child with special needs has children of their own. Again, it is vital that the parent to that adult child supports them to be a responsible parent rather than enables them to forego those responsibilities. This can be a blurry boundary but if your adult child is using their illness or disability as an excuse to delegate all parenting to you, this is not helping anyone, not least your grandchild. The odd wobble may be OK but a pattern of irresponsible behaviour (not turning up at the school gate on time, leaving a child unattended, deliberately embarrassing them in public, etc.) will need to be addressed quickly.

Perhaps you could offer to attend a local parenting class with them so you can support them in developing the skills they will need to be a 'good enough' parent?

For more guidance, read:

When our Grown Kids Disappoint Us: Letting Go of Their Problems, Loving Them Anyway, and Getting On With Our Lives - J. Adams

Don't Let Your Kids Kill You: A Guide for Parents of Drug and Alcohol Addicted Children - C. Rubin and Tom Zingarelli et al.

Under Our Roof: A Son's Battle for Recovery, a Mother's Battle for her Son - M. Dean and H. Cunnane

CHAPTER 59

FOUR GOOD DAYS AND TRAINSPOTTING: HARROWING PERSPECTIVES OF THE PARENTING ROLE IN AN ADDICT'S LIFE

"Struggles with the devil: no warm blood runs here."
- Michael Padraig Acton -

Four Good Days is a film adaptation of a 2016 Washington Post newspaper article. The film is about a girl (Molly, played by Mila Kunis) who abuses drugs and turns up at her mum's house for help. Her parents are healthy enough, but Molly has burnt her bridges. She only ever comes back when she needs something, and this has been going on for 10 years. The whole story is about her relationship with mum (Deb, played by Glenn Close) who is horrible to Molly at first but relents, telling her she needs to go to a centre and go through rehab again.

As the story unfolds, you realise that mum's given Molly everything. She's sacrificed her life in many ways, so many times. Molly's lied and done bad things. She's stolen her mother's engagement ring; she's sold her shoes. She's just wreaked havoc and finally mum says, "Enough! I can't do it."

Molly completes the rehab, and she must complete four days clean before she can get her shot of naltrexone, an opioid antagonist that will prevent her from getting high. These are the 'four good days' of the title and we follow Deb experiencing getting her daughter back.

I won't spoil the ending, but the film is about the struggles of a parent putting in boundaries with an adult child who is having problems. Parents naturally love their children. They may not like them or respect them, and they might be scared of them, but it's very difficult for any parent to put in a boundary when they're seeing their child die. And that's what drugs and alcohol do–they kill people. But parents can't just be a punch bag, so it's about putting that boundary in and saying, "I matter too!"

Four Good Days is very moving, and it is a good portrayal of the struggle that a parent goes through when a child is just taking from them: the lies, manipulation, deceit, and pain. Irrespective of how much money, how much education, etc. a person has, a child who is a drug addict or an alcoholic is addicted and married to the drug. They love the drug more than anything else and will drain everything to keep that relationship with the drug or drink going.

Danny Boyle's *Trainspotting* is mainly focused on a group of Scottish heroin addicts but there are several scenes that depict the terrible situation parents find themselves in. When Renton (played by Ewan McGregor) is spared jail, his parents hold a celebration in the pub, but this facade of normality is revealed in Renton's voiced thoughts–he wants to get a fix more than ever. The small size of the parents at the end of the bed while Renton is going cold turkey is particularly excellent. It not only shows the viewer the hallucinations that withdrawal causes but also depicts the lack of importance the parents have to a drug addict while they are hooked.

It doesn't matter how old or young your child is, it's so important for you, as a parent or caregiver, to put on your oxygen mask first before you help anybody else. I am so tired of seeing parents that have drained their bodies and souls to keep their child going, living in fear that they may not have done enough if their child ever dies.

If you don't protect yourself, if you don't put boundaries in such as those put in by the parents in both films, you are not going to survive. You did not have children to commit suicide by not having boundaries. Nobody can manage this on their own.

The films are chilling in the way they depict this behaviour. If you are having issues around drugs with your children, you must take care of yourself. Your children are living their own lives and making their own journeys. It may sound harsh but there's only so much we can do for them. And if you think about how many people depend on us being alive: our husbands, our wives, our partners, our other children, our nieces, our nephews, our work. . . there are other things we need to be responsible for also.

People on drugs are married to the drugs. People on drugs will terrorise their parents in order to feed their addiction. You do not exist to them. Only the drugs and alcohol exist. Heed my warning. If you don't protect yourself, you are going to be useless to your child. You are not saving them, you are enabling them and enabling a child kills them faster than you putting in boundaries and giving them support.

CHAPTER 60

10 TIPS
FOR PARENTING YOUR ADULT CHILD WITH AUTISM

"Gifted, beautiful and tough."
- Michael Padraig Acton -

For more insight into the subject of this chapter, go to my YouTube channel and watch my discussion with somebody I diagnosed with and treated for Autistic Spectrum Disorder (ASD). It was created in collaboration with the NHS, which is the British hospital system, for Autism Awareness Week in 2021 to help spread the word about how to support employees with ASD.

Parenting an adult child on the autistic spectrum brings unique challenges. This chapter provides some useful tips for helping your child lead a positive, happy life.

Be mindful that we're talking about the high functioning end of the spectrum including geniuses and gifted adults. If your adult child is at the low functioning end, that's a very different subject and we sadly can't look at low functioning autism within the scope of this book. However, there are amazing centres that can look after your child and bring their gifts out of them.

Here is what you can do to support an adult child at the high functioning end of the spectrum:

One: Help them to develop coping mechanisms.
Perhaps the biggest challenge for people with autism is that people dehumanise them because they generally can't maintain eye contact really well and don't know how to be socially gregarious (or are sociable enough but can't manage chaos). As a parent, you can help your adult child with autism to understand, build and manage coping mechanisms for chaos or noise. It's about establishing a routine and keeping them safe. Even if your adult child has a well-paid career in the city or is a professor at a university, there are aspects of their life that will need management. They need to find ways of understanding how to soothe themselves and choose responses that will help and be good for them rather than destroy them or put them in awkward situations. Take a party. It's OK for your child to leave for 15 minutes, calm themselves and return rather than staying and becoming snappy or frustrated (or hitting themselves: people don't realise how many adult people with autism on the high functioning end of the spectrum harm themselves or don't parent themselves very well). So, a lot of your role is about helping your adult child parent themselves as an adult on the ASD.

Two: Invite them to consider therapy with a qualified and experienced counsellor or therapist.
This will be someone your child can talk to in confidence about their feelings and concerns. They may also need medical input from a GP/ physician if they are also experiencing mental health issues such as anxiety or depression. Make sure the therapist is versed in and understands ASD, cognitive-behavioural therapy (CBT), transactional analysis, and systemic family work. It needs a village to help a person manage ASD effectively.

Three: Find support groups for parents of adult children with autism in your local area.
Ask your nearest autism society for help as they will usually be able to put you in touch with a group. If there are no local services, join an online forum or social media group. You will feel less isolated and may even

pick up some useful tips. Meetup.com is another option for finding other parents in your situation.

Four: Locate specific support for adults with autism.

Your local autism society can also help you to find local services and agencies that will help make life for your adult child that bit easier.

Five: Consider family therapy.

Family therapy is an effective way to improve the dynamics between all family members. Having an adult with autism in the family, especially if you are all under one roof, can place a strain on siblings, partners, grandparents, and the interactions between them. Look for a family therapist with experience of working systemically and with adults with autism.

Six: Support them–don't enable them!

The biggest thing when you've got an adult child with autism is knowing the difference between supporting that child and helping them move forward and enabling them. This is tough. ASD is a huge spectrum and if your child is on the high functioning end, it can be very difficult to think about their struggles in life and find that balance between support and enabling (e.g., letting your adult child sit in their room playing video games all day when they could actually be having a purpose in life). Another aspect of this is knowing that you cannot change the adult child or apply norms to them such as, 'You need to be working and have a girlfriend/ boyfriend.' You have to think, 'This is them. They're wired differently. They have different strengths.'

Seven: Take a 'can do' approach.

Following on from the previous point, always focus on what your adult child can do rather than what holds them back. By reinforcing and strengthening the skills they have, they can achieve more on their own than you might have thought possible. You might want to read/re-read the chapter *Caring By letting go: supporting versus enabling revisited.*

Eight: Investigate educational support. If your adult child with autism is in education, find out what support is available from their college or university. All further and higher education institutions have facility to support students with disabilities. They may be able to support your child by, for example, substituting elements of the course that they might find challenging (e.g., residential schools).

Nine: Research financial support.
Find out what is available through the government or your local authority. You may be eligible for support with finances through tax breaks, benefits, housing support, etc. If relevant, you can also get advice on trusts, power of attorney and other financial vehicles that might be relevant to your situation.

Ten: Educate yourself.
The more you understand of your adult child's psychology, the more able you will be to help them live their best life. Read widely around the subject of adult autism. Research the latest scientific developments but also read case studies from adults with autism and their families. Stick to authentic and reputable sources.

Always remember to show compassion, understanding and love for your child with ASD. They may struggle but they are loyal, kind, loving and gifted people.

For more guidance, read:
Knowing Why: Adult-Diagnosed Autistic People on Life and Autism - Autistic Self Advocacy Network and E. Bartmess
Understanding Autism in Adults and Aging Adults - T. Regan and M. Goldsmith
An Adult With an Autism Diagnosis - G. Drew

CHAPTER 61

ADULT CHILDREN IN THE MODERN-DAY FAMILY

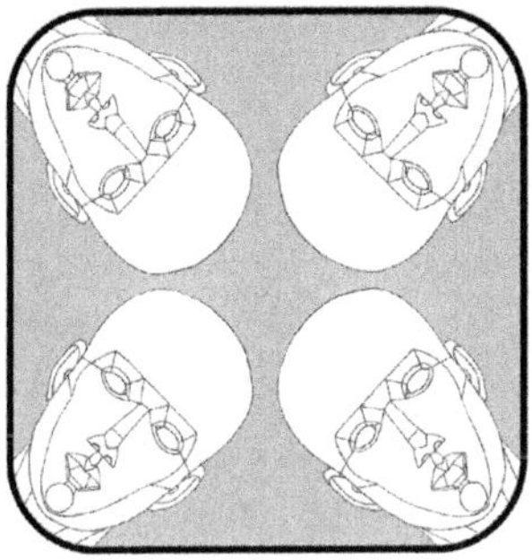

"If you feel that you're investing more than the rest of the family, start to question it. Never be scared of speaking your truth to your children."
- Michael Padraig Acton -

Some modern-day families can have as many as eight parents/grandparents depending upon how many divorces and break ups there have been. The term 'blended family' is used commonly, but some families blend well and others are terrible. Every individual is different, and every family brings with it its own uniqueness. We're trained in therapy - and I'm putting it over to you - to never expect the same situation as you had when you were growing up, or the same experiences as you have previously had in your life, because there are all different kinds of families that work with the people involved. For example, there may be two mums and one dad and it works out really well with that family. Who are we to judge if the children are healthy? It's not for us to put our moral stamp on it. This book's all about health, not morals. If the parents are in an open relationship and the children are thriving that's great. All families take management, 'blended' or not. It's a fiction to think that we have to add 'more' to a family.

It's important to understand our position in an extended, modern family and what we want out of it. With adult children, we don't have to do anything or give them anything anymore. We're not obliged to take care of them or offer moral guidance. They are adults now. They can make their own decisions and they have the legal right to make those decisions. The only time you ever step in as the parent of an adult child is if they are threatening their own life or wellbeing or that of somebody else—and I mean severe threats such as suicide planning or thinking of hurting, harming, or murdering somebody.

So, what do we want from the extended family?

It is often the case that one set of parents feels they are not getting fair treatment. This can lead to resentment and a rift in the extended family. If there are four sets of parents/grandparents and your adult child is choosing to do Christmas with one, birthdays with another, Halloween with another and you're not getting your bite of it, tell them! It might be that your adult child's partner is very strong-willed and is saying, "We should do that," "We shouldn't go there," or, "I don't want to do this."

You could say, "I feel it's unfair that we're not getting to celebrate anything. What could we do to make sure we celebrate something each year?" Give them some suggestions, "I'm wondering if we could do Easter or celebrate a mini-Christmas before Christmas or New Year's?"

Make them realise that you're not going to be the quiet one in the corner and don't be frightened of saying, "We'd like to be involved."

The modern-day family and money

It's not uncommon for one set of parents/grandparents to be asked for more contribution and investments than others. It is often the case that they are seen as a 'soft touch' and the others have all said "No."

The advice I've given some people over the years is: if the children need something and there are four sets of parents, explain that you'll contribute exactly what the other three sets of parents are contributing. Have your boundaries in place from the start.

For example, if you are in an extended family and your adult child comes to you and asks for $800 towards a car, which they are struggling to pay for, you could say, "It would be a great thing if all four sets of parents could contribute $200 each. Let me know when they've done that, and I will give you my contribution."

Investment needs to equal return and if you feel that you're investing more than the rest of the family, start to question it. Why and how is that happening? Maybe there is a degree of inequality regarding incomes or wealth, and you may be a bit more cash-heavy than most. You may accept you will need to contribute more cash than the others. But what about things such as babysitting or cutting the lawn or making a meal? Could the other parents contribute in another way? Just check that you're not the only one giving out of that group. Make sure that you're not being taken advantage of and there is equal investment from all parties. You also may want to make sure, at this point, that your adult child is not playing games with you, that there really is a contribution from each party and it's not a scam.

If things are uneven, be honest about it. Tell your adult child your truth. Use the 1, 2, 3 we covered in the first part of this book:

1. I feel like I'm contributing an awful lot and it's feeling unfair to me.
2. Nobody else seems to be doing much and we don't see you as often.
3. To resolve this, we'd like to create new traditions in the family that we can look forward to each year.

Never fear speaking your truth to your children. Adult children can sometimes be scary and challenging, and sometimes we just don't know what to do.

Unfortunately, we never stop caring. I say 'unfortunately' because it would be a peaceful world if we could just turn off the caring at times, but we don't if we're healthy parents. We always care and love our children. We just want the best for them, so when things aren't going right, we need to challenge them on it. We need to ask them, "Why did that happen? Why is this happening this way? How can we do it differently?"

Do not suffer in silence. It's not your job as the parent of an adult child.

For more guidance, read:
The Modern Grandparent's Handbook: The Ultimate Guide to the New Rules of Grandparenting - Dr G. Witkin
The Step-Parents' Parachute: The Four Cornerstones of Good Step-Parenting - F. McEvedy

CHAPTER 62

ADULT CHILDREN IN THE FAMILY BUSINESS

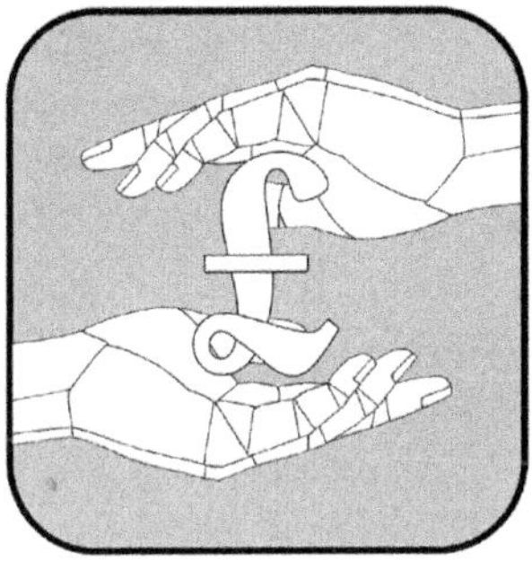

"Business doesn't incorporate friends and family."
- Michael Padraig Acton -

Whether you have a private family office and are extremely wealthy or run a humble family bakery, you have to understand that a business is a business. It's about money, it's not about relationships.

So, if you're entering into business with a family or you're in business with your adult children, you need to put in clear boundaries around what you require or expect. As much as employees of any business need a job description, that is even more of a requirement when working in a family private office or a family business. Duties and responsibilities have to be clearly delineated. So, if there are 10 members, you have to understand what's reasonable from each other and agree to a certain standard of conduct and level of accountability. There are always consequences to good and bad actions so as a healthy family, you will need to work as a team and draw on legal advice for your business when necessary.

Also, boundary your time within the business or family. Don't be sitting there watching a movie and all of a sudden think, 'Oh, I need to talk to you about that business plan.' One of the most successful things I've taught families in business is to have weekly business meetings. Just set aside half an hour where you can sit and anchor all your concerns or issues or thoughts about the business's progress or employees. Anchor it for once a week so you all know it's coming.

Remember, business is about money, it's not about family relationships. You have to make sure there are boundaries because no one is immune from greed, anger or frustration. So, we need to protect the business from the family dynamics. You don't have family members–they are colleagues. Get that right and you'll be fine.

For more guidance, read:

In the Company of Family: How To Thrive When Business is Personal - M. Mitchell-Blitch

Family Business on the Couch: A Psychological Perspective - M. Kets de Vries and R. Carlock

Dirty Little Secrets of Family Business: Ensuring Success from One Generation to the Next - H. Hutcheson

CHAPTER 63

LESSON ONE REVISITED: IT IS ABOUT ALL OF US

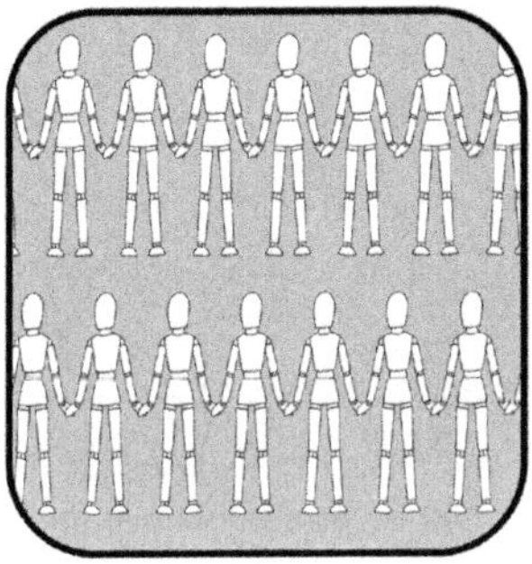

"We can let go of control when our children are able, at any age.
We can tighten the control when our children are less able. . .
drugs, mental health issues, illness, etc.
However, we can let go of control and at the same time not let go
of loving and caring for them."
- Michael Padraig Acton -

The battleground of parent versus child control is common to most families. This chapter looks at the many cases where one or more of the parents have a habit of trying to control everything around them. The popular term for such parents is 'control freak,' although this label suggests that there is something innate about the need to control. This is not normally the case. Most of the time, this behaviour is a learned habit and can be worked with.

For some parents, and you may be one of them, we only realise that our 'control freak' habit isn't working for us when our children have cut themselves off. Young children may distance themselves emotionally. Adult children may make that distance physical. Sometimes they might cut themselves off completely.

How controlling behaviour affects our relationship with our children

As children become older and more independent, they are more likely to resent their behaviour being controlled. As the emotional tension builds, they may choose 'fight' or 'flight'. For a child living at home, flight might include disengaging (the silent treatment), spending lots of time in their bedroom, or even running away.

Adult children (and even younger teenagers, in some circumstances) can make the choice to leave home. If they have the skills to manage a parent's controlling behaviour from a distance, the relationship can work. However, if they lack these skills, physical distance can turn into estrangement.

When we realise we have become estranged from our adult children we can feel angry, but beneath that anger is often a cocktail of other emotions: guilt, hurt, shock and more. We might also feel judged by friends and family, as we imagine what they might be thinking or saying about our parenting.

Where control freak behaviour comes from

The need to control is based on the fear of what happens when we let go. No human is comfortable with complete chaos, but we all have different thresholds when it comes to how happy we are to 'go with the flow'. This comes from both individual psychological and biological differences, as well as our lived experiences.

Rarely, controlling behaviour is part of a personality disorder such as narcissistic personality disorder (NPD) or borderline personality disorder (BPD). Or there may be an underlying mental health condition such as obsessive-compulsive disorder (OCD) or generalised anxiety disorder (GAD).

However, in most cases, control freaks have learnt this behaviour as a general coping mechanism for feelings of anxiety.

The symptoms of being a control freak

Control freaks are rarely at peace with themselves. Since they feel that they are responsible for everything that happens around them, they can never let up for a minute in their management of people and environments.

Here are some of the common signs that someone has an unhelpful need to be in control:

- They don't work well in teams. They either prefer to work on their own or dictate what everyone in the team is doing.
- They hate delegating, as they feel they will need to spend even more time fixing what goes wrong. When they do delegate, they micromanage the person carrying out the task.
- They are unforgiving of mistakes, in themselves or others.
- They often appear busy yet may not be very productive.
- They often seem irritable or stressed.
- They catastrophise, fearing the worst is about to happen.

Dealing with your need to control

One of the first things you can do to curb your controlling behaviour is recognise when the impulse to take charge rears its head. This can be hard to do, especially at first, so congratulate yourself when you do recognise it and gently, with compassion, ask yourself whether you really do need to exert control.

Knowing the difference between what needs to be controlled (taking your son to school on time or making sure your adult daughter pays the rent) and what you want to control (telling your daughter what book she should read next or making your adult son come back home before ten at night) is key.

As you waste less energy trying to control the people and things around you, you will find you have more to spend on what really matters.

If you feel overwhelmed with uncertainty, learn to calm yourself with small areas of control. Choose the restaurant you want to go to or which outfit you will wear. Make lists and choose tasks you can delegate.

Getting your child back

If your child has chosen not to engage with you because of your controlling behaviour, trying to make them change their mind through guilt-tripping or manipulation is like throwing fuel on a fire to put it out.

Recognise that they have made a choice to disconnect and that blaming them, or your parenting, for that decision is not going to change that.

What can you do to help repair the relationship? Here are some tips:

- **Don't cut them off to spite them.** Often, 'cutting off' is an immature response to emotional intensity. As an adult, it is more constructive to be a role model of how to repair a damaged relationship. Reach out to them occasionally in a non-intrusive way. Leave messages, remind them that you love them and want to fix things. Send birthday cards and gifts.
- **Get support.** Talk to friends and relatives you trust about what you are going through. Join a parents' support group. Avoid the temptation to dwell on anger or your feelings of betrayal.
- **Hear your adult child.** If your child talks to you about the reasons behind their estrangement, be prepared to swallow your pride. Even if they have misunderstood the situation, there may be grains of truth in what they say. Accept their perception of what has happened and work with them on a way forward that suits everyone.
- **Change yourself.** Whatever happens between you, know that you can never change your adult child. You have to accept them as they are and not the idealised adult you may have been trying to mould. Your focus should be on changing your own behaviours and thought processes.

When the time is right, your child may surprise you by responding positively to your olive branches. They may realise that the only way to inner peace is to face the issues between you and untie those knots.

In the meantime, the best thing you can do as a parent is to let them live their lives while letting them know that the door is always open. You will never let go of loving them, but you can make a space for yourself to live in peace.

CHAPTER 64

PAUSE, REFLECTION AND CONCLUSION

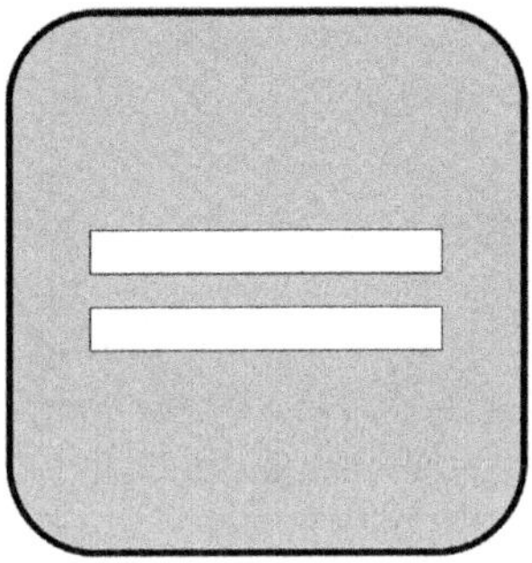

"Is familiar hell better than unknown heaven?"
- Janne Bjorkroth and Elise Widemark -
(Battle Beast 'Familiar Hell')

What a journey writing this book has been. I have questioned and challenged every bone and tissue in my body and brain. Being a father for 36 years and a grandpa for 15, I am not sure of the exact details of everything I did, when or how. All I know is that I did the absolute best I could, given the knowledge and resources I had at that time. I also realised I have struggles with relationships and repeating my own unhealthy patterns. Becoming a parent did not solve these. I became a codependent parent who was threatened and held to ransom. I beat myself up over how I 'should' or 'ought' to do better.

Never be held to ransom. Whether you are being held to ransom by a two-year-old over food management or by an adult child withholding access to your grandchildren, it is without doubt wrong.

I too have been held to ransom, as all parents have if we're honest. It takes me all the power I can muster sometimes to not write a cheque.

Remember, we can give our children the best tools for them to succeed in any environment. It is up to them to make that work or not. If our children are successful, we can be proud, but we must not own that achievement because it is theirs. Similarly, if our children turn out abusive and disrespectful—and even if they become murderers or rapists—it is equally not our fault. Now, if we train them to be dishonest, takers and manipulators, that is definitely not a good thing and can rub off on how they are. Equally, if we instil high morals, politeness and a giving nature, that can rub off on them too.

You may be reading this book as part of your studies or because you are questioning your own parenting or the parenting of someone near to you. Always remember, parenting is about relationships. Yours with others. They have choices and they follow their own journeys. What you must do is separate yourself out from your children, healthy or otherwise, and give them space to see you differently. Have a good, hard look at yourself. The keys to successful parenting, successful peace in your life are within you—not in how they are.

Again, as previously mentioned, Mrs Obama said a very powerful thing. The press caught her on the stairs and asked her, "Are you happy Ma'am?" She very quickly replied, "I am as happy as my most unhappy child." Yes, this may be very true, but it is dangerous if taken to the extreme. When our children grow up and we have this attitude, we will never be at peace or happy because we have not separated out. We need to tell our children that if they need us, they must ask clearly what they require and describe honestly the situation that they are in. If they don't, we will always be interpreting their lives, and I must emphasise, you will be setting yourself up for failure. No life is without its ups and downs and sometimes there are catastrophes.

A successful parent is a peaceful parent asking for forgiveness when things could have gone better, learning from those mistakes and allowing their children to be good or bad, better or worse than they themselves were - it is their journey.

The purpose of writing this book is to help fill gaps in people's knowledge and skill sets. Parenting is a career. It evolves and changes. If we do not develop along with it, we are going to fail.

Everything we do as humans, if we really think about it, is about relationships with other people and things. There is no such thing as perfect when it comes to parenting but there is a lot to be said for simply being the best we can possible be. I must stress that this attitude does not excuse selfish behaviour or neglect. Parents that do not give a damn cannot call themselves parents. Those that take more than they give do not deserve to call themselves parents. Those that use and manipulate their children for their own gain do not deserve the title of parents.

Our young children depend upon our guidance. I emphasise again that education, health and wellbeing are not negotiable. To earn the title of parent, it is our duty to help our children achieve their best given their context and ability.

On the other hand, adult children need to earn the title of 'my child.' Does this sound harsh? It's true. All relationships are a two-way street. When it becomes one-way, it is abusive. In times of harsh trials there is give and take, but if this is the usual pattern, put on the brakes and bail. Your child can come back or good riddance.

Take money as an example. We either work hard for our money or receive it as a right. This does not entitle anyone to it and that includes our children. If we choose to give, donate or share our money, that's our given right. Our children are entitled to zero, especially if they are poorly behaved. It is our job to support and guide our children the best we can.

I hope I have helped clarify the thin and dangerous line between supporting and enabling. Supporting helps them to help themselves. Enabling helps them to take from others.

It will always be painful, but parenting is not about sacrificing our wonderful gift of life and peace. If you are a parent who has earned the title, you deserve to have a peaceful and fulfilled life.

Honesty is what helps us change relationships. If we are getting it wrong, the biggest change we need to make as parents is to change the relationship with ourselves. There is no love like the love for our children. There is no pain like the pain our children can bestow upon us.

Remember, the people that purport to be the best parents in this world, and the ones who give the most advice, are the dishonest ones or those without children. The honest ones say, "There are grey areas. We can only do our best. It takes a village to raise a child."

'We are never young enough to know everything' is my favourite mantra. However, age is no guarantee of wisdom either. So many people go through life and do not develop, do not change.

Why do some develop, others regress and some destroy? Whatever our position in life, it is our human condition that dictates that we can do better. What should always preface this is the right of children–all children–to have a voice and vision.

As parents we can all pivot, change, evolve and most of all enjoy our lives! We figure too!

We don't always reap what we sow in life and that is not important. It's what we do. It is about our intent, and how we manage the crop, that matters most.

Having said all this, worked through all these chapters, thought long and hard and turned myself inside out writing and editing, I couldn't claim this book as complete without sharing with you the reward I have collected for being a good enough parent: looking into my daughter's and grandchildren's eyes, seeing them be and engage and develop, all fills me with warmth, love and awe. . . every time.

How can you arrive at that same blessed place? I leave you with an analogy I use with people I work with who are struggling with their life journey.

Working through life is exactly like doing a jigsaw puzzle. We set up all the corners, add the edges and build our frame for life. We then find the pieces and put them in their rightful places. What a satisfying feeling it is when we find that one elusive piece and put it in its rightful place. However, jigsaws are truth. When we find a piece that 'sort of' fits, we often try to force it to work. But if it is not the right piece for that space then it is not the right piece. We have to concede that it is the wrong piece, take it out and work hard at finding where that piece does fit (maybe it does not belong in this jigsaw at all). Once we remove that piece, we start to feel better and can resume looking for the correct piece of the puzzle. As we build the different parts of the jigsaw, a picture starts to emerge. The more we add, the more we can see the bigger picture.

We always finish the jigsaw. We put our last piece in the day we pass over.

Our picture is complete, and we have fulfilled our short time on this Earth. Don't sweat the small stuff; there is a place for everything.

PLEASE LEAVE A REVIEW AND GIVE US YOUR FEEDBACK

Thank you for reading this second book in the Power of You series.

- What did you like?
- What additions would you like to see?
- What topics would you like me to write about next?

I want this to continue to be the most helpful and informative book of its kind on this subject.

Please contribute to helping others by leaving a review and feedback via my contact page on my website, on Amazon, on Goodreads, and share on social media. Tell us what you feel needs to be included. We read all feedback and, where needed, will make changes to future editions of this book.

Connect with me online:
Twitter: www.twitter.com/mpamind_com
Facebook: www.facebook.com/mpamind
Instagram: www.instagram.com/mpamind_com
YouTube: www.youtube.com/channel/UCHGfUjqfS2ERjjKtPaQcQ5w
LinkedIn: www.linkedin.com/in/michael-padraig-acton-1045562b/
Website: www.mpamind.com
Email: office@mpamind.com

GLOSSARY OF TERMS

American Psychiatric Association (APA): The largest professional association of psychiatrists and trainee psychiatrists in the world.The APA publish the *Diagnostic and Statistical Manual of Mental Disorders.*

Artificial Intelligence (AI): An umbrella term for various technologies designed to mimic human intelligence.

Attachment Disorder: A broad term covering a range of disorders rooted in the lack of typical socialising care and attention in early childhood.

Autism Spectrum Disorder (ASD): A disorder characterised by the inability to make and sustain two way social communication and the performance of restricted or repetitive behaviours.

Borderline Personality Disorder (BPD): A disorder characterised by unstable relationships, emotional outbursts and distorted self-image.

Codependency (CD): A disorder characterised by enabling behaviour in a relationship. The codependent takes responsibility for the other person's behaviour and wellbeing. See my book: *Learning How To Leave: A Practical Guide to Stepping Away from Narcissistic and Toxic Relationships.*

Counselor/Counsellor: A person who works with individuals and groups to promote optimal mental health and wellbeing. In many territories, the word is unprotected. It is therefore advisable for people to choose a counselor who is an accredited member of one of the country's professional bodies.

Dopamine: A brain chemical connected with reward-motivated behaviour. Some drugs and addictive activities stimulate or block the absorption of dopamine.

DSM-5: The latest (2013) edition of the *Diagnostic and Statistical Manual of Mental Disorders*. Published by the APA, it standardises and classifies mental disorders.

Elaborated codes: A form of language characterised by the use of a wide vocabulary designed to provide thorough explanation.

Enabling: Taking responsibility for the development or problems of another person.

Family Estrangement: The loss of a physical and/or emotional relationship between family members. This loss causes pain to at least one of the parties involved.

Gaming disorder: The compulsive playing of video games, leading to problems functioning in daily life. First defined in the ICD-11.

Generalised anxiety disorder (GAD): A disorder characterised by chronic, excessive and sometimes irrational worry.

ICD-11: The latest (2022) edition of the *International Classification of Diseases*. Developed by the WHO, it provides diagnostic codes for the classification of diseases.

Internet Watch Foundation (IWF): A non-profit organisation dedicated to finding and removing images of child sexual abuse from the Internet.

Narcissistic Personality Disorder (NPD): A disorder characterised by exaggerated self-importance, lack of empathy and craving for admiration. See my book: *Learning How To Leave: A Practical Guide to Stepping Away from Narcissistic and Toxic Relationships*.

Obsessive compulsive disorder (OCD): An anxiety disorder characterised by repetitive behaviours.

Psychiatrist: A medically trained professional who specialises in the study, diagnosis and treatment of mental disorders. All psychiatrists hold a medical degree, but professional requirements vary by country.

Psychologist: A person trained in the workings of the mind. In many territories, the word is unprotected. It is therefore advisable for people to choose a psychologist who is an accredited member of one of the country's professional bodies.

Psychotherapist: A person who helps treat disorders of the mind and personality. In many territories, the word is unprotected. It is therefore advisable for people to choose a therapist who is an accredited member of one of the country's professional bodies.

Restricted codes: A form of language characterised by the use of a narrow, shared vocabulary. It is designed to instruct rather than explain.

Safeguarding: A term, used in the UK and Ireland, for the protection of individual health, wellbeing and human rights, especially those of children and vulnerable adults.

Social gaming: Playing video games that require interaction with other players.

Socratic questioning: A method of extracting information by the posing of carefully constructed open questions. Originally devised by the Greek philosopher Socrates.

Suicidal ideation: A symptom of some mental disorders characterised by thoughts or fantasies about suicide. Suicidal ideation can progress from passive thoughts to active planning.

Stages of Change (model): A five stage model used in the treatment of various addictions. Patients progress through the following stages: pre-contemplation, contemplation, preparation, action and maintenance.

Sexually Transmitted Infection (STI): An infection that is usually transmitted through sexual contact.

Transactional Analysis (TA): A theory and therapeutic method, whereby social interactions are analysed by the ego state of the participants (whether this is parent-like, childlike or adult-like). The concept was developed in the 1950s by Eric Berne.

Transgender: Having a gender identity that is different to the sex assigned at birth.

World Health Organisation (WHO): The United Nations agency dedicated to promoting global health.

FURTHER READING

CHAPTER 1

Eyes Wide Open: Help! With Control Freak Co-Parents - D. Wingfield

Stop Being Controlling: How to Overcome Control Issues - B. Gain

Recovering from Control Issues: How to Rebuild Your Self-Esteem & Confidence - C. Loving

CHAPTER 2

I didn't do it. A book about telling the truth - S. Graves

Teaching your children to tell themselves the truth - W.D. & C. Backus

Lying Up a Storm - J. Cook

CHAPTER 3

Loneliness in Childhood and Adolescence - K.J. Rotenberg and S. Hymel

How to be Alone - S. Maitland

Mama, I'm Lonely! - R.C. Sood and D. Joglekar

CHAPTER 4

How to Tell When Kids are in Trouble with Alcohol/Drugs - Parenting for Prevention

Teens, Alcohol & Drugs: Adventures in Single Parenting - L. Mooney

Parenting for Prevention: How to Raise a Child to Say No to Alcohol/Drugs - D.J. Wilmes

Teenagers, Alcohol and Drugs: What Your Kids Really Want to Know About Alcohol and Drugs - P. Dillon

CHAPTER 5

21 Lessons for the 21st Century - Y.N. Harari

The Tech Diet for Your Child and Teen: The 7-Step Plan to Unplug & Reclaim Your Kid - B. Marshall

Are Your Kids Naked Online: How to Protect Your Tech-Savvy Kids from Online Self-Destruction - C. Good and L. Good

CHAPTER 6

Where did I Come From - P. Mayle

It's NOT the Stork - R. Harris

21st Century Guide to the Birds and the Bees - B. Messer and R. Luik

CHAPTER 7

Calmer, Easier, Happier Homework: The Revolutionary Programme That Transforms Homework - N. Janis-Norton

Ending the Homework Hassle: Understanding, Preventing, and Solving School Performance Problems - J.K. Rosemond

Homework Help for Mums and Dads: Help Your Child Succeed - K. Dolby

CHAPTER 8

Balanced Parenting Guide: How to Balance Between Love, Nurturing and Enabling Your Child - M. Viskovich

Kind Yet Firm: Discipline Your Toddler the Positive Parenting Way - G. Stockholm

Parenting: The Ultimate Parenting Manual. How to Promote and Support the Physical, Emotional, Social and Intellectual Development of Your Child - A. Kats

Detachment and Enabling: Seven Simple Steps – J. M. Knowlton and R.D. Chaitin

CHAPTER 9

There's No Such Thing as 'Naughty' - K. Silverton

The Young Child: Development from Prebirth Through Age Eight - M.B. Puckett and J.K. Black

Brighter Futures: A Parents' Guide to Raising Happy, Confident Children in the Primary School Years - Dr L. Dawes, N. Gorringe, Dr L. Russell, Dr K. Hodson, Dr J. Swanston and Dr S. Wimshurst

CHAPTER 10

Safeguarding Children Exposed to Narcissistic Parenting, Coercive Control and Parental Alienation - A. Smith

Living Without a Father: Heal from Dad's Rejection - S. Tonder

Overcoming Parental Rejection & Hurts - E. Middleton

CHAPTER 13

An Introduction to Coping with Anxiety - B. Hogan and L. Brosan

Helping Your Anxious Teen: Positive Parenting Strategies to Help Your Teen Beat Anxiety, Stress, and Worry - S.A. Josephs PhD

The Opposite of Worry: The Playful Parenting Approach to Childhood Anxieties and Fears - L.J. Cohen

CHAPTER 14

Wonderful Ways to Love a Child: Inspired Ideas for Raising Happy, Healthy Children - J. Ford and A. Ford

Am I Yelling: 45 Highly Effective Strategies to Control and Manage Anger for Parents - T. Zaid and J. Green

Calm Parents, Happy Kids: The Secrets of Stress-Free Parenting - Dr L. Markham

CHAPTER 15

Parenting Isn't for Cowards - Dr J.C. Dobson

Raising Boys in the 21st Century - S. Biddulph

Parenting 101 - M. Miller and HowExpert

CHAPTER 16

The ABCs of Diversity: Helping Kids (and Ourselves) Embrace Our Differences - C. Helsel and Y.J. Harris-Smith

The Gender Affirmative Model: An Interdisciplinary Approach to Supporting Transgender and Gender Expansive Children - C. Keo-Meier and D. Ehrensaft

Why Are People Different Colours? Big Issues for Little People Around Identity and Diversity - E. Waddington and C. McCurry

CHAPTER 17

Chess for Success: Using an Old Game to Build New Strengths in Children and Teens - M.G. Ashley

The Seven Spiritual Laws of Success for Parents: Guiding Your Children to Success and Fulfilment - D. Chopra

Let Them Play: The Mindful Way to Parent Kids for Fun and Success in Sports - J. Lynch

CHAPTER 18

Parenting: The 7 Secrets of Spending Quality Time with Your Children - N. Ghostleaf

One Million Minutes: What My Daughter Taught Me About Time - W. Kuper

Dad Can Do: Build, Make, Do. . .The Best Way to Spend Quality Time with Your Kids - C. Barnardo

Guides for Family Quality time: Series 1: Indoor Sports - S. Guo and A. Guo

CHAPTER 19

The Good Parenting Food Guide: Managing What Children Eat Without Making Food a Problem - J. Ogden

Healthy Food, Healthy Gut, Happy Child: The Real Dirt on Raising Healthy Kids in a Processed World - *Dr M. Shetreat-Klein*

Help Your Teenager Beat an Eating Disorder - J. Lock PhD and D. Le Grange PhD

CHAPTER 20

Twins & Multiple Births: The Essential Parenting Guide from Pregnancy to Adulthood - Dr C. Cooper

The First Year is Survival: The Essential Guide to Parenting Twins and Multiples - L. Hule

OMG It's Twins! Get Your Twins to Their First Birthday Without Losing Your Mind - A. Perry

Having Twins and More: A Parent's Guide to Multiple Pregnancy, Birth and Early Childhood - E. Noble, L. Sorger et al

CHAPTER 21

Sorry, I Forgot to Ask: My Story About Asking for Permission and Masking an Apology! - J. Cook

Ellie Jelly and the Massive Mum Meltdown - S. Naish

I'm Sorry: The Art of Apology & the Gift of Forgiveness - A. Krusinski

CHAPTER 22

Primal Leadership: Unleashing the Power of Emotional Intelligence - D. Goleman, R.E. Boyatzis and A. McKee

How to Win Friends & Influence People - D. Carnegie

The 7 Habits of Highly Effective People - S.R. Covey

CHAPTER 23

The Language of Parenting: A Parenting Guide Designed to Help Parents Meet the Everyday Challenges of Parenting - S. Schumer M.A.

Fowl Language - Winging it: The Art of Imperfect Parenting - B. Gordon

Small Talk: How to Develop Your Child's Language Skills from Birth to Age Four - N. Lathey and T. Blake

CHAPTER 24

Negotiation Parenting: Or How Not to Raise a Brat in Today's Complex World - F.K. Hean

Talks and Negotiations with My Child - Dr P. Jednaszewski

Negotiation Generation: Take Back Your Parental Authority Without Punishment - L. Reeves Griffin

CHAPTER 25

Black Sheep: This Can't Be Happening - R. Scholl

The Parent Gap: Tools to Keep Your Cool, Stay Connected and Change Unhealthy Patterns - R. Rubenstein

The Practice of Family Therapy: Key Elements Across Models - S. Midori Hanna

CHAPTER 26

Stop the Lecturing Start the Conversation - S.H. Sidsworth

The Socratic Parent: How to Raise a Child of Any Age by Asking the Right Questions - P. Sweetow

The Case Method Miracle - A. Jones

CHAPTER 27

Bullying: Real and Lasting Ways to Stop Bullies, Stand Up for Yourself & Overcome Fear - A. Caldwell

Bully-Proof Kids - S. O'Malley

The Bullying Antidote: Superpower Your Kids for Life - L. Hart and K. Caven

CHAPTER 28

Overcoming the Co-Parenting Trap:Essential Parenting Skills When a Child Resists a Parent - J. A. Moran PhD, T. Sullivan and Matthew Sullivan PhD

The Co-Parenting Survival Guide: Letting Go of Conflict After a Difficult Divorce - J. Zimmerman

Co-Parenting 101: Helping Your Children Thrive after Divorce -D. Philyaw

CHAPTER 29

The Legal Adoption Guide: Safely Navigating the System - C. Alexander-Roberts

How to Annihilate a Narcissist: In the Family Court - R. Watson

CHAPTER 30

Single Parenting That Works: Six Keys to Raising Happy, Healthy Children in a Single-Parent Home - K. Leman

I am the Parent Who Stayed: Joyfully Parenting Alone N. Farr

CHAPTER 31

Parenting Forward: How to Raise Children with Justice, Mercy and Kindness - C. Wang Brandt and R. Held Evans

A New Alphabet for Humanity - L. McGregor

CHAPTER 32

Three Pearls: Transactional Analysis Fairy World - M. Naubert

TA for Kids: Powerful Techniques for Developing Self-Esteem - A.M. Freed

CHAPTER 33

Parenting Out of Control: Anxious Parents in Uncertain Times - M. K. Nelson

Anxious Kids, Anxious Parents: 7 Ways to Stop the Worry Cycle and Raise Courageous and Independent Children - R. Wilson PhD and L Lyons

CHAPTER 34

Dibs in Search of Self: Personality Development in Play Therapy - V. M. Axline

The Simple Guide to Attachment Difficulties in Children: What They Are and How to Help - B. de Thierry

CHAPTER 35

Families and How to Survive Them - Dr R. Skynner and J. Cleese

Finding Forgiveness: A 7-Step Program for Letting Go of Anger and Bitterness - E. Borris-Dunchunstang

CHAPTER 36

Money-Savvy Kids: Parenting Penny-Wise Kids in a Money-Hungry World - J. Raymond Albrektson

The Wisest Investment: Teaching Your Kids to Be Responsible, Independent and Money-Smart for Life - R. Taub

CHAPTER 37

The Parent's Guide to Self-Harm: What Parents Need to Know - J. Smith

Self Harm: Why Teens Do It and What Parents Can Do to Help - M. Mitchell

The Mindfulness Workbook for Teen Self-Harm: Skills to Help You Overcome Cutting and Self-Harming Behaviors, Thoughts, and Feelings - G. M. Biegel MA LMFT and S. Cooper

CHAPTER 38

Hot Mess to Mindful Mom: 40 Ways to Find Balance and Joy in Your Every Day - A. Katz

My Cape is at the Cleaners: Choosing Happy Over Perfect - W. Elover

CHAPTER 39

Parenting a Child with Asperger Syndrome: 200 Tips and Strategies - B. Boyd

Parenting a Child with Emotional and Behavioural Difficulties - D. Hughes

CHAPTER 40

Parenting ADHD: What ADHD Child Wants from You - G.P. Clifford

Mindful Parenting for ADHD: A Guide to Cultivating Calm, Reducing Stress, and Helping Children Thrive - M. Bertin M.D.

Mental Health in America: Misdiagnosis of ADHDIn Young Chillren - I. Azirayah (presentation)

ADHD: Not Overdiagnosed, Misdiagnosed - K. Graham (presentation)

ADHD: Current Concepts and Treatments in Children and Adolescents - Various (2)

CHAPTER 42

How to Teach Your Child Responsibility: Nurture Self-esteem - Kidbizu

Blame the Child - It's Easier: Learning Difficulties Can Be Solved - H. Blumenthal

Parenting with Love and Logic: Teaching Children Responsibility - F. Cline

CHAPTER 43

The Day No One Played Together: A Story about Compromise - D. Helsley and S. Harkey

Why Can't You See it My Way? Resolving Values Conflicts at Work and Home - A. Estes

Mastering Confrontation: Become an Expert at Effective Communication. Master the Art of Dealing with Conflict - R. Hunt

CHAPTER 45

Helping Your Child Recover from Sexual Abuse - C. Adams and J.J. Fay

Freedom's Flowers: The Effects of Domestic Abuse on Children - P. Craven

CHAPTER 46

Day by Day: Emotional Wellbeing in Parents of Disabled Children - J. Griffen

Shattered Assumptions: Towards a New Psychology of Trauma - R. Janoff-Bulman

CHAPTER 47

Virtue, Success, Pleasure and Liberation: Four Aims of Life in the Tradition of Ancient India - A. Danielou

Raising Children: Surprising Insights from Other Cultures - D.F. Lancy

CHAPTER 49

Setting Boundaries with Your Adult Children: Six Steps to Hope and Healing for Struggling Parents - A. Bottke

25 Ways to Stop Enabling Your Adult Child and How to Set Boundaries - E.S. Addington

CHAPTER 50

The Hands-On Guide to Surviving Adult Children Living at Home - C. Newberry

The Crowded Nest Syndrome - K. Shaputis

CHAPTER 51

How To Really Love Your Adult Child: Building a Healthy Relationship in a Changing World - G. Chapman and R. Campbell M.D.

Doing Life With Your Adult Children: Keep Your Mouth Shut and the Welcome Mat Out - J. Burns

CHAPTER 52

Setting Boundaries with Your Adult Children: Six Steps to Hope and Healing for Struggling Parents - A. Bottke

When Parents Hurt: Compassionate Strategies When You and Your Grown Child Don't Get Along - J. Coleman PhD

CHAPTER 54

Learning How To Leave: A Practical Guide to Stepping Away from Toxic & Narcissistic Relationships - Michael Padraig Acton

When Your Adult Child Breaks Your Heart: Coping With Mental Illness, Substance Abuse, and the Problems That Tear Families Apart - J. Young and C. Adamec

CHAPTER 55

Walking on Eggshells: Navigating the Delicate Relationship Between Adult Children and Their Parents - J. Isay

The Parallel Process: Growing Alongside Your Adolescent or Young Adult Child in Treatment - K. Pozatec

CHAPTER 56

Rules of Estrangement: Why Adult Children Cut Ties and How to Heal the Conflict - J. Coleman

Reconnecting with Your Estranged Adult Child: Practical Tips and Tools to Heal your Relationship - T. Gilbertson

CHAPTER 57

Restoring Family Connections: Helping Targeted Parents and Adult Alienated Children Work Through Conflict, Improve Communication, and Enhance Relationships - A. Baker, P. Fine and A. Lacheen-Baker

Mending Fences Healing Hearts: The Top 10 Keys to a Better Relationship with Your Adult Children - Dr C. Lynch

CHAPTER 58

When Our Grown Kids Disappoint Us: Letting Go of Their Problems, Loving Them Anyway, and Getting On With Our Lives - J. Adams

Don't Let Your Kids Kill You: A Guidefor Parents of Drugand Alcohol Addicted Children -C. Rubin and Tom Zingarelli et al.

Under Our Roof: A Son's Battle for Recovery, a Mother's Battle for Her Son - M. Dean and H. Cunnane

CHAPTER 59

Four Good Days (movie) - Screenplay by E. Saslow and R. Garcia, directed by R. Garcia

Trainspotting (movie) - Screenplay by I. Welsh and J. Hodge, directed by D. Boyle

CHAPTER 61

The Modern Grandparent's Handbook: The Ultimate Guide to the New Rules of Grandparenting - Dr G. Witkin

The Step-Parents' Parachute: The Four Cornerstones of Good Step-Parenting - F. McEvedy

CHAPTER 62

In the Company of Family: How To Thrive When Business is Personal - M. Mitchell-Blitch

Family Business on the Couch: A Psychological Perspective - M. Kets de Vries and R. Carlock

Dirty Little Secrets of Family Business: Ensuring Success from One Generation to the Next - H. Hutcheson

ENDNOTES

1. Hartney, E. (2011), The Stages of Change Model of Overcoming Addiction, https://www.verywellmind.com/the-stages-of-change-model-of-overcoming-addiction-21961, last accessed 5/12/21

2. Drechsler, R., Brem, S., Brandeeis, D., Grunblatt, E., Berger, G. and Walitza, S. (2020), ADHD: Current Concepts and Treatments in Children and Adolescents, Neuropediatrics 2020; 51(05): 315-335

ABOUT DR. MICHAEL ACTON

Michael Padraig Acton (B.Ed., M.Ed. (Psych.) Hons., M.A. C.Psych., P.D. C.Psych., AFBPsS., BACP (Accred), MICF) of MPAMind.com is a consultant, psychologist, counselor, clinical supervisor, legal consultant, systemic life coach, trained scientist practitioner and author with over 30 years of clinical experience. Michael is also a world-wide, high profile celebrity therapist to the rich, famous and titled. Working globally, with his main offices in London (UK) and Miami (USA), originally from England and Ireland, Michael specializes in helping couples, families and individuals. He has extensive training in therapeutic approaches including applied clinical and counseling psychology, CBT, psychoanalysis, and psychodynamic, Jungian, Gestalt, systemic and transactional analysis, as well as holistic forms of therapeutic alliance such as mindfulness and shamanism.

As mostly a single parent for his daughter's upbringing, and having no parental support as a child, Michael left home and the Catholic church behind at the age of 17 having spent months struggling to survive meningitis. Despite being homeless and sleeping rough in a friend's car, Michael had a moment of realization that for the first time in his life he was completely free. He moved into a tiny rented room with a shared kitchen and bathroom in Kent, England, working as a waiter and barman to make ends meet, before deciding to pursue a career as a teacher. This took him around the world.

After experiencing counseling psychology in Australia, both as a client and a pastoral care provider at the college where he taught, he soon realized his future lay in that direction. He applied for a conversion course to become a graduate member of the British Psychological Society and went through clinical training at Dundee University.

Michael's first clinical role was at Dundee Royal Infirmary, before moving to Sussex to study, work and research alongside Dr Mick Burton and Professor Mic Cooper on psychodynamic and family/young person's therapy.

Michael has worked within the British NHS in pain management and drug dependency units, adolescent and young people's clinics and with Relate's couples counseling programs, in addition to counseling HIV and AIDS patients for a non-profit.

In 1998, Michael was asked by The London Institute to set up a private practice in West London based upon his work experience with families, couples and substance abuse; identity issues; life crises, and gender dysphoria, as well as his research and work with lesbian, gay and bisexual issues. In 2004, he took a sabbatical to work and travel in America and Australia. During this time, he researched suicide prevalence and prevention and worked with shamanism alongside native people. After his sabbatical, he returned to the UK to resume his practice. He now continues to divide his time between the UK and the USA. Michael still travels worldwide to support people in his consultant's role. Michael is a genuine, caring and thoughtful professional, father and grandpa with scholastic and real human values. He is humbled by how much he has learned from those that have sought his help and is dedicated to paying this forward.

For more information: www.MPAmind.com.

Printed in Great Britain
by Amazon

19417577R00193